THE ART OF DECEPTION

THE ART OF DECEPTION

Elizabeth Ironside

Hodder & Stoughton

First published in Great Britain in 1998
by Hodder and Stoughton
A division of Hodder Headline PLC

10 9 8 7 6 5 4 3 2 1

A CIP catalogue record for this title is available
from the British Library

ISBN 0 340 71684 3

Typeset by Avon Dataset Ltd, Bidford-on-Avon, Warks

Printed and bound in Great Britain by
Clays Ltd, St Ives plc

Hodder and Stoughton
A division of Hodder Headline PLC
338 Euston Road
London NW1 3BH

500 296321

For Prue and Andrew

Contents

'The mind of a killer is a fascinating study,' Prisca remarked.

She was eating a trout, concentrating on piercing its crisply fried skin, slicing along its back and separating it into fillets, having already removed its head. She was the sort of vegetarian who, somehow, categorises fish among plant life.

'Can one tell, do you think?' she went on. 'Not after the event, but before. Not who did it, that's an obvious question, but who will do it? Could you? Did you see?' She did not look at me.

'No, of course not,' I said. 'There was a lot I didn't see.'

'Before now I've only ever known murderers retrospectively.' She was lifting out the backbone and removing it fastidiously to the side of her plate. 'That is, they'd already killed when I met them, when I was a prison visitor. I never knew them before the act. And that's the interesting bit.'

'Beforehand I had everything wrong. All the information was there, but I simply didn't read it properly.'

I had chosen a steak, because I couldn't be bothered to consider anything else on the menu. I cut through the encrusted surface and the reddish edge was gently weeping onto my plate.

'To do you justice, some of the information was faked.'

'You know I don't accept that.'

'Nicholas, you were duped, tricked all along the line. Either that or you're fooling us.'

She selected a forkful of pink flesh, dabbed it with sauce and put it in her mouth.

'Why aren't you eating? Isn't rare enough for you? You ought to write it up. It would be therapy, get you started again. You needn't bother with who did it, we know all that. The view you want is not who, but why. Could you see beforehand? Should you have guessed what was going

1

on? You were the only person who had the information, who knew everybody, or at least knew about everybody.'

'It's not just a question of who is going to be the killer. It's also who is going to be killed.'

'The victim was always pretty obvious. Asking for it, in my opinion. Not that I dreamt . . . But I didn't know the half of it.' Prisca helped herself to a piece of French bread. She stabbed a curl of butter and pasted it into place.

'I can't write any more. I've been trying to work on my book on art and perception, but I can't concentrate. I think I need a holiday.'

The steak was tough. It required some energy to saw through it. Human flesh was equally fibrous, dense, knit together in a durable web of tissue. To puncture the skin and pierce the muscle was the work of force. I put my knife and fork down, wishing I'd chosen something else.

'Nonsense.' Prisca never took holidays and did not see why anyone else should. 'You've just got to get the whole thing out of your system. Write it up. Then you can come back to your academic stuff later. Refreshed.'

She ate the last mouthful of her fish and took a sip of wine. All that remained on her plate was a framework of fine bones.

'I suppose I could try. I'd want to explain how it seemed at the time, the signs that were there, but which I didn't understand, to do it without hindsight, innocently.'

'However you want to tackle it,' Prisca said, 'the important thing is to cauterise the past.' She took the menu from the waiter. 'Now, what shall we have for pudding?'

After some thought, she chose an arrangement of exotic fruit. I had roasted figs.

'I think it's quite important for you,' she said, 'to come to some kind of understanding of what happened, why it happened, why it happened to you of all people.'

The figs, three fat black bulbs, sat in a raspberry sauce, which made a pink pool in the centre of the white plate. I broke into the first fruit with the side of my fork. It opened up like a wound to reveal its centre, a milder red, fibrillous, speckled with golden seeds. Food had recently taken *on an extraordinary power to return itself to raw materials in front of my eyes. And not just the form of its origin, but transubstantiated into flesh, open, throbbing, bloody, female. If writing about what had happened would put an end to this, it would be worth doing.*

'It all began like this,' I said.

'What do you mean?'

'It began that night two years ago, when you and I had dinner together to talk about Emily. Do you remember? That's when I met her.'

Part 1

Girl in a Fur

1

'I don't see. I simply don't see what she wants. What *do* women want?'

' "What do women want?" ' My cousin repeated the question in her faintly American accent. When I spoke, in exasperation, it had been a simple query; in her mouth it became something different. The tone of her voice, reflective rather than interrogative, suggested that she was more concerned with assessing why I asked than with giving an answer. Her dark, Nefertiti-like face wore an expression of compassion.

'The usual things, I would have thought. Home, job, children; love, power, comfort; respect, justice.' She stopped to think of a third, matching quality. 'Revenge,' she finished.

'In fact, everything, at once, all the time, right now.'

'Like men.'

'No, men are more reasonable. We know that certain things are impossible, so you have to make choices.'

I don't like conversations like this, pretentious, generalised. I like particularity; whoever said God is in the detail was right. Prisca has always been one for the abstract approach. On this occasion it was my own fault for asking the question in the first place. It must have been the benign effect that Prisca has always had on me that had allowed me to voice such a Freudian query.

We had been talking about Emily, my wife, my soon-to-be-ex-wife, whose behaviour in the past few months I had found incomprehensible. Prisca had acted as mediator on several occasions. I trusted her honesty and good will and she had proved herself exemplary in this difficult role.

It was Emily's behaviour that had produced my irritable question. Only by assuming that there was some fundamental need that had been left unmet could you account for what she had done. I should say at once there was no other man. At the time of her atom-splitting statement, that she and the children were going to leave, I was convinced there must be a lover. Only sexual infatuation could explain why a woman would abandon her home and husband with such ruthless abruptness. She denied it and no one else had appeared to claim her when we finally separated. So one obvious explanation failed. Outsiders may have drawn other conclusions. They may have thought that I was pathologically jealous, a woman-chaser, but I, at least, knew that this was not the case and that Emily had no reason to leave.

She had made known her wish to go without preliminaries. There had been no period of tears and scenes to warn me of what was coming. I had known Em for twelve years; we had been married for eleven. She had been an uncertain teenager when I first met her, a nineteen-year-old drop-out from university. Within a year we were married and she was expecting our first child. She settled into marriage and motherhood at once. It was obviously what she was created for. Her vagueness and uncertainty of purpose disappeared and we had our three children within five years.

There was nothing wrong with Emily's life or our marriage, as far as I could see. We were well off. I earn a decent amount from my writing and academic work, but the truth is that my earnings are irrelevant. My great grandfather, a buccaneering capitalist of the nineteenth century, who founded our family fortune with a great drugs and cosmetics empire, made flexible and prudent dispositions for the transfer of money between generations. Neither taxation nor inflation nor my father's alimony payments had seriously harmed his arrangements. We lived in a large house in Holland Park and Emily had all the nannies and helpers she required. She had a generous allowance for herself which she spent without any accounting to me. When she decided the children needed more space, we bought a house in Dorset where we went for weekends and holidays. She ran our lives. Love, power, comfort. She had them all.

Then one day last spring she announced that she was leaving me. It was Sunday and we had been in the country for the weekend. We arrived home at last after a hot, fractious journey, during which sibling rivalry could not be contained. Cordelia had been annoying her brothers and they, to have their own back, stole her favourite toy, a very old doll which had belonged originally to Emily as a child. She had soft limbs, a rigid, hydrocephalic head, large eyes and masses of dark hair. She was known, in spite of plentiful signals of her femininity, as George.

We began to unpack the car. Among the bags and baskets in the hall Sholto noticed George. Emily and I, laden with suitcases and boxes, saw him seize the doll and run upstairs with her, shouting to Cordelia, 'George is coming with me. She doesn't want to live with you any more.'

Cordelia shrieked like a siren and pursued him.

Emily shouted, 'Sholto, Delia,' and tripped over the edge of the Persian rug, spilling the vegetables we had picked in the garden that morning over the hall floor. 'For goodness sake, Nicholas, do something.'

I looked at the asparagus and beans and new potatoes rolling over the marble and walked upstairs after the children. At the top of the stairs Sholto was hanging over the bannisters, holding George out over the void.

'She's going, she's going.' He was keeping his sister off with his other arm. She was grappling with him, pushing him outwards against the balustrade

'Cordelia, Sholto,' I said sharply.

Sholto, his attention diverted for a second, drew in his arm. Cordelia, undeflected, seized the doll.

'Well, I don't want her any more,' she said and threw the beloved toy who had betrayed her, with all her force. By the time I reached them and had grasped an arm of each, they were both leaning out to look down at where George lay on the marble tiles of the hall. She had landed face down, her hair thrown up above her head and her soft limbs twisted into impossible contortions.

Sholto said with satisfaction, 'Look what you've done. You've killed her. She's broken her neck.'

Delia let out a wail of grief. Emily was coming up the stairs with Angus behind her. This was her opportunity.

'Nicholas,' she said, 'I've something to tell you.'

It is no wonder that, months later, I was still trying to understand what women wanted. Emily had decided she needed to 'fulfil' herself, to 'be' herself, and to do so she would be leaving me and enrolling on some university course. Paradoxically, she did not reject the children. They were to be hers exclusively.

I felt I was entitled to feel a little aggrieved at Prisca's reaction to my question.

'In so far as your abstractions have any bearing on real life,' I said, 'I would have thought that Emily had everything you mention. Love, power, comfort, whatever.'

The waiter set down the plate containing my main course in front of me. I looked down at the comforting heap of steak and kidney and the piled mashed potato.

'I would have found it easier to cope with if she had taken a lover,' I said. 'At least I could have understood that.' I chewed the combination of textures, firm and soft, with relish.

'You may be right. These problems often just come down to sexual compatibility. But if she had, you would have been devastated.'

I decided not to argue with Prisca's first point. It wasn't true; there was nothing wrong with sex in our marriage.

'No, no.' I said. 'I'm not possessive. I'm not physically jealous at all. If she had had a lover and stayed with me, I would at least have had the children. I still think that Emily should let me have them, if she wants to launch herself on her new life of self-fulfilment.'

'Nicholas, you say you are not possessive, yet you do everything to keep her. You and Em have been very civilised and I hope you'll go on being so. I still hope for reconciliation, as I know you do. And it's far more likely to happen if we avoid rows.'

I said, self-pityingly, 'I miss the children.'

It was true. There were times in my solitary life now when I realised that if I had been at home I would have been looking at Sholto's homework or listening to one of Cordelia's interminable stories. For, although Emily had originally said that she wanted to leave with the children, it had been clearly much more sensible for me to move out. When all the factors of the children's busy lives had been taken into account, it looked as though I would have to buy the house next door. So I left instead. I had behaved well in every respect. What I did not admit to Prisca was that I did not miss them much. I was surprised how quickly I had settled down to a bachelor life again.

'Of course you do.' Prisca looked at me over her spectacles, with an expression that made me uneasy, as if she was reading my real feelings.

An obese peer approached us on his way to his table. Seeing Prisca he stopped and, bending over her as closely as he could, began to talk about the proceedings of a committee on which they both served, with the barest acknowledgement to me of his interruption of our conversation. I had chosen a restaurant within the Division Bell area, not far from her office in the Lords, for Prisca's convenience.

Prisca requires some explanation. She had, for a short period, been the wife of my cousin, Montfort. The unlikely marriage between a Scottish landowner and a half-American, Sorbonne-educated Barbadan with a PhD from Harvard can be accounted for primarily by the fact that Prisca was extraordinarily beautiful and, then, socially inexperienced. The mix of races in her ancestry, African, Indian, Caribbean, even Caucasian, had produced someone strikingly sexy. My cousin loved showing off and Prisca was the coup de theatre of his career of marriage and remarriage. As for me, I fell for her wholeheartedly, a situation she handled with great tact, even though she was barely nine years my senior. She is very clever, far too clever for Montfort, with whom she rapidly lost patience. She divorced him as soon as she could and went on to public life, teaching law at London University, doing voluntary work, sitting on committees, chairing a Royal Commission on education whose findings were ignored and finally being made a Labour peer in 1988. In discarding my cousin, she did not give up on his family and for years I had found in her a friend whose loyalty I never doubted and whose perspicacity I sometimes feared.

When she had finished talking to her colleague, she turned back to me to explain what Emily wanted in particular rather than in metaphysical terms. This time it was a question of Sholto's school.

A couple of years ago I had suggested that the boys should go to boarding school. Emily had been vehemently against the idea. Now, Prisca explained, Sholto had raised the subject himself: he wanted to go away to school. I hope that I did not betray the rage that erupted in me. Emily had double-crossed me. She had got the house under false pretences by insisting that the children's routine should not be disturbed, and now she was packing them off to school, to enjoy her new life of 'fulfilment' and irresponsibility. I hid my feelings and appeared all reasonableness, as we discussed what to do. But even as I agreed that Emily and Sholto should go to look at one or two schools, I knew, deeper than reason, that I had been fooled again.

Prisca was pleased with me. She watched me indulgently while I ate sticky toffee pudding, which she refused. Finally, I saw her to her little car and closed her door for her. She wound down the window as she started the engine. I stood on the pavement waiting for her to drive away.

'Nicholas,' she said, hooking her fingers with their pale oval nails over the edge of the glass. 'Perhaps it's time to let go, to let her go.'

'I have let her go,' I said angrily. 'I've let her do whatever she wanted, just as I always did. I would simply like to understand.'

Prisca turned the wheel and began to manoeuvre out of her parking spot. Then she stopped, the nose of her car jutting into the road.

The Art of Deception

'What women really want,' she said, 'is the last word.' She closed her window and waved goodbye, her yellowish palm making a curious circular pass. Then she shot away down Marsham Street. I set off home, walking.

2

Home for me now was my mother's flat in Knightsbridge. My poor mother was ill most of her life. Years ago, after my father left her, (he was, like my cousin Montfort, a much married man) she took up hypochondria as her main interest. When she began, a year or so ago, to whisper about a pain in her side, I took no more notice than of the other fake syndromes she had cultivated over the years, and nor did she. She did not realise that this was the real thing at last; she had cancer and it was going to kill her. The last stages were rapid and merciful. If they had been more protracted, she might in any case have died of astonishment at the experience of pain.

Her apartment had been unoccupied for several months, waiting for Emily to organise the packing up of its contents, which she had unaccountably failed to do. So when my family life was thrown into upheaval, the decision that I should leave rather than she was made easier by the fact that I had somewhere to go. One weekend in May I packed up my clothes, some books and CDs, put them in the back of my car and drove them to Knightsbridge. And that was that. I moved into my mother's old-ladyish apartment, with its eau-de-nil carpets and pink and green chintz, changing nothing. It was comfortable enough, but it was not the kind of place you hurried back to.

As I approached home, my pace slowed and I finally halted in the square itself. I was standing by the railings of the central garden, looking up at the fanciful facade of the building, making up my mind to go in. I hated entering a dark house, something I had never had to do when I was married.

The square was quiet. A black BMW slid past at about five miles an hour. The heads of both occupants were turned away from me towards the houses, searching for a number. It disappeared on the opposite side of the square. From the street came the purposeful click of a woman's stride. I was aware that I made a suspicious figure by lurking there; that a woman alone, after eleven at night, might well feel afraid to see me, immobile, under the shadow of the trees. Yet I still could not persuade myself to behave normally, to propel myself across the road to my front door.

The woman turned into the square. I saw her glance at me and continue resolutely onward. She was wearing a fur coat, though the night was not cold and she folded her arms in front of her, defensively. I could hear another car drifting round the one-way system, coming slowly from my left. I decided to go home at last. I stepped forward to the edge of the pavement and waited for the car to pass. As it glided in front of me, I saw it was the same BMW, still circling, still searching.

A dark-clothed jogger appeared in the left of my vision, running on the opposite side of the road, towards the woman. He covered the ground fast, noiselessly. I was too far away to hear his breathing; his trainers struck no sound from the paving stones. He was close to her now, but instead of passing one another, two unconnected atoms, they clashed, as if a meteor had been pulled into a planet's orbit. I watched the unexpected meeting, as they revolved in a balletic embrace, a joyful reunion of friends long-separated. I felt, simultaneously, identification and exclusion at the sight.

The woman gave a little cry and slid out of the jogger's arms. He bent over her abruptly. I was reinterpreting what I had seen. They had not recognised one another: these were two strangers who had become accidentally entangled in the darkness. The sound of my shoes on the tarmac made the jogger aware of my presence. It was only when he pulled away from the fallen woman and raced off, that

I realised that he had not accidentally run into her, nor was he attempting to help her. What I had assumed to be a happy meeting was, in fact, a mugging; the embrace had been an attack.

I ran across the empty road. The black BMW, on its third circuit, accelerated furiously. I heard the sudden gunning of its engine and caught the flicker of movement in the corner of my eye. It was coming straight for me. I made a spurt to reach the protection of the pavement, crashing to the ground in the gutter between two parked cars, banging my shoulder on the rear bumper of a Ford estate. I heard the dull slam of a door and the car made a half revolution of the square at speed.

The woman in the fur coat still lay on the ground, like an animal hit by a passing lorry and left on the side of the road, a vigorous machine of muscle, bone and hair reduced to a slack bag of burst intestines.

But it was not that bad. As I bent over her, I could see she was making an effort to rise. She was face down, her hair, almost the same colour as the fur, spread out around her. Her head swayed as she pushed herself up on her wrists. She was making brief animal grunting noises.

'Are you all right?' I said. I put my arm round her back and my fingers slipped through the thick fur to grasp her armpits. The attempt to resurrect her was against all reason. As a doctor, I knew I should leave the injured undisturbed, but she was struggling upward and I wanted to restore the striding creature to herself. She had lost the shoes that had clicked with such determination, but regained her balance on her bare feet and at last turned round to face me.

I shall never forget that first sight of Julian. A fur coat and Knightsbridge meant old ladies to me. Perhaps I had seen my poor mother being attacked. I was not prepared to see a young woman, still less one who had a physical presence that struck like a knife. I saw a strong face, bleached by the street-lights, large dark blue eyes, a shocked, half-open mouth.

'Are you all right?' I asked again.

17

'I don't know. What happened?'

'You were mugged. Did he take your bag?' I could see no sign of one.

'No.' A quilted pouch on a chain hung over her shoulder. I bent to pick up her shoes.

'We must call the police. I live just here. If we go in, the porter can phone.' I indicated the door of my building just in front of us.

'Yes, I'll go home.' She had not understood me. She staggered and I put my arm around her again. I opened the front door and saw Victor, the night porter, sitting behind his desk in the warmly lit entrance hall. He stood up, his worn face like an old leather jacket, creased into an expression of concern.

'Miss Bennet. Mr Ochterlonie.'

'Could you call the police, Victor. There's just been a mugging outside our door here. Will you sit down?' I tried to lead her to the sofa beside the gas fire.

'No, no, I'll go up.'

I had by now realised I was dealing not with a passer-by, but a neighbour in my own block, whom I had never seen in all the years my mother had lived here, nor in my own few months' tenure. She made for the lifts.

'Will you phone, Victor?' I said over my shoulder. The doors closed and she began to sag, leaning heavily against me, her head hanging down. I was afraid that she was more severely injured than I had first thought and I wished I had asked Victor to call an ambulance as well.

'Fourth,' she said.

I pressed the button for my own floor. By the time we had arrived she was moaning softly on every out-breath.

'Here.' She produced a key from the pocket of her coat. I dropped the high-heeled shoes and unlocked the door opposite my own.

'Is there an alarm?'

'No.' She was gasping now. 'I don't bother.'

The door swung inwards and with my free hand I groped for the

18

light switch. My companion, in one movement, shrugged off her fur coat and me. Stepping forward into her home, she fell headlong once again. She was wearing black trousers and some kind of dark top, so only when I knelt beside her and put my hand on her prostrate body, was I aware of the soaking blood, its colour concealed by the dark clothing.

The next few hours were occupied by the ambulance, the casualty department, the police. I filled in forms on her behalf with an authority born of two minutes' conversation with Victor, out of whom I managed to squeeze her name.

'Miss Julian Bennet,' he had said as we waited for the stretcher to come down the stairs. 'She's lived in that flat for about three or four years now. She used to go and see your mum, do a bit of shopping for her when she wasn't feeling too good. I'd've thought you'd've met her.'

Even at the time I wondered why I was getting myself involved. Once she had been loaded into the ambulance, I could have waited for the police at home, sunk in my own armchair with a glass of brandy to soothe the shock. Why I accompanied her to the hospital, I could not explain.

I did not leave until she had come out of the operating theatre. I met the usual reluctance of professionals to commit themselves to an opinion. Eventually, I captured the nurse with stout calf muscles and ham-like hands who had first dealt with her, cutting off the remains of the blood-soaked top. There was a knife wound in her right side, she told me. She had lost a lot of blood. It was nothing to fuss about. It was simply a question of sewing her up and pumping her full of new blood. She would be out of theatre soon and then they would be able to tell me more. And so I waited longer, until I heard she was in the recovery room and would be put on a ward in the morning.

In the meantime a policeman came in the early hours of the morning to interview me. We sat in the entrance hall. Teams of lifts moved silently up and down, occasionally arriving at the ground floor, opening their doors for a second or two before closing themselves on emptiness and rising to an inaudible summons. I had never had anything to do with the police in my life, not even a motoring offence, and at this stage suspicion and guilt had not entered my consciousness. I was willing to be helpful, as long as I was put to no special trouble. I had nothing to conceal. So when things went less than well, it was not from any defensiveness on my part.

His tone was adversarial. I found my initial neutrality hardening into dislike which focused on his appearance and voice. He was short and stocky with thick curly brown hair. His voice, corrected Sarf London, had a tough, sceptical tone. He could see I was not telling the truth. But the truth I was not telling had nothing to do with Miss Bennet and the crime. The 'truth' about why I had been standing on the edge of the square that evening was impossible to tell: it was the whole history of dinner with Prisca, Sholto's school, Emily's defection. So I just said, unconvincingly, that I was enjoying the fresh air.

He stared at me incredulously. 'Fresh air? At eleven o'clock at night?'

'More or less.'

'The black car. Remember the number plate?'

'No.' That was not the kind of thing I ever noticed, let alone remembered.

'It was a BMW?'

'I thought so. But, you know, at night . . . I wasn't concentrating on it. It didn't seem important. Until afterwards.'

'The jogger. Did he wear a hat? What sort of clothes? Jeans? Track suit? What sort of trainers?'

'Yes, a ski hat, at least, he could have had a hat, or dark hair.' I struggled to recall. 'I can only tell you he wasn't bald and he wasn't blond. His head was dark.' The jogger reran his track in my memory. I could only see speed and force. 'He was fit,' I said. 'He ran well, fast.'

As an observer, I was a failure, a wilful one. My record became more suspicious when I denied all knowledge of Miss Bennet.

'She used to do errands for your mum, your porter says. And you'd never even heard of her.'

'No.' There was no point in explaining.

'And you've lived there how long?'

I counted. 'Four months.' Since Emily threw me out and took over the Holland Park house.

'And in that time you never once saw her, never shared a lift with her?'

'No.'

He looked at me belligerently. I stared back.

When I got back I found Victor had turned off the ceiling lights in the entrance hall, which was now only lit by his desk lamp and a light by the fire, where he was reading a paperback. He took off his reading glasses as soon as I came in.

'You stayed a long time, sir. I rang to find out how she was.'

'What did they say? They may have told you more than me.'

'Oh, she'd had an emergency operation and was comfortable now.'

I sat down wearily in the sofa on the other side of the fire. The building had been refurbished some five years ago and at that time the hall had been fitted out like a miniature country house hotel, with a gas fire and masses of chintz.

'What exactly happened out there, sir?' Victor asked.

'She was mugged by a jogger.'

'But the blood. Where did that blood come from?'

'She was stabbed.'

'They're trying to kill her.' He was more upset than I had at first realised.

'There was only one man, Victor.' Then I remembered the BMW. 'No, you're right, there were three of them. Who would want to kill her?' I asked rhetorically. 'Who is she? How is it that I've never heard of her, never seen her in all these years?'

'I can't account for that. Once seen never forgotten, it's true. But you're always very absorbed. And they were always very keen on

21

their privacy. But she's going to be all right?' He was genuinely anxious.

'Oh, yes.' It was the first time it had occurred to me to think of his feelings. With his mask-like politeness and inscrutable black face beneath his grey crinkled head, his personality was impossible to assess. I looked down at his shoes. He had a dandyish streak, for they were expensive loafers, with tassels.

'And it was just a mugging?'

'Yes, what else could it be?'

'Nothing, sir.'

The whites of his eyes were beige, as if the deep brown of the irises had somehow leaked out. He gazed defiantly back at me. I was not going to learn from him who Miss Bennet was, nor who might want to kill her. I dragged myself out of the sofa.

'Goodnight, Victor.'

3

The evening following the mugging I was due to deliver the first of the Coulounieix lectures at London University. I had been preparing them, off and on, for the last year, and my preoccupation with them had, I suppose, obscured the signs of Emily's disenchantment with me.

The lectures are given bi-annually, usually by philosophers, and it was unusual to invite someone like me who spanned the world of art history, psychology and medicine. Strictly speaking, I am not an academic, though during this time I held the post of visiting professor of History of Art at the University of London. When pushed to define my occupation, as, for example, on a passport application form, I call myself a writer, for writing is how I spend the bulk of my time, though it does not provide the bulk of my income. I trained as a doctor, a profession that seemed socially useful, which was my ambition when young. However, I was distracted from my aim by psychology, in which I specialised after completing my training. I studied questions of vision and perception, which directed my attention to art, where we have an external rendering of an internal vision, a point of access to what others see. I'm interested in the physical processes in the brain that allow artists to deceive the eye in order to produce three-dimensional effects in a two-dimensional space; and in the symbolic and associative codes by which the mind endows chosen objects with significance.

I was also drawn to art because my great-grandfather and my

grandfather had been among the great British collectors of the nineteenth century. They had been newly-moneyed men and had concentrated on modern styles of painting.

Their collection is a mixed one. My great-grandfather was very taken by Loiseau, a minor Impressionist whose work has never been as highly regarded as his fellows'. Nonetheless, they admired and bought Monet, Matisse, Cezanne. They began collecting in the 1880s and continued through to the 'thirties. The First World War gave a boost to the family fortune, which resumed its growth in the 1940s, allowing my father to indulge his expensive enthusiasm for American art. I grew up with paintings and the visual arts made a natural focus for my work.

While shaving that morning, I found it difficult to concentrate on my lecture because clips of the previous evening replayed themselves in disconnected bursts.

The fur-coated woman, her arms folded around herself, walked into the square. This time, in memory, I noticed that her stride was too long, even in high heels, for her to have been the elderly lady I had taken her for. Preconception had interpreted vision. The black BMW saloon passed me, once, twice. As the driver braked to turn right, only one rear light appeared. I hadn't recalled that detail for the police last night. Had I made it up? Was the mind re-interpreting vision after the event, too? I leaned forward to the mirror and felt the stiffness in my shoulder where it had hit the rear bumper of the parked Ford. I saw not my own face but Julian Bennet's, once seen never forgotten, as Victor had said. This clip was a still, in black and white, a Magnum photograph rather than a movie. Tricks of the light, deceiving the eye, leaching the colour from the face, blackening the hair, eyes and mouth, making a two-dimensional image of a three-dimensional person.

What I was about to become involved in with Julian I had no possibility of guessing beforehand. The lectures were another matter. I knew that they would be controversial, indeed, I wanted them to be provocative. I anticipated it would be my theoretical exposition that would excite interest, but it produced nothing like the passion that was fired by an example I only interpolated at the very last minute, as the result of a chance sighting that day.

The lecture was to be delivered at six in the evening in the Senate House. I had arranged to see Minna Horndeane, the director of the Litvak Foundation, in the middle of the afternoon. I arrived a quarter of an hour early and when I learned that Minna was out, I decided, rather than wait in the secretary's cramped office, to look at the pictures in the gallery.

The Foundation had been established in the 1940s; its core works had come from Germany in the 'thirties, retrieved, along with his family and his fortune, by a German Jew who had been lucky enough to get a visa to escape. After the war he had endowed the Foundation with the lease of his attractive Mayfair house, his collection of seventeenth-century paintings, silver and textiles. It had evolved into an important centre for research, in the forefront of technical developments for restoration. The collection was not large, but it was particularly fine, containing three Rembrandts, survivors of the scrutiny of the Rembrandt Research Project which has rejected so many of the master's works in the last few years, a Rubens, a Vermeer, among other favourites.

I went down with the intention of looking at a Pieter van den Bergh and found it had been moved from the position it had occupied when I last examined it several years ago. As I wandered idly through the neighbouring rooms, not bothering to ask where it had gone, I came across another painting which had moved, the Vermeer, *Lady in a Pelisse*.

The little picture glowed, hanging alone on its own wall. I hardly need to describe it, the image is so well known. It shows the head and shoulders of a woman who is turning her head over her left shoulder, gazing directly at the viewer, with a faintly questioning expression. One hand is raised to her breast, holding the lapels of the eponymous jacket together, revealing the underside of the reveres. The air is filled by a cold, clear light falling through an

25

invisible window on the left side of the panel. The handling of the paint produces a soft luminosity, which seems to surround the woman on all sides. Tiny dabs of paint along her nose, on the fullness of the lower lip, on the pearl in her ear, give a vibrant radiance to the painting. The pelisse is of golden brown silk and the light glosses it and picks out fine individual strands of its fur lining, so that they shine like gold wires. All the recognised qualities of the painter are there.

In its new position, literally seen in a new light, the picture had a different aspect. Had it been cleaned, I wondered. It was stupendously beautiful, and yet, and yet . . . I felt uneasy, as if a trick was being played on me. The woman's gaze was too limpid, too innocent. There was something wrong. I stepped closer, to search for a reason for my gut feeling and noticed the coarseness of the brush strokes on the face, the uncharacteristic clumsiness of the rendering of the hand.

A heavy footstep could be heard. I turned from Vermeer's harmonious world, now dissonant, to see Minna Horndeane. I glanced at my watch.

'Minna, am I late? I was distracted by your pictures.'

'Not late yet,' Minna said. 'But I decided not to let you be. I've a busy afternoon ahead.'

I had known Minna for years and our relationship had always been amicable but not close, partly because she was a good twenty years older than me and partly because I was not beholden to her. She was an example of a female academic of her generation, extremely clever, probably cleverer than most of her male contemporaries, with the self-confidence to back her artistic judgements. She had adopted the strategy of androgyny, you could almost say drag, and wore grey suits and black brogues. Her cuboid body was topped with a wild brush of brindled curls. She was often seen in the company of her dog, Berenson. I am not sure of his breed; with his rough grey-brown coat, deep bark and overpowering personality, he was uncannily like his owner.

The Art of Deception

Minna was by now extremely eminent, almost pre-eminent, among art historians in London. She belonged to a certain generation and the radical interdisciplinary interpretations of the feminist or social anthropological schools had barely penetrated her consciousness. Yet she was still highly honoured for her extensive and often pioneering work in the past and for her power. She sat on the boards of museums and government heritage committees. She had produced throughout her working life a steady stream of publications, including one major three-volume work on Dutch genre painting of the Golden Age. She had also developed a highly regarded postgraduate seminar at the Foundation. In this way she knew generations of young art historians, had hand-picked many of those who had continued in the discipline, whether as academics or with the great sales houses. She and her ex-pupils formed a powerful clique in the art world. In short, Minna was a formidable woman, important to placate, dangerous to offend. As I have explained, I came to art history in an indirect fashion, through medicine and psychology and through my family's art collection. I did not need Minna's patronage, but nor did I want to antagonise her.

She led me away from the *Lady in a Pelisse*, saying, 'You've just been visiting my favourite, I see.'

'I was looking for the van den Bergh *Courtesan* which you've rehung.'

'A long time ago. It shows how often you come here, Nicholas.'

We had reached the lift and stepped inside, joining a slight man, carrying an elegant leather folder under one arm. He had a thick head of wavy grey hair and a distinguished face, with flaring, up-cut nostrils. The doors slowly closed on us, trapping us uncomfortably close within the steel box.

'Do you two know one another?' Minna said in her abrupt manner. 'Nicholas Ochterlonie; Anthony Watendlath. He's come from America to be my deputy. He's a great computer man, wants my job.'

Her remarks, unintelligible in detail, were eloquent about the state of relations between them. We acknowledged the introduction with

27

nods. He so studiously refused the initiative that I wondered if they were on speaking terms.

'How are the applications going?' Minna went on. 'Anthony's starting up an undergraduate course.' Still no reply from her deputy.

'Remind me, Minna,' I said, to fill in the awkward pause, 'of the provenance of the Vermeer.'

Scholars on the whole have slow reactions. They take time to absorb new material, working out the implications for their own ideas. My enquiry was, I suppose, an implicit questioning of Minna's favourite, but it was voiced in the most casual way. Her reaction was one of rage, impressive for its immediacy and disproportionate force. Her broad face, too close to mine, became even more florid.

'You're wrong,' she said. 'All those questions were settled years ago. No one, but no one, has queried that picture in thirty years.'

I saw Watendlath looking drily from her to me and back. He smiled, a reverse smile, formed by turning down the corners of his mouth.

The doors opened on the fifth floor. Watendlath ostentatiously permitted me to precede him out of the lift. Minna marched ahead, shouldering open the door to her office. Berenson was lying beneath his mistress's desk. He got up, wagging his tail in foolish amiability. Long-practised, I warded him off as he rushed forward to thrust his nose into my genitals. Minna accepted his greeting, patting his rough head, and sat down heavily, regarding me masterfully from behind the desk.

'I'm telling you, Nicholas, not to start on this.'

'Minna, I'm not starting on anything. I just asked where the picture came from. Let's leave it. I can look up the literature any time.'

She did not look mollified and our meeting, about something quite different, a conference to be held in Moscow the following year, did not pass compliantly.

That evening I gave my first lecture. As usual, the Coulounieix committee gave a drinks party beforehand to open the series, and many of the eminent and even the smart turned up. Probably because of the events of the previous night, I felt more than usually detached from what was going on around me. I shook hands in a vague professorial way with people who had crowded into the hall in the Senate House to drink warm white wine. Fortunately, my sense of experiencing everything at long range diminished once I stood at the podium and looked around the lecture hall. The semi-circular tiers were well filled. My cousin Jamie and his wife, Sibyl, were there in support. I saw Anthony Watendlath settling, with a look of bright expectation, into one of the seats on the front row, which are always the last to be filled in English lecture halls. Just before I began, Prisca swept in and joined him there. No Minna.

The *Lady in a Pelisse* must have made a deeper impression than I realised, coalescing with other questions of identity, of another woman in a fur coat, playing one of those mental tricks that artists exploit. For as I was speaking, I saw how my reaction to the picture illustrated a point about the visual judgement of a work of art. It was a passing example, an unscripted remark, when one looks up from one's notes for longer than usual in order to speak directly to the audience, fixing one's eyes on a particular face. I could not see the one I was looking for.

'. . . Take the Vermeer in the Litvak Foundation that we all know so well. When we look at it, are we really seeing what we think we see? Do we revere it because of the label attached to it or for what it is? Is it by Vermeer, or someone else and if the latter, does it matter, in the aesthetic sense, rather than the financial, of course. It is this question which, with the growth of popular culture in this century has teased artists in producing and reproducing: Marilyn Monroe, cartoons, baked bean cans . . .'

Because it was delivered in this manner, it was not part of my text and I could never remember afterwards exactly what I had said. But what I had meant and what had been understood was clear: the *Lady in a Pelisse* was not what it was believed to be. I moved on to the rest of my discourse, thinking no more about it.

4

The lecture was over. It had been well received and I was almost satisfied with it myself, but I needed someone with whom to share my triumph. As I dropped my keys into the drawer of the hall table in my mother's flat, a loose key, a stranger, fell with the others. As soon as I saw it, I knew what it was. I remembered slipping it awkwardly into my pocket as I pushed open the door of the flat opposite, just before my companion stumbled out of my arms and onto the floor. I picked it up again, resolving to go down later and give it to Victor, or at least ask him who was in charge across the landing.

As I moved around the flat, turning on lights, the television, pouring myself a drink, I was aware of the key in my pocket. After I had eaten, I telephoned the hospital to ask after Miss Bennet. At last, I let myself out of the flat. On the landing, in front of the lift, I hesitated, though I don't know why. I had intended all along to do it.

I am a prudent man and I began by ringing the doorbell, twice. I could hear its sound within, but no answering footsteps. This precaution taken, I inserted the key into the lock and opened the door.

The hall was dark, but a lamp shone in the corner of an adjoining room. I stepped in and closed the door behind me. I found myself in a large space rising to double height, with a gallery on the floor above, reached by an open, curving staircase. The previous night I had not had time to observe that it was furnished with statues, each of exceptional quality. There was a boddhisatva with a tranquil moon

31

face standing almost four feet tall to welcome new arrivals. On a plinth was a pregnant woman sitting cross-legged, carved in smooth, dark green marble. I stroked each one suspiciously, unwilling to believe that they were what they appeared to be.

I walked through an archway into the drawing room and in the half-light I could only make out certain details: a Turkey carpet in ruddy pinks, large sofas, a glass coffee table, a huge vase of lilies like sculpture, a marble fireplace and gilt mirror above it. The room was conventional enough. What lifted it above what could be expected in every other drawing room in the block was the painting on the inside wall above one of the sofas. The vibrant colours of Matisse were unmistakable.

I saw that an area the equivalent of double my mother's flat had been completely opened out and redefined. The design was excellent and there were some superb pieces. Or were they copies? Doubt assailed me, at seeing so much in one room. The place had been put together by someone with a passion for colour and a strong sense of space and mass. There was, however, something synthetic about the whole, as if one had stepped into a stage set, the falseness lying not so much in its inauthenticity as its theatricality.

When I had opened the door I had meant to learn what I could about the beautiful Julian Bennet by peering into her flat. I had almost forgotten about her in the interest of the apartment itself and I could see no reason, now I had made the first step into the forbidden, to halt in the entrance hall.

After visiting the kitchen and dining room, like a tourist in a National Trust house, I started up the stairs to the gallery. The first room I came to was an office. A computer sat blankly on the desk with its modem and fax. Filing cabinets were marshalled along the walls, with shelves of box files above them. I could gain no idea of what business was carried on there from loose papers or jottings on the telephone pad, faxes recently arrived: there were none. Everything was filed away with fanatical neatness. I only glanced around, before walking back along the gallery to the bedrooms, flicking on lights with the confidence of a resident. Even here, I was glad to see, whoever had designed the place had not lost his grip. The first room was strongly coloured (a rather acid blue-green, that I was not sure I could sleep with) and contained one important piece of furniture (an inlaid French bed with scrolled ends placed lengthways to the wall). The second bedroom contained a tallboy with oval medallions on the doors and, as I saw when I looked inside, a magnificent array of drawers and pigeon holes.

I opened the final door, which I took to be Julian Bennet's own bedroom, with some anticipation. I had no chance to admire the decoration, for the first thing I saw was a naked man lying face-down on the bed, asleep. The room was not lit, but the curtains were undrawn, so light from the square lay across the room, drawing it in black and white.

I am not someone who is stimulated by shock or fear. Instead, I become icy cold, slower in my movements while my brain races. I began my retreat immediately, with great care. At the same time I observed all the details of the scene. He was a tall man, as tall as me, with fine pale hair and very white skin. He was thin, with hollows on the outer curve of each buttock. One knee was drawn up, the foot tense, about to kick out. I could not see his face at all. His arms were thrown above his head, his hands loosely rolled into fists. Clothes were strewn around the room, as if he had torn them off and thrown himself down: a leather jacket, a pair of black jeans. Even his watch lay on the floor beside the bed. I retreated from the room backwards, not taking my eyes off him, as if by looking at him I could compel his unconsciousness.

Closing the front door, I remembered the rectangular box on the bedside table, with a tongue of foil sticking out from between the open cardboard flaps. He must have taken a sleeping pill, which had obliterated the natural defences of recognition of unaccountable noise. I stood innocently in front of the lift, feeling my heart beating above its normal rate and my breathing more rapid than usual.

Downstairs, Victor was reading his book. I laid the key in front of him.

'I held onto this last night. Is there anyone I should give it to?'

He made no attempt to touch it. 'I don't know who it'd be.' We looked at the object between us. 'If I was you, I'd keep it and hand it back to her when she comes out of hospital. You're as trustworthy as anyone.'

I picked it up again. Did Victor know about the man asleep in her bedroom? Had his discretion reached the point of complete non-involvement? And if so, why, in this case? He had always revealed himself so helpful to my poor mother. A guarded expression descended on his face when I asked him directly if there was anyone else living there.

'No,' he said without hesitation. 'She's alone. There's no one else there.'

'Has anyone enquired after her?' I asked. 'Any family who should be told?' He stared back at me.

'No one, sir.' Then, as if he could not prevent himself from asking, 'Any news, is there?'

'I phoned this morning and they said she was comfortable. Whatever that means. They never tell you much, hospitals.'

'No, well, they can't be too careful. You never can tell, can you?'

His conventional phrases seemed loaded with significance that evening. His expression was bland, refusing to know.

That experience, my first essay into if not criminal, at least dishonourable, behaviour, should have warned me to abandon my interest in Julian Bennet. I should have sent flowers to the hospital and returned to the comfortable London condition of not knowing my neighbour. If we had met in the lift from time to time we would have greeted one another as good friends, for people who have been through a mugging together are bound to feel a certain camaraderie. But nothing more than that was called for. And I did try to behave in this conventional fashion. I did not go again to the hospital, though I couldn't prevent myself from phoning daily to ask about her progress.

34

The Art of Deception

Looking back at this period, I ask myself where I stepped over the line, when did I cease to act reasonably. The key had tempted me. I took it and opened the door voluntarily. The action was not only wrong, it was unwise, but I could not stop myself. Time and again, in the weeks that followed, I made resolutions that I would not do something that was unreasonable. Yet I found myself, as if without my own volition, acting in ways quite contrary to my overt determination, as though a subterranean personality, with a force much stronger than my usual self, emerged at crucial moments and took over my actions. The first time that this happened, when I clandestinely entered Julian's flat, I told myself it was an aberration, which would never happen again. Far from being an aberration, it was the start of a pattern.

5

In the days immediately after my first Coulounieix lecture several people reacted to my comments on the *Lady in a Pelisse*. A curator from Edinburgh said in passing, as she congratulated me afterwards, that she, too, had always had doubts about the work and weren't there any tests. Anthony Watendlath rang me the next day to applaud my lecture and say that more work was needed on the Vermeer.

Minna had had her spies there. Who had reported to her with a summary of what I had said, including my unscripted remark about the Vermeer, I do not know. It could have been any one of the considerable number of her ex-students, fellow-trustees, -board and -committee members among the audience. Whether Minna took the next step herself or encouraged someone else to do it, again I never discovered. My cousin's wife, Sibyl, a sculptress and always well informed about the art world, alerted me to what had happened. She rang early the following week and I know the eagerness with which I answered the phone was not because I expected to hear my cousin's voice.

'You saw that piece in the *Standard*, about your lecture?'

'No.'

'It sounds as if you've done something to offend Minna Horndeane. What have you been up to?'

'What was it about, Sibyl? What did Minna say?'

'It was just one of those diary pieces, saying that you attacked London's favourite painting, the Vermeer, they call it *Girl in a Fur*,

37

"without rhyme or reason", yes, I promise you, "without rhyme or reason".' I could hear the disdainful quotation marks enclosing the cliché. 'Then they asked Minna for her opinion.' There was a rustling of newspaper. 'She says nothing to defend the picture; she just says, well basically, that you don't know what you're talking about.'

'Oh, to hell with Minna,' I said irritably. 'What's the *Standard* got to do with it?'

'What have you done to annoy her?'

'Nothing. It was that remark I made about the Vermeer in my lecture you came to.'

'I don't remember anything unduly outrageous that evening. I don't even remember anything about Vermeer.'

'You were probably asleep.'

'Very likely. I was only there to support you, darling; you know, in case no one else came. Anyway, I wanted to say, watch out for Minna. She didn't get where she is without fighting.'

So I had a choice. I had made an instinctive judgement about the painting which I could now try to validate and either prove to my own satisfaction that there were grounds for doubting the attribution, or that I was mistaken in my view and acknowledge it to Minna. Or I could retreat from the field, simply abandoning the question. There were plenty of reasons for doing so. I was already very busy; I had never before involved myself in a debate about authenticity. I knew that, in persisting in questioning the work, I was taking on a formidable woman. But this reasoning carried no weight. I wanted to know if I was right.

Judgement of the genuineness of a work of art is a complex business. In the first place authenticity is a concept which is not always useful. The painting may not be what it appears or purports to be, but the fallacy is interesting in itself, whether it lies in a forger's intention to deceive or in the viewer's wish to see what he desires. This area, lying close to my work on perception, has always been of interest to me. However, I was now not concerned with what the mind, subjectively, made of the picture but with the scientific evidence that objectively supported its identity.

Such proof falls into two categories, historical provenance and scientific analysis. Once the supposed artistic quality of the work is put on one side and the baggage of association, mythical, religious, sexual and poetic, is discarded, the treatment of the object should be purely forensic. However, only in exceptional and fortunate cases can the history of a work of art be traced without doubt, from its source to the present day. Painstaking historical research is needed to trace its passage in contracts and wills, bills of sale and bankruptcy papers, inventories and travelogues.

For most paintings, documentary references, often uncertain ones, have to be supplemented by scientific analysis to produce a balance of probability, which is combined with the experience and judgement of the critic. However, scientific tests promise more than they can deliver in many cases. Experts argue about the interpretation of the data. They do not even agree on some of the basic criteria. One will say that a certain pigment was not used before or after a certain date; another will insist it was. So its presence or absence need not necessarily prove conclusive.

The forger has existed as long as men have valued art and when there is an abundance of money in the hands of wealthy patrons, private or public, there will be forgers willing to supply them with what they are looking for. Museums have sometimes spent millions on a work that later has had to be quietly transferred to the basement, with its label removed.

A modern forger's purpose is straightforward: to deceive for financial gain. All the scientific techniques of analysis are available for him to bend to his contrary purpose. He can use old panels and scrape down old canvases. He can mix his paints according to ancient receipts. However, earlier painters had less mercenary motives for doing much the same thing as the forger, copying masterpieces. Artists themselves, their studios and followers, often made copies of admired paintings, with no thought of fraud. Authenticity is a spectrum that runs from a Leonardo fresco, still on the wall for which it was commissioned, to a Tom Keating forgery. One is undeniably what it is meant to be, the other painted to deceive. On the line between these points come many stages: the honest copy, restoration, touching up, adding new to old, fusing two separate works. A large space is left for disagreement in which the reliability of scientific tests, as well as artistic judgement, can be violently disputed and the reputations of academics and the prestige of museums are at stake. This would be the battlefield on which Minna and I would be fighting. And it was war. Her campaign, which had begun with the *Standard* diary article, was getting out of hand.

There were two more articles, in the *Standard* and the *Mail*, and then a longer and much more reasoned piece appeared in one of the weekend broad sheets, discussing how a painting, like the *Lady in a Pelisse* becomes an icon, rather than examining its authenticity. Newspapers love a forgery or misattribution. There are wonderful opportunities to mock authority for wasting public money on a worthless square of canvas, and for being caught out by a con. However, in this case there was little to be done on these lines. The painting had been in the public domain for decades and had been a gift, too. So no one had been fooled, at least recently, and no public money wasted. There was no incentive to ask any questions. The article ended with a brief paragraph on the question of attribution, personalising it into rivalry between Minna and me. She was depicted, approvingly, as the clear voice of traditional scholarship, while I was a dilettante media 'personality' bringing the fuzzy thinking of psychology and relative values to the matter. This was an infuriating distortion. It was I, after all, who was looking for scientific clarification of the hazy view of connoisseurship. I was irritated, too, by the inverted commas, which suggested a fraudulent claim on my part.

I spent a day in the Courtauld Library gathering references to the literature that accumulates around any work of art, discussing its physical and metaphysical properties. I had imagined that a painting belonging to the Litvak, an institute of world reputation, must have an impeccable provenance, a virginal past accounted for in every detail, or, at the very least, a respectable history. My reading suggested that this was not the case. The *Lady in a Pelisse* had only appeared on the scene in the 1920s and had been acquired from a 'private collection' by the fashionable Parisian dealer, Schall. He had sold the work to Litvak; that was all there was to it.

Here another warning bell rang. Between the wars Schall had been one of the great dealers. Only in the 'fifties had the genuineness of his old masters been questioned. Some of them, five I could recollect, and three of them Dutch masters of the seventeenth century, had been exposed, not simply as misattributions, but outright frauds. The fact that he had been misled, like other experts, did not necessarily make him a cheat. But few other dealers had so high a score of forgeries, suggesting he was particularly unlucky, particularly unskilful or had his own supplier of fakes.

There were no scientific data, as far as I could see, and all discussion so far had been based on historical and aesthetic discrimination: old-fashioned connoisseurship. In the past the question of judgement often had a moralistic tone to it. Can you recognise an authentic Vermeer, or are you taken in by the meretricious imitation of a minor artist? Can you recognise integrity in a fellow human being or are you deceived by a deceitfully beautiful face?

It was at this point that I made my decision to continue with my research. I had doubts about the painting on stylistic grounds; it had passed through the hands of a questionable dealer; there was no scientific support for its date or attribution. I had seen how lightweight was the evidence that permitted the Foundation to attach the label of 'Jan Vermeer of Delft' to the painting. It was enough, it seemed, that an authoritative person said so for everyone to accept the declaration.

6

I made a point of asking Victor every evening if there was any news of Julian's return. One evening later that week he looked up from his book when I came in.

'She's back,' he said.

The next morning I scribbled a note to congratulate her on her return from hospital. I had planned what I would do that evening, but my excuse of delivering her key was redundant. When I opened my door, I found a message with her telephone number, asking me to ring her when I was free to allow her to thank me, et cetera. I had no objection to being thanked, et cetera. The key lay on the hall table, waiting to be redeemed. I picked it up and rang her doorbell.

Seeing her again, this time in normal circumstances, confirmed those first disjointed impressions I had received at the time of the attack. Although she was not strictly beautiful because she lacked symmetry, she was enormously beguiling in both appearance and personality. Her face, with its strong jaw and full mouth was uneven in its expression. When she smiled one corner of her mouth stretched wider than the other; when she laughed, one eyebrow rose higher.

She led me through the hall, which was lit by lamps trained on each of the statues, to the drawing room where a fire burned. As she poured us both a drink, I noticed only a slight stiffness in her movements and a precaution in lowering herself into her chair. She evidently wished to make light of what had happened to her.

'It was mad,' she said. 'I was hurt because I held onto my bag. I know in theory you should give them anything they want in order to save your skin. But I didn't have time to act reasonably. By instinct, I clutched my bag closer. I was damned if anyone was going to take it away from me. Insane. Do you know what it contained? About fifty pounds in cash, my credit cards and a lipstick. All this to save fifty pounds.'

So it was settled between us: it was a failed bag-snatch, the motive: money. The idea that someone was trying to kill her was absurd, a product of Victor's nervous imagination.

I looked round at the room I had explored a few days earlier. No reference had been made to a husband or partner, but the masculine style of the furnishings confirmed my illicit knowledge of the other occupant. You would not assume that the owner was a single woman. I leaned back to look at the double height of the hall and said, 'Your flat is a stunning contrast to my own. I had somehow assumed that all the apartments in this block were as old-fashioned as mine.'

'Your flat suited your mother very well, though I can imagine you might feel a bit out of place in it.'

'Have you been here long?'

'About four years. I bought two apartments, one above the other, and put them together. I did them myself, about three years ago.'

'You designed them?'

'Yes. It's my profession: I'm an interior designer.'

'Ah, well, that explains it then.' In fact, it explained nothing. It did not explain the Hepworth statue or the Matisse on the wall behind her, which drew my eyes upward when I felt I had been staring too fixedly at her. When I left, I realised that I had told her all about myself without receiving any information in return. Nor had I given back her key. I hesitated on the landing, wondering whether to knock on the door that had just closed and decided it would be importunate. There would be another opportunity.

But seeing your neighbour in a London apartment block is not a casual matter, as I had proved, so I had to invent excuses to see her again. Calls about her health provided the occasions I needed over the next week. I asked her advice on what to do with my mother's flat. I was perfectly capable of deciding what I needed, but that was not the point. She came and listened to my ideas, but evinced no eagerness for the commission. I asked her what she was working on; she replied vaguely that she had just finished a project in Paris, for 'a friend'.

'I don't do anything in a big way,' she said, 'just for people I know.' She paused, then said, 'I started off wanting to be an architect and I began the training, but I dropped out.'

We fell into the habit of having a drink together in the evening, usually in her flat, several times a week. This was not simply by my manoeuvring. Very often she would say as I left, 'What about Wednesday, about eight?' It was never a matter of more than an hour or so and never more than a drink. She didn't suggest dinner and indeed didn't look like the sort of woman who cooked very much. If we didn't meet for a drink, we would call one another in the late afternoon and talk for fifteen or twenty minutes.

I didn't think too hard about what I intended at this stage, although I expected to return to Emily and the children eventually. But Emily, even though she was apparently living a chaste life herself, could hardly be surprised, after the way she had behaved, if I found some temporary companionship elsewhere. As for Julian: she was beautiful, I found her deeply desirable, and she seemed as eligible as it was possible to be: unattached, independent. I refused to think about the mysterious knife attack, the man in her bed or any of the other indications that stated as clearly as possible that she was dangerous to know.

I wanted to know her and to know about her. The former was not so difficult, I thought. Given enough time with someone you quickly build up the pattern of her character. To know about her was more difficult. Her origins and her past did not feature in our conversation. Information of provenance isn't necessary, but it is usually exchanged in the early stages of a relationship, to authenticate and solidify it.

Julian contributed nothing. She existed now, without a past, without a future. Our conversations were always about the present. My one useful discovery was that she was passionately musical and went to concerts every week. I am tone deaf, but I was even prepared to face opera in order to spend an evening with her.

Oddly, I thought, in the light of his reticence about her, she had a close interest in Victor. She reported to me almost daily on what he had told her about his family life: it was a living soap opera, an unending human interest story. He lived, it appeared, in an all-female household. His partner, his woman Julian called her, was white. His daughter shared their house, living there with her little girl. The daughter and the woman did not get on. They gave Victor hell, Julian reported.

Since she told me nothing about herself, I was forced to look elsewhere for information. I could find no one we knew in common, apart from my mother and Victor. Since my mother was not available for questioning, I was forced once again to try Victor. This was no more of a success than my previous efforts. I am not the sort of person who chats to taxi drivers and porters and receives confidences about their lives, as Julian was. Before I met her, I had never exchanged more than a few words with Victor, on the weather or cricket results. I had difficulty, too, in framing my questions. What does she do? I wanted to ask. Where did she come from? Who does she sleep with? Who *is* she?

I took my opportunity to speak to him when I returned late one evening. There was no one about and he was reading his paperback with his usual absorption. His response to my questions, which obliquely paraphrased what I really wanted to know, was strange. He fidgeted, riffling the top edge of the pages.

'Mr Ochterlonie,' he said, his eyes cast down, not meeting mine. 'It's better not to ask, do you see what I mean?' He glanced up and, seeing my surprise, continued, 'I don't mean anything against her. She's a very nice lady, very friendly and considerate. It's not that. But people here like their privacy. That's why they live here.'

'Ok, Victor.' I picked up my umbrella, which I had leaned against his desk. 'I just wondered. It's, er, nice to know something about one's neighbours.'

'No, you didn't mean that, sir.' I looked even more surprised. 'I know what you mean. But some people pay us extra, a tip, know what I mean, not to talk to no one. No journalists, no fans, no one.'

'I quite understand, Victor. I shouldn't have asked you. Goodnight.'

'Goodnight, sir.' I had started across the hall towards the lift when he added unexpectedly, 'Watch how you go.'

I tried making enquiries about her among my friends, but the world of interior design was not one I had ever had much to do with. No one I knew who employed interior decorators had heard of her, and none of their pet decorators knew her either. What I learned at this stage came from Julian herself, as the result of a comment about her unusual name.

'I invented it.'

'But why Julian?'

'I had, well, I suppose you could call it a religious upbringing, so I knew about Julian of Norwich. And it seemed to fit. It was optimistic, determined, or it could be made so in a secular sense.'

'*All will be well. All manner of things will be well,*' I quoted.

'Yes, that sort of thing. I was determined that all would be well, for me at least. And it was close to the original.'

'And what was that?'

'Can't you guess? Impossible to live with. Julie Anne, I'm afraid.'

I felt that I was failing in my technique of seduction, or rather attraction, for women are not seduced nowadays. From the start we fell into a pattern of companionableness and I realised that it was going to be hard for me to develop this along the lines I had in mind. I was out of practice. It was twelve years since I had married Emily and since then I had been a faithful husband. Winning Emily had been easy. She had been young and impressionable. I was much older than her, experienced, rich. None of these advantages worked with Julian. She was admittedly much younger than me, about Emily's

47

age, but she was not easily impressed and was evidently very well off herself. No friendship between a man and a woman is without its sexual element, I suppose, and most social arrangements go to diffusing such attraction. The problem now was how to concentrate it. Julian seemed glad of friendship of an easy, conversational kind and made no signals, apart from ones that were implicit in her beauty, of requiring more.

We might have gone on for some time like this. I became more and more reluctant to make a pass, for fear that it would put an end to something that still looked promising, if distantly so, and that I valued for itself. She filled the period in the evening that had been taken up by Emily and the children, and I looked forward to the time spent with her with an eagerness that Sholto's homework and Cordelia's chatter never aroused, however devoted to them I was.

About six weeks after our original violent meeting the situation changed. I went, as usual, at about seven thirty for a drink in her flat. We talked for about an hour and just when I was on the point of leaving, she said. 'I'm starving. Shall we go and find something to eat?'

As a bachelor now, I had become an expert on all the restaurants in the neighbourhood. She was too, and ignoring my suggestions, she led me to one I had not found. Her cheerfulness evaporated as we walked. She seemed preoccupied and paid little attention to what I was saying. She stopped on a corner and turned to look back down the street we had just taken. I realised that there had been an echo, doubling our footsteps, and that this must have troubled her. Within two minutes the footsteps behind us reverberated again between the facades. Her pace picked up to reach the restaurant. I opened the door for her and when she had passed through, I dropped my hand onto her shoulder, feeling the bone through the fur coat, like an animal's moving under its pelt.

'Should you be wearing this?' I asked as I helped her off with her coat. 'It's sable, isn't it?' The fur coat was as beautiful and sexy as she was, of a particularly glowing dark brown, and she wore it like a living fleece, a part of her.

'You mean it's too grand for where we are?' The restaurant was small and crowded and had the atmosphere of a student haunt. The risk could not have been a new idea to her, but she looked at me as blankly as if it had never occurred to her that there might be those who disapproved of wearing fur, to the extent of using violence.

'Well, perhaps it is, but what I meant was, don't you risk a can of paint or abuse?'

I had not meant that either. The link in my mind, an entirely illogical one, was that if she hadn't worn the coat, she wouldn't be hunted herself.

'I don't think so. Round here.'

'This is exactly where you'd come, if you wanted to make a point.'

Emily disapproved of fur coats. She thought they were grannyish in any case. She was sentimental about animals and did not eat veal. Julian shrugged. Her coat was by no means grannyish.

'It's a risk. But I'm a risk-taker.'

'And does it worry you?'

We had been pointed to a small table and sat down at such close quarters to our neighbours that our elbows almost touched. I had forgotten such places existed. They had passed out of my consciousness with age and marriage. To follow Julian through the door, to be enveloped by the atmosphere, smoky with candles, was to return to the dark clubs and restaurants, smoky with cigarettes and dope, that I had frequented twenty-five years earlier. The contrast and the similarity with my pre-marital life were rejuvenating.

'You mean cruelty and all that?' Julian was looking at the menu. 'No, not at all. It's no different from wearing leather shoes or eating meat. I'm a natural carnivore. I'm going to have the ris de veau tonight.' Then she added inconsequentially. 'In any case, in cold places like Russia, you need furs to keep you warm.'

All the sensations of that evening come so vividly to my mind: Julian's ris de veau, creamy and succulent, lying on her plate and opposite it, my daube, glistening, dark and aromatic; her narrow hands lifting her fork to her mouth, revealing the inside of a wrist so

49

pale that I could trace a network of blue veins running up to her elbow.

When we made our way home, tension re-emerged. I felt the nervousness that entered her as a van, parked outside the restaurant, started its engine before we had reached the end of the street. She lengthened her stride, taking a less direct route home. Behind us, footsteps rang hollow on the pavement. She quickened her pace and darted along a pedestrian passage, cutting between two roads. She had her key ready to unlock the door without delay. All this took place without comment from either of us.

Once inside, she greeted Victor as if there had been nothing odd about our walk and made for the lift. I followed her closely.

'Julian, what was all that about?'

'Nothing. I'm just being stupid. Sometimes I'm nervous at night. I imagine things. It must be the effect of the mugging. I thought I'd settled everything.'

'Will you be all right? Let me come in and check the flat for you.'

'No one could possibly get in,' she said. 'We've got Victor on the door. I'm fine.'

We got out of the lift and the doors closed behind us, boxing us into the landing with out two front doors opposite one another.

Then she relented, 'But come in anyway.'

And once inside I found it was easy, as easy as when I was young. I took the key from her and relocked the door and passed the chain across. The air was full of the scent of lilies. She was standing on the spot where she had fallen on the first night. I took her in my arms and the fur slid beneath my fingers. It had a tremulous, silky warmth, as if it were alive. I kissed her and, although she responded with conviction, she still stood apart from me, her arms by her side, making no attempt to embrace me in her turn.

I put my hands inside the coat and pushed it off her shoulders onto the floor at her feet. As if she had been released, she stepped out of it and, taking my hand, led the way upstairs, along the corridor. She undressed at once, her clothes falling off her like leaves, much quicker than I could manage. She was naked and I could see how thin she was. Her shoulders, neck and wrists were attenuated, fragile, her breasts disproportionately large, with long dark-red nipples, the shape and colour of mulberries.

She was moving about, turning off a lamp, putting on the music by which she lived. She had taken control, which she was willing to hand back and share. This time she held me, putting her hands on my back, running them down my sides, drawing me into her. She was not soft, pliable, passive, someone whom you could sink into, to be enfolded and enveloped. Her skin was smooth and her body hard, with all the muscles, tendons, bones, making themselves felt below the surface. I groaned, my face in the hollow of her neck, as she fell forward onto me, and I heard for the first time her strange animal cry, like the mewing of a buzzard, or the yelp of a fox.

Sex is sex and its variety is not infinite and its detail is boring. What is strange, though, is why it works so extraordinarily well with one person and so dully with another. Thought of her filled my day, at my desk, in meetings and seminars, I would find myself recalling the side of her face, her mouth, the nape of her neck when her hair fell forward, exposing the vertebra like a victim on the scaffold. My fascination with Julian now came to comprehend a form of sexual obsession, a never-sated desire.

7

I learned no more about Julian once we had become lovers than I knew before. I never entered her flat except by invitation, nor she mine. However, now I had penetrated to the upper regions of her apartment, which I had secretly explored, and had certain rights there, if temporary ones, I could look for signs of that other man. But I found nothing. No shaving foam stood among her hairsprays and deodorants. No electric razor was tucked into any drawer that I opened, stealthily, when I went into the bathroom to pee or to shower.

One evening I was sitting beside the fire in her apartment waiting for her, when I saw on the table beside her chair an open box file crammed with papers. I sat down cautiously and crooked my head so that its contents came into view. Below the top two sheets of paper, bank statements, the address Geneva, lay a sheaf of photographs. They were of different sizes and looked as if they had been gathered up, unsorted, and pushed into the box to tidy them out of the way.

Brazenly, I lifted the pile from the box and shuffled through the photographs. They were all of one man, but not, curiously enough, the man I had already seen. This one was of different build, solider, older, about my own age, with a well cared for complacency radiating from his smile.

Julian descended, unheard, as I reached this point of analysis, or fabrication. Guilty, I made no attempt to hide the incriminating documents.

'So you're spying on me, too,' she said. I laid them down on the table; the face with its even teeth and moustachioed upper lip, unmoved at being caught in flagrante, smiled up at us.

'It's my job,' I said, 'I'm a psychologist and a historian. I'm researching you.'

'That's my past. He's an old boyfriend.'

'What's his name?'

I thought she might refuse to answer. Then, pulling on her fur coat, she replied, 'Anatoli. Let's go, Nick.'

So I learned his name and nothing more. I had to make what I could of it, just as I had to deduce what I could from her name. She was standing by the door with her keys ready. I replaced the photographs, slipping the last one into my pocket. She had started using her alarm and she was punching the code into the keyboard. With a Matisse on the wall and a Swiss bank account, she had a lot to lose.

We went to see a concert performance of *Otello* that night. The torrent of love and jealousy on stage must have reminded her about Victor's tempestuous home life, for she had another episode to tell me on our way back.

'Victor had a terrible weekend,' she said in the taxi. 'His daughter and his woman had a frightful row. They argued and shouted at one another all afternoon and, Josie, the daughter, deliberately smashed a set of plates that Victor and Mary bought when they went to Majorca.'

I tried to imagine a life in which disagreement resolved itself in the breaking of china, and failed.

'What did Victor do?'

'He watched the football. It was Arsenal versus Liverpool.'

'Did he mind?'

'Of course he minded. Not the plates and the noise, but the situation itself. You see, he adores his granddaughter. She's the love of his life. He's afraid that Josie will move out and take Rose with her.' We were drawing up outside our house. 'It's all right. I've got cash.' She was already flourishing a twenty-pound note.

Victor said goodnight to us with his usual impassivity. None of his intimate conversations with Julian took place in my presence. I looked at him furtively. He must know about Julian and me; I now knew about him. We hid our secret knowledge of one another.

On our common landing Julian turned automatically to her own door, saying, 'Goodnight, Nick.' She was turning her key in the lock. I put my arms around her. I heard a small intake of breath, but I had not caused it.

'The lights must have fused,' she was saying. 'Damn.'

I realised that there was no sound from the alarm.

'Let me find a torch.'

I had entered my own flat by now and was rummaging in the drawer of my mother's hall table for the torch that, with a timid precaution, she had always kept there for going out at night and other emergencies. Even before I had reached her with a light, Julian had realised that something was seriously wrong.

'I think there's been a break-in.'

The thread of light from the torch could not comprehend the destruction, the overturned furniture, the heaps of books that had been swept onto the floor.

'Wait.' Her voice sounded perfectly natural, detached. 'If our eyes can just get used to the dark, we'll manage better.'

'Where's the fuse box?'

'In the corridor outside the kitchen.'

'We need some light on this.'

To reach the kitchen corridor was impossible. The doors of the china cupboard had been opened and the contents poured on to the floor where they lay in a mountain of shards, wedging the door and preventing our passing. The frail beam revealed the door blocking our way. When I pushed it, the broken glass and porcelain grated in resistance.

I found an extension cord, which I ran from my flat to hers and Julian plugged in a lamp from which she had removed the shade. The undirected light radiated blindingly. She held it aloft to reveal an unimaginable chaos.

It was evident at once that this was no casual burglary. The arch between the hall and the drawing room was filled with upturned chairs. The sofas had been tipped forward, but not before all the cushions had been razored, so that there was a fall of feathers like snow on all the surfaces. Over and around these basic blocks of disorder, books, lamps, shades, ornaments lay jumbled. On top of them were papers, slithering down the slopes, fanning out from the crevices, one piece of computer paper balanced like a hanging rock on one of the summits. Oddly, in all this destruction, the works of art remained untouched. The Matisse still hung on the wall above the slaughtered sofa. The Hepworth I found, undamaged, beneath a heap cushions and papers. Julian's response was of preternatural calm.

'My God, what a mess,' she said.

'It is rather.' My reply sounded inadequate because my mind was already engaged in finding hypotheses to explain the attack. It was the counterpart of the mugging. The direction of the violence had been transferred from Julian herself to her creation, but the meaning of both was the same. It was a threat, perhaps, a punishment, or revenge. Only Julian herself could interpret what had happened. I bent down and lifted some of the papers.

'Why?' she said. 'Why would anyone want to do this? Why didn't they just take the video and run.'

'I don't think this was a burglary.'

'The first thing is to put the electricity on.'

'The first thing is to phone the police.'

'I suppose we have to. They'll take all night.'

'Certainly we must.'

'I just want to see what else they've done.'

She climbed through the rubble towards the stairs, which were deep with fabric, a waterfall of material, which I recognised as curtains, their tracks still attached, chunks of plaster hanging from them, showing they had been hauled from the walls. The corridor was strewn with clothes. She picked up a dress in passing, and let it drop again at the sight of the slash cutting through it from neck to hem. The bed had been pulled away from the wall and its pillows, sheets and covers dragged to the bathroom, piled into the bath and the water turned on. The taps were now nose-deep below the surface, still running, the water overflowing onto the floor in a steady stream. I turned them off and went back with the idea of checking the other bathrooms.

In the middle of her mattress, which had been slashed to ribbons with a manic, industrial thoroughness, was a small hill of dollar bills. Julian had seen them at once and she was already kneeling on the bed, gathering them up. She looked up at me, saying nothing, and continued with her task. I went out, and when I returned, having found the other bathrooms dry, she had regularised the cash into a brick-like block, which she was inserting into her handbag. They were, I noticed, notes of a hundred dollars. Whatever the purpose of this break-in, it wasn't theft.

'We'd better get out quickly. The floor could come down any minute. God knows how long the water's been running.'

We went to my flat to phone the police. I was beginning to engage with the details. 'I wonder if anyone heard anything. It must have sounded like a gang of navvies at work.'

I poured her a generous glass of brandy. She was sitting on my mother's chintz-covered sofa, her legs crossed, one flat shoe half-off her foot, swinging with deceptive casualness, swinging, swinging.

'Unlikely,' she said. 'The flat is double height, after all. I've never heard noises from above or below, so the sound-proofing I put in must be reasonably effective.'

'How could they have got in? Why did the alarm not work?' Julian did not answer these questions. She refused speculation.

Although dealing with the police did not take all night, it did occupy a very long time. The report of a break-in at a flat did not sound like a matter of the greatest urgency and we waited for an hour or so before a pair of officers turned up.

The one who took the lead, introducing himself and his companion, was tall and heavy, with a double chin that haloed his jaw line. Inside his gross face was a prim mouth. The other, who only reached his shoulder, was compact and wore his hands gathered into permanent fists. They asked at once to see the damage, polite boredom written on their obedient, doggy faces, bulldog and terrier. When they opened the door and saw the state of the apartment, they registered at once that they were looking at something out of scale. The first, the bulldog, whistled through his teeth when I turned on the lamp and shone its beams over the heaps of furniture.

The other made a kind of hooting sound in his surprise, 'Oh-wo-wo, did they find what they were looking for?' he asked.

The terrier was already muttering into his radio, his eyes flicking round as he described the devastation.

I did not reply to the bulldog's question. This was Julian's business. She was standing on the landing, as if she could not bear to re-enter her home.

'There was nothing to find,' she said. 'Nothing special. It was just an ordinary flat.'

Both of them directed sceptical expressions at her. 'They must've been looking for something,' he insisted obstinately.

The terrier shook his head in disbelief. 'I've got a scene-of-crime officer coming round straight away. He'll make a start on finger-printing. You haven't seen how they got in, sir?'

I remained silent. Julian said, 'No, I've no idea. I haven't been able to look everywhere in any case.'

'He'll find whatever there is.'

We went back to my mother's drawing room to give them the details they required, while the scene-of-crime officer examined the debris next door. The questions were initially addressed to me, with instinctive chauvinism. I disclaimed the role of principal and listened to Julian's replies. She spoke precisely, answering their queries, giving no background information or gloss to set what had happened into any kind of context. However, towards the end of the interview one of the police officers, the terrier, looking over his notes, said, 'Julian Bennet, odd name for a woman. Didn't you have an accident or something recently?'

'Not an accident exactly. I was mugged just outside here in the square.'

'I remember the name. I was on duty that night at the station and I noticed the name. I collect them,' he added.

'Collect names?' The full force of Julian's smile was directed at him for this diversion.

'Yes, odd ones, you know. Only this month I've had Blanche Black and Joy Comfort and Laurie Carr. I mean you can't forget names like that, can you?' His face was illuminated with interest. I thought he was going to flip over the page in his pad and read us a list of idiosyncratic nomenclature that he had come across recently. Then the light died and his professionalism took over.

'I was just struck by a woman with a man's name. A mugging, was it? What happened?'

'I wouldn't let go of my handbag and got myself stabbed.'

'You're not lucky, are you? You'll have to watch out. They say these things come in threes.'

'Did you say you were the owner of the flat opposite, madam, or the tenant?' The bulldog got back to work.

'I'm the owner.' Julian's voice was firm and business-like.

'You've lived here long?'

'About four years now.'

'And you live alone?'

'I do.'

The bulldog had been slapping his next question on to her reply, like a child playing snap. Now he stopped, as if to allow her to elaborate.

Silence.

The bulldog closed his pad. 'I'll have to ask you not to disturb things. Your insurance assessor may want to have a look. Destruction like that is unusual, to say the least. We'll go and have a word with the porter now.'

I saw them out and returned to the drawing room. Julian was still sitting on the sofa, nursing her glass. She did not turn around as I came in.

'I'll have to beg a toothbrush from you, Nicholas.'

'That's no problem. I'm sure I've a spare one.'

'And a bed to go with it.'

8

The following day the police and the representatives of the insurance company continued to sift through the wreckage. Julian refused to pay attention to what was happening next door, so I remained at home to take the burden off her. I wandered into her apartment from time to time with offers of tea and coffee, hoping to glean some information for myself. It was an opportunity to see things that were normally inaccessible to my curiosity and I decided to take it.

Miraculously, the ceiling of the drawing room had not crashed under the weight of water from Julian's bathroom. Only isolated lumps of plaster had flaked, like scurf, onto the general debris below. I moved from room to room, searching for something I would recognise only when I saw it. I was rewarded by a gleam of gold in the corner of the bedroom. I bent down to pick up a single cuff link. I walked to the window to look at it in the light. AΦ was inscribed on it. I held it in my hand, warming it, before tossing it back into the melee.

I learned that Victor had heard and seen nothing. Nobody unaccounted for had entered the building. There was only one exit to the street, past the porter's desk. The fire escape, which zigzagged down through the central well of the block, led to a small Italianate courtyard, tiled in marble with a lion's head wall fountain, thence into the entrance hall. On one of my coffee-bearing expeditions I met a scene-of-crime officer returning to the kitchen from the fire escape. He was a lanky, bearded man, red-haired and Celtic, with long arms and bony, prehensile fingers.

61

'Very funny, this,' he remarked. 'It looks as though the window might have been cut from the inside.' He held up the bag in his supple jointed hands.

'How do you know,' I asked.

'Most of the damage was done from the outside. We can tell by the remains inside the kitchen from which direction the force came. But they might have wanted to make it appear so. And this glass on the fire escape could have been from the first cut they made, with glass cutters, to let them out there.'

'So how did they get in, if they went out there by the window?'

'Ah, you tell me. There's our problem. There may be a little question of keys and access here.'

I thought guiltily of the key I had never returned, which lay in the drawer in my hall. Then of the naked man on her bed. If the police knew about either they would suspect him, or me. I quickly asked about the alarm which had not gone off, which he dismissed as irrelevant.

'Decoration,' he said. 'A skilled professional can disable one of those in seconds. They're deterrents to the casual thief, but they don't worry the serious criminal for a second. And whatever else, these guys were serious.'

'They were?'

'Knife-men, razors. You see how everything's been slashed.'

'And fingerprints?' I asked. 'Are they going to help?'

He laughed. 'Give us a break. I just said, didn't I? These were professionals. There aren't none. They aren't giving any help at all. We'll do you and her and that'll account for anything we find.'

We lived together now, but there was none of the intimacy of marriage nor the slovenliness of flat-sharing. Julian maintained her independence of life, areas that I was never to reach, zones of radio silence from which no signals were ever emitted. She never permitted me to make assumptions about her, living alongside rather than with me.

My flat was transformed by her presence. Previously it had been a bleak and temporary space. She changed things at once. Furniture moved; some objects disappeared altogether; others took up new stations. Her cat-like presence, made up of a combination of indolence and intensity, filled the apartment. When I returned home in the evening, which was earlier and earlier, I would find the lamps on, the fire lit, music, which she played constantly, filling the air, and Julian herself lying on the sofa, propping a magazine on her crooked knees. Her moving in was unplanned by either of us, and so I could have no expectations of how long she would stay. There was always a half-formed fear in my mind, as I unlocked my door each evening, that she would have vanished.

She made no attempt to analyse what had happened and why. She referred to the wrecking of her flat as 'the burglary', although what, if anything, had been stolen was unclear. It was obvious to me, as it was to the police, that the mugging and the burglary were directed against her personally, but since she refused to accept this interpretation and would accuse nobody, it was impossible to guess from where the threat came and what motivated it.

I had abandoned any attempt to find out about her and added to what I knew when, very occasionally, she let slip something about herself. I could guess that she had been brought up in a provincial lower-middle-class home. I imagined a strict upbringing, an authoritarian father, an only child, who had rebelled and escaped, recreating herself. Then, unexpectedly, I had my first glimpse of her past, from an unsolicited source. It was as if I were walking in the street and, glancing down, I had seen through a lifted drain cover the stream of sewage that flows incessantly beneath the city.

I was at a reception held in the Oxford and Cambridge Club for a friend from Cambridge who had just been awarded a prize for his research in physics. I did not recognise many people when I entered the room and I had just taken a drink and was looking round when I was greeted by a pink-faced, silver-haired man whom, after a second, I recognised as a friend of my father-in-law, a powerful figure in the City. We talked for a while until, loosening up, he said that he had seen me the other day dining with a beautiful girl who was not my wife. I explained that Emily and I were separated, and found myself reiterating, though with some reluctance, my usual piece about its not being my choice and that I hoped we would be together again soon.

'Oh, yes,' he said, dismissively. 'I knew about that already. No, it was the girl. I'd seen her before somewhere, but I couldn't for the life of me think where. I'd've come to say hello to you both, but I was with my wife and thought it was more discreet not to.' He paused, apparently for congratulation on his tact. 'Then, in the middle of the night, three o'clock in the morning, it came to me where I'd met her.'

This time I was forced to show interest before he would continue. 'Where was it?' I asked. I knew from the pleasure he was taking in telling his story that I was not going to enjoy hearing it.

'It was years ago, in the 'eighties. I had a big deal on with some Arabs at the time and I gave a dinner for the prince involved and some of his entourage. I'd heard that it was sometimes necessary to provide, how shall I say, extra services for them when they were in London. But I really didn't want to get into that game. There's quite enough going on with private bank accounts without that. In the event, we didn't have to because they'd made their own arrangements, as we realised when they asked if they could bring along a few extra people to the dinner.' He had an irritating laugh, which he interjected here. 'And that's where I saw her.'

I had known that this was to be the denouement when he had begun the story. I didn't want to listen to him, but I wanted to know. His childishly pink lips had a little gathering of mucus in each corner, as if he was salivating more than necessary for his whisky and canapés.

'There were about five or six of them, the Arabs, and not quite as many girls. God, they were stunning. The head girl was Lebanese or Egyptian and loaded with stones. I remember I noticed your girl right away.' He was enjoying himself, spinning out his story with sips of his whisky. 'It was quite funny.' He laughed, while I looked on with a social smile I wished I had refused to concede. 'My wife was there and she didn't have a clue what was going on. She told me afterwards that the Princess had been charming and that one of the wives had had an English education, because she had studied architecture in London. Where they found them I have no idea and, I must say, we'd probably have lost the contract if it had depended on us to provide them. I can't imagine where you go to get that sort of service . . .'

I let him maunder on, hoping for, fearing another view of Julian. It could have been a mistake. He had only seen her once before, several years ago. But I knew it wasn't. As Victor had said, if you saw her once you were unlikely to forget her. And the story immediately filled in the blank of her previous life, which was so noticeably lacking the husband or boyfriend or career that should have taken up those years. I stood passively, my drink untouched in my hand, allowing him to talk about himself, until he had forgotten Julian and why he had spoken to me in the first place.

I set off home, on foot, because I needed time to absorb what I had been told. I had said to Prisca that I would not have minded if Emily had had a lover, if she had stayed with me. And what I felt now was not jealousy of the men of Julian's past, the Arab prince, the Russian Anatoli, it was curiosity, I told myself. I wanted to know. To know her, to comprehend, was to hold her, in some sense. I would then possess her in a way that I did not have her now.

Why was she living with me? The acceptable explanation was that, finding ourselves thrown together by chance, we had been permitted to succumb to a strong sexual attraction by the absence of wife and partner, an attraction that I found ever more bindingly powerful. But was it really the same for her? Was it likely? Sexual attraction is an odd, random and immensely powerful force. It is not necessary to seek rational explanations for it. The rational explanation came back to me, nevertheless, pat this time, provided by the spittle-edged mouth of my father-in-law's friend.

Because she needs you. She's moved in with you to evade the pursuers who mugged her and wrecked her apartment. She planned everything from the start and allowed you to become her lover for no other reason than to prepare for the moment which she knew might come, when she was forced out of her flat. She's faking it and has been all along.

But, if she'd really wished to go into hiding, she'd have done better to leave the area entirely.

She needs to be close. For whatever reason, she can't go far: that's why living with you is convenient for her.

But she didn't have to do it this way. She didn't have to live with me. She didn't have to sleep with me.

The level of internal argument was not very high. I scrutinised the memory of every meeting, from the beginning, examining the stages of our short relationship, each day marked in my mind by some advance towards her that I had engineered. Or had she been in charge? Had she simply seen a fool and an opportunity and seized them adventitiously? And sex? Could she fake it to that extent? Was I being tricked, as men throughout the ages have been tricked, by her claims, which I had thought involuntary? The cherubic face of my father-in-law's friend seemed to look pityingly at me.

Come on, man. She's a woman who battens on men. And as for faking it, with the experience she's had, she'd have no problem in fooling you.

The house was warm, the lamps lit when I entered. There was an enormous bunch of narcissi on the table behind the sofa and the sharp medicinal smell pierced my nostrils, overpowering her scent. She was out. Immediately I felt the fear of her loss, and realised I could not confront her. I wanted her and I wanted her to stay. I would accept the fake for the real.

Part 2

Fake

9

'I want you to take me to see your *Girl in a Fur*,' Julian said.

Although I knew so little about her life, she entered completely into mine. She was always interested in my work, the seminars I was giving for my visiting professorship, the Coulounieix lectures, my book, the conference in Moscow, now scheduled for March. She had been following my row with Minna as if it were a spectator sport.

'You can see it any time. Have you never been to the Litvak?'

'I must have, years ago. But I want to go with you.'

I was avoiding the Foundation and any meeting with its director. I offered Julian postcards and art books. She rejected my suggestions.

'I want the real thing, or the real fake, and I want to see it with you.'

'I suppose Minna is unlikely to be there at the weekend,' I said, doubtfully.

'Why are you afraid of her?' Julian asked. 'Why stop going there? It's a public gallery, after all.'

'I don't like personal confrontations. If I have a disagreement, I prefer to keep it to scholarly journals.'

'I want a personal confrontation with the *Girl in a Fur*, and I want you to explain it to me.'

So we went, walking to the Foundation through the park. It was a clear blue winter afternoon. The sun shone coldly, glossing her sable coat and her hair with the same metallic sheen.

'Victor's daughter's left home,' she told me as we crossed the peaty surface of Rotten Row.

'That'll give him some peace at last, won't it?' I tried to remember what happened last.

'Not really, because she's left Rose, her little girl, with Mary. There's still plenty of opportunity for them to quarrel about her.'

'I thought she hated Mary.'

'She does, but her new boyfriend doesn't want the child. Or there's no room for her where they're living. I'm not sure which. Anyway, Victor's very relieved. He didn't want her to be taken away.'

Julian added enormously to my life. She made me experience things so intensely that I realised that for twelve years I had been living in a dream, drugged by the comfort of marriage. As we walked that day, she said, 'Have you ever noticed how the world is full of missing halves?'

The single cuff link, marked ΑΦ. Emily. I no longer wanted her back, just yet at any rate. My lawyer was stalling on everything. We were still arguing about Sholto's schooling, and I had gained a slight advantage, since Emily and Sholto liked different schools.

'What on earth do you mean?'

'Look,' she said triumphantly, as if she had proved her thesis, and pointed to a woman approaching us pushing a double buggy. On one side sat a fat child of about two, plucking discontentedly at the webbing straps that confined it. Its companion seat was empty.

'So?' I said. 'There's an explanation for it. The other child is at a party, is sick, is having a day with its grandmother.'

'You don't understand. Of course there's always a reason for it. I see it everywhere, the missing half.'

I could not understand what she was talking about at the time, but her words like her presence, had an evocative power. Just as Julian herself reappeared so vividly in my mind when she was absent, so her odd ideas took hold of me.

When we reached the Foundation, I let her buy our entrance

tickets while I skulked in the hall, halfway between the ticket office and the postcard stand.

'You look so guilty,' she said as she joined me at the foot of the staircase. 'Like a caricature of a spy about to meet his controller, or a hit and run thief about to make off with one of the paintings.'

'It's the effect that Minna has on me. I feel that I'm entering enemy territory and that every one of her fluffy old ladies is a secret agent watching and reporting on me.'

The old ladies of the Foundation were a standing joke. The security officers who patrolled other galleries had not yet taken over here. Instead, in every room sat a stout middle-aged woman. The one in the Vermeer room was knitting. Julian looked at her out of the corner of her eye and said, 'If you try anything here, she'll stab you with her needle. It must be worse than a knife. She's probably trained in marksmanship and can throw it like a javelin at the backs of retreating thieves.'

The west-facing windows were screened with translucent cream blinds and to obtain the best view of the painting it was necessary to stand a little on one side and look at it obliquely.

'What do you think?' I asked.

'She's very beautiful,' she said. Not it, but she. It was the person, not the thing she had seen.

I looked again and saw that she was right. She was beautiful and mysterious. Her eyes met mine with an aching sensuousness. The jacket was not the gold silk and ermine one used in many of Vermeer's other canvases. The fur was dark brown, forming the lining of a golden brown quilted silk robe, only revealing itself at the edge and the neck, ideal for the damp north European winter, the pelt enclosing the body, trapping the warmth.

'That's not the point,' I said. I was seeing more of the little signs that had made me uneasy in the first place: the awkward hand, the odd perspective of the back of the chair.

'I'd have thought it was the whole point. The painting is what it is, whoever did it.' She moved away and I heard her heels on the bare boards as she walked slowly round the room.

Art criticism depends on exactly what I was doing: close study of the painting, in which experience, taste, knowledge of other works by the master and his contemporaries and of the craft of painting are all brought to bear on the quality of the work. But part of my study of perception was on precisely this question: the subjectivity of appreciation, how the eye creates what it sees, how it selects, arranges and interprets, according to pre-formed patterns. The eye is not innocent, it is already committed.

I took my eyes off the face, the central focus of the picture and swept the peripheries of the panel. I stopped at the dark corner where the signature J VER MEER was just visible.

I stood there for a long time. Julian disappeared. The gallery was not crowded. Little groups, couples, teenagers, stood beside me and passed on. Sometimes I was alone, except for my guard clicking her needles, not moving her eyes from my back. I sighed. The visit had tested my reactions once again. The answer to the painting's origin lay in balancing the provenance, the scientific data, the artistic quality. I had already looked up the controversy of the 'sixties, and Minna's refutation of the case against it, and I would go over it all again. What I needed was scientific data. It was strange nothing had been done, especially in an institute which had specialised in restoration from its earliest days. I did not rate my chances of persuading Minna to have the painting tested. But, with or without the tests, the problem in essence came to this: it did not feel right to me.

Julian, when I rejoined her, was standing in front of the Pieter van den Bergh's *Courtesan*.

'You're writing about this one?'

'I find him interesting. He's a not-much-admired painter, too facile for modern taste. He could adapt himself to almost any style, and he usually did so at the command of a patron. Though it's hard to see who would have ordered this one.'

The courtesan lay back on her disordered pillows. Her hair, hanging over her shoulders in a mass of tousled curls, was painted with bold, free brush strokes. Her flesh was tawny, rather than pink, and its curves and folds were rendered joyously in a loose, painterly style, so that its soft palpability was transferred through the eye. You could almost sense its firm and yielding qualities under your fingers. The censorious tone that the Dutch liked to give to such scenes was absent here.

'A besotted patron, artistic and amorous,' Julian suggested. 'She looks like the other one.'

'Like the Vermeer? There's no comparison.'

'Yes, there is. It's the same woman. It's just that she's seen through different eyes.'

Her words astonished me. I had been so concerned with the technical qualities of the work that I had not looked at the model as a person. The position of the head, in profile, was different from that of the *Lady in a Pelisse* so it was not easy to compare the features. The hair was different. Most telling of all, the moral atmosphere of the Vermeer was a world away from that of the *Courtesan*. I looked again, trying to school myself to see a person not a painting, a woman not an idea. Julian was moving on, and I followed her.

10

The story of Julian and the Arab princes haunted me. Once again the need to know more about her took hold of me. Because I knew she sometimes feared she was followed, I had the idea of stalking her myself. I had entered her flat without permission, looked at her photos, glanced at her bank statements; to track her was only another stage in my research. I could not afford the time to watch the house all day and see what she did while I was at work, so I chose an evening expedition. Just one, I told myself, a random sample, to give me an idea of how she passed her time when we were not together.

I began with her diary, which I took out of her handbag one night while she was in the bath. The door of the bathroom was ajar, but the noise of Radio Three and of running water combined to cover the sound of my opening of the bag and digging through the detritus that all women carry around with them. Emily's bag was the history of her life. Julian's was more rigorously controlled. It contained a make-up pouch, a wallet and cheque book, credit cards, a phone, a pen and notebook, the diary. I opened the soft leather covers and, with instinctive egocentricity, looked for her appointments with me during those first weeks. I featured as N.O.: N.O., 7.30; then as N.: N, 7 Wig. Hall. Looking ahead, I saw for the coming week Monday 12.30, I; Wednesday, 8.30, Fr.

On Monday I waited outside the flat from midday, wondering if she had already left. At a quarter past a taxi drew up outside the house and a few minutes later Julian emerged and got in, holding the

75

back door handle as she spoke to the driver. They moved off round the square and my will failed me. I couldn't follow a taxi round London. I would lose it within five minutes and during that time Julian, alert to being watched, would have noticed me. I went indoors gloomily and saw from his expression that Victor had seen my odd behaviour. Reason had won, but I felt no better for it.

In the end I followed Julian by mistake. I was returning later than usual on Wednesday, and, as I approached the square, I saw her at the end of the road, unmistakable in her sable coat. She crossed the street and disappeared. I looked at my watch. It was eight twenty-five. Wherever she was expected at eight thirty, it could not be far away if she was going on foot. Because I knew the area, I could keep well back. In Walton Street there were more people about and I felt safer. She was making slower time now, glancing in shop windows. I watched her turn left and, cautiously rounding the corner, I thought I had lost her, for there was no one on either pavement. Then a rectangle of light silhouetted her on a doorstep. She embraced the person who opened the door, a woman, and went in. I walked slowly past, noting the number, 15. I retraced my steps on the other side of the street. From this angle I could see into the basement kitchen where a table was laid for three. A woman's hands were placing a basket of bread between the wine glasses. I felt elation mingle with my guilt, as if I had proved something. Spying was unpleasant, but it was worth it to be reassured by an innocent evening with a girlfriend.

I arrived home, cheerfully and almost immediately the phone rang and a voice I did not know said, 'Could I speak to Mrs Ochterlonie?'

I did not explain my mother's death, simply saying, 'This is Nicholas Ochterlonie.'

The tone was not that of the academic world, still less of a friend or acquaintance. There was authority in the pronunciation of my name, slightly threatening, which jarred with the ostentatious civility with which the speaker went on.

'This is Tom Naish of the CID. I wondered if we could have a brief interview.'

I knew at once what it was about. Since meeting Julian, I had had two encounters with the police. It was becoming routine. I began to get out my diary, thinking of when I could fit him in during the next few days.

'I wondered,' he was saying, 'if you're free, if I could pop in now.'

I looked at my watch and agreed. His arrival was so swift I realised he must have been phoning from his car somewhere nearby. He probably knew I was at home and unoccupied. He must have been watching me, as I had been watching Julian.

He introduced himself again and insisted on showing me his identity card. I offered him coffee or a drink, both of which he refused. He took out a pocket organiser, turned it on and kept his eyes fixed on the screen, giving the impression he was comparing my words with some technologically authenticated version of the truth. His first words were a surprise.

'I'm making some enquiries about one of your neighbours, a Russian business man called Vozkresensky, and I wondered whether you would be able to help us.'

'I don't know anyone called Vozkresensky.'

He looked disappointed, even sceptical. 'He's your neighbour.'

'Maybe, but I'm afraid I don't know everyone who lives in the blocks of flats around me.'

'But he lives literally opposite you.'

Now I understood. It was about Julian after all.

'And you've lived here so long, I thought there might be a chance . . .'

'I've lived here long?'

'You haven't? The electoral roll has the name of Ochterlonie since . . .'

'My mother. She died last year. I've only been here a few months.'

'And you know nothing about your neighbour, nothing reported to you by your mother? I'm thinking of personal habits that neighbours might know about: noisy parties, rows, loud music, anything at all.'

'No, nothing like that. The residents around me are so quiet I wouldn't know if they were there or not.' Which was true as far as it went.

He snapped shut his organiser. 'I can see I've drawn a blank. But that's police work. Sorry to have bothered you, sir.' He stood up.

'I suppose this is all to do with the break-in?' I said. I was filling in the time while he got himself ready to leave.

'What break-in's that?'

'In the flat opposite.'

'Mr Vozkresensky's flat?'

'I suppose so.'

'I don't know about any break-in.' He was looking puzzled and so was I.

'It was some time ago now, say four weeks. The place was totally wrecked. I assumed you'd come to talk about that.'

He sat down again and his voice was more conciliatory. 'Perhaps we ought to begin again.'

His call was unrelated to Julian, and I had just revealed her to him. I was uncertain whether to regret this or not. If I had said nothing about the break-in, I would have been rid of him, at least for a time; but I would have learned nothing.

'Tell me about this burglary next door,' he was saying.

'It'll all be on record. I have the crime number somewhere if you want to find out about it. I gather you are not the local bobby checking up on a minor detail.'

He laughed. 'Let me give you my card. It's more informative than an identity document. He passed it to me. *Detective Constable Tom Naish CID (Fraud)* I read. I held it, studying its terminology, as I described to him the destruction that had been inflicted with such creative energy next door. I said nothing about Julian. I wanted to hear about Mr Vozkresensky, the owner of the flat.

'How did you come to be enquiring about my mysterious neighbour if you hadn't heard of this?' I posed the question before he could ask me to fill in some of the gaps in my story. I had him at a disadvantage. I had revealed a hole in his knowledge and then I had given him, apparently freely, the information he needed. I had some kind of credit, but he was still unwilling to give anything away.

'I'm afraid I can't go into detail. We have been alerted to certain aspects of Mr Vozkresensky's business activities. That's as much as I can say.'

I had to mention Julian now. He would find out in any case, as soon as he looked up the records of the break-in, and I would look extremely devious if I had said nothing.

'I should tell you,' I said to him in the hall, 'that though I've never met or even heard of Mr Vozkresensky before this evening, there was someone living next door, a woman called Julian Bennet.'

He shook my hand firmly and took the stairs to the ground floor. I poured myself a large whisky and wandered with it into our bedroom. I opened cupboard doors, put my hand into the pockets of a jacket. I drew out the drawers of a chest. I was not systematically searching. I was waiting for something to show itself. And it did. On a shelf I found a tortoiseshell jewellery box, unlocked. I lifted the lid as idly, speculatively, as I had opened the cupboard and the drawers and this time I was rewarded, or punished. It contained the dollars, the ones I had seen Julian gathering up on the night of the break-in. On top of them lay a pistol, black, business-like, no lady's weapon. I did not touch, but just looked at this store before putting it away.

This visit and my find decided me on two initiatives. One was to learn something about Tom Naish CID (Fraud) and the other was to employ a private detective. I had never called upon the services of such a person before, but I revived from the depths of my memory an account, heard months ago, before I had split up with Emily, of a friend who had a case of industrial espionage in his office. He had described to an enthralled dinner table how the firm he had employed had tracked down the culprit among his employees.

I rang him and asked for his firm of detectives and whether he would recommend them.

'Obviously, yes. They did a brilliant job for us, but, well, Nick, you know they're not cheap, not that you're short of a bob or two, but what I mean is . . .'

'What do you mean, Simon?'

'I'm not sure they're what you're looking for. They'll do marital stuff, but it would be a bit like buying a Rolls-Royce when you need a country runabout.'

'It's not for marital business,' I reassured him. My disagreements with Emily must be known to all the world by now, I thought. 'It's something, er, financial. You'll understand that I can't say much about it.'

'Of course, of course. Well, if you want the best and are prepared to pay for it, these are your men. The guy who dealt with us was called Colin, Colin Trevor, or was it Trevor Colin? I'll look it up and fax you the details.'

I kept the phone number of Colin Trevor on my desk. It was a bit like the key to Julian's flat. I knew I would use it, but as long as I didn't, I was innocent of spying. In the meantime, I managed to achieve a little more on my own.

I was invited to lunch at a bank in the City, a networking meeting with no obvious theme to the guests, apart from the fact that we were all old friends of our host. Opposite me at the table was someone I had not seen since our university days together at Edinburgh. He was called Mills-Millais now and worked in the Home Office, although then he had been plain Charles Mills, reading some fashionably sociological subject. It was somewhere in the middle of the smoked salmon that I realised he could help me, which was what such lunches were for. I waited for coffee, until he was unwrapping a chocolate mint, before starting my story of the visit of Tom Naish of the CID. I drew it out a bit, emphasising the suddenness, the lateness of the hour, the mysteriousness of the fellow.

Then I said, 'I'd really like to know what sort of outfit he's working for and what they're investigating. Can you find out for me? It must be the sort of thing that comes within your empire. I don't want you to tell me anything confidential, naturally. It's just if one receives a mysterious visit from an agent of some unspecified unit, one likes to know who and what one's dealing with.' I handed him Naish's card. 'This is who he claims to be.'

People always like to show off their power, and he had all the meticulousness of the bureaucrat. Once the demand was fed into the system, I was sure that a reply would emerge, in time. He made no promise to help, but he put the card away with a small grunt, which I felt was a good sign.

About two days later he called me at my office.

'I've got something on Tom Naish. I don't know why he was being so uncommunicative. It's quite hush-hush, but he could still have told you a bit more. It seems that a section was set up in Scotland Yard to deal with economic crime in an international context. It's called the International Economic Crime Intelligence Unit or IECIU. It's been going for about three years now. The Americans have been very keen in the last few years to prevent drugs profits from entering the white economy. They've forced the Europeans to pass legislation, obliging banks to notify deposits and movements that they suspect might have a drugs-related origin. The unit monitors this sort of thing, but it's not just drugs-related crime. Its remit is any kind of large-scale international financial scam. It's such a major problem nowadays that the PM felt that it needed concentrated attention. Is that any good to you?'

'Excellent. Couldn't be better. Many thanks. I don't suppose you discovered what in particular our Mr Naish is working on at present?'

He did not reply at once. I realised he knew, but was not going to tell me.

'That's an area we can't go into. Sorry, Nick. You can see why.'

'Indeed. Thanks for all you've done.'

I put down the receiver and looked for Colin Trevor's number. If Mills-Millais wouldn't tell me, someone else would. The information was there. Somewhere there were traces of Julian Bennet and Vozkresensky. I stopped. The cuff links: AФ. Surely, if Vozkresensky was Anatoli, the Cyrillic monogram would have been AB? So

Vozkresensky was perhaps the other one, the sleeper. For some reason, I nursed a hostility to that invader of Julian's bed that I did not feel towards the smiling, moustachioed figure in the photograph. Colin Trevor would find all this out for me.

We met the next day in his office in a modern building near Blackfriars. I was suffering from residual unease, determinedly suppressed, about spying. The clinically orderly offices, with their silent, blinking screens and glass partitions reassured me. There was a combination of light and silence. Nothing could be heard, everything could be seen. It was at once open and unsleazy and private. Colin Trevor sat opposite me behind his desk, in his shirt sleeves, like an accountant or a management consultant. What I was doing was perfectly normal.

I explained I wanted to find out anything I could about Miss Julian Bennet and Mr Vozkresensky and Anatoli, who might be Mr Anatoli Vozkresensky. I stipulated very carefully that I did not want any attempt made to follow Miss Bennet. I had already seen Julian frightened by this possibility and I did not want to make her more nervous, still less to discover that I was spying on her.

Colin Trevor had the fresh face of a twenty-two-year-old, which was probably a disadvantage to someone approaching forty. He was, nonetheless, business-like, emotionless. He must have cultivated his manner to defuse the rage and anxiety and tension that routinely filled his office. He explained his firm's system of charging and the length of time he would expect his enquiry to take.

'Time is often the most important factor for some of our clients,' he said. 'So we can set a date for a preliminary report, say a week from now. This would enable us to work out how much info we are likely to get, even if we have not been able to obtain everything you want by then. After that we can go on until we have got what you need, or until we have exhausted our possibilities. Or you can set a deadline and we can present you with as much as we can within that time.'

'Time is not an overriding consideration for me,' I said. 'I mean, I don't want this to go on for months, but I don't need the information tomorrow. I would rather you took longer and were more thorough. Anyway, let's say a month. Let's see what you can come up with after Christmas.'

11

Julian had stimulated my ideas about the *Lady in a Pelisse*. I was now even more certain that there was something wrong with the painting. In some respects, it was too good to be true. It was Vermeer pared to the bone, with what we expect and nothing more, just the light, the face, the earring, the colours, dark gold and dark blue: Vermeer without ambition or difficulty. Vermeer in essence. The *Girl with a Pearl Earring* in the Mauritshuis has the same poignant simplicity and perfection, but it does not have the coarseness of the brush work, the weakness of the shoulders and hand.

I looked over the texts to find my point of departure. I began with Minna's monograph of the 1950s in which she suggested 1666 as the date of execution on stylistic grounds, which had been generally accepted. She cited an entry in a 1696 sale catalogue, which offered *A Lady in a Fur signed I MEER* as the earliest reference. This seemed a reasonable starting point for the story. The painting had always been known by that name and indeed the fur was its distinguishing characteristic. If I had not just visited the Foundation with Julian, I might have accepted it. But the signature that I had looked at the previous weekend had not been I MEER. Vermeer used different styles at different times of his life and there was no reason why a variation should be suspicious. However, since the signature I had seen had clearly been J VER MEER, the painting mentioned in 1696 could not be the Litvak *Lady*. And since a gold and ermine jacket figures in at least five other paintings by Vermeer, several of which are signed, the cursory catalogue description must have referred to one of them. It did not take much further enquiry to establish that the sale catalogue quoted by Minna was also used, by other scholars, as provenance for the Berlin *Young Lady with a Pearl Necklace* which really is signed I MEER. I noted Minna's sloppiness and the fact that it had gone unremarked for all these years, with some astonishment, and then told myself I should not be surprised. In intellectual matters the mind works no differently from the eye in visual ones. Preconceptions mould the evidence. Trustingly we accept authority. Only when we are driven to it, do we check that reality corresponds to the label. The question was whether Minna's error was careless or deliberate.

Then I turned to the question of scientific analysis. In all the documentation I had assembled, I had found no record of any scientific tests being carried out. This seemed to me to be almost incredible. X-ray analysis was available for authenticating paintings even in the 1920s when the *Lady* had first appeared on the market. Evidently the judgement of experts had been regarded as so secure that no additional endorsement was considered necessary.

However, there had been some fuss in the 1960s. The incident had occurred when an American post-doctoral student called Skaekbekker had aimed at tenure at an American university by writing an article on false Vermeers. In this group he included the Litvak *Lady* and the *Girl Holding a Flute*, along with several other works, which were now agreed to have been optimistic attributions made by earlier experts. His article had been published in a prestigious British magazine, so he had had some influential backing from somewhere. I remembered that the editor of the day, a certain Timothy Goldie, now dead, had once crossed swords with Minna. The board had removed him from the editorship sometime afterwards. Perhaps this article had appeared during his defiance of Minna's rule. Skaekbekker's reasoning was entirely art historical, not scientific, and his analysis of the weaknesses was not dissimilar from my own.

Minna had quickly regained the scholarly upper hand. I found an off-print of her reply to Skaekbekker's attack. She, too, argued on grounds of technique and artistic quality, although I remarked one sentence of significance. 'All scientific tests support a mid-seventeenth-century date for the work.' This was very odd. It would have been normal for the author to give the details of the tests undertaken and the results obtained. Admittedly, even in the 'sixties scientific evidence was regarded with less esteem than connoisseurship. If a work was a blatant forgery and an x-ray showed it to be such, that was one thing. If the test did no more than confirm an approximate dating that an expert could make without resort to science, it still seemed that technical tests were only stating the obvious in a time-consuming and expensive way. Today science was regarded with more respect, and even if an analysis did not say more than was already known, it would not, for that reason, be omitted. Why did Minna not make more of the tests if they were favourable to her argument, I wondered.

The question, unanswerable but useful, remained at the end of my research. Minna was so enraged with me that there was no possibility of gaining access to the Foundation's records by the usual means of asking permission. I had placed a request to see the papers held there. So far no reply had been forthcoming and enquiries by my secretary had been met with evasion.

I had recently had a phone call with no apparent purpose from Anthony Watendlath, who had asked about how my researches into the Litvak *Lady* were progressing. When I had taken the opportunity to complain of the lack of co-operation from the Foundation, he had replied, 'But what do you expect? You'll have to make a less direct approach.'

'I'll need some help,' I said. But he had not volunteered. I found his attitude distinctly manipulative.

A few days later I received an intriguing e-mail message on my computer in the university. It was headed: *Subject: Litvak Vermeer*, and read *Go for the tests*. It had come from within the university and its originator was 'gill'. I e-mailed her in reply, asking her to phone me, and had a bewildered call from an administrator in the Admissions Office who denied any message. I said there must have been a mistake and rang off, without commenting to her that someone had gained access to her terminal. I was hoping for more from the same source.

'The tests', if they existed, could only have been done by the Litvak Foundation, so the data must be held under Minna's guard. I must somehow see what was there. So I devised an indirect method of seeing the archives and Julian came to my mind at once as an assistant. Never in all my marriage would I have asked Emily for help in my work, still less in something a little disreputable, but I saw Julian immediately as a fellow conspirator. What I had in mind was not, in fact, anything dishonest. Since I could not see the files on the *Lady* myself, I wanted someone whom I could trust to do so for me, and Julian, intelligent, adaptable, seemed an ideal agent.

To persuade her to help me was not a difficult task. It was done, as usual, at a meal. I had begun, in desperation, to cook, or at least to assemble food. Julian was no housewife, making no attempt to prepare meals or take over the running of my flat when she moved in. She would order cases of wine or water, by telephone, and take delivery of them. She bought flowers, nothing more. So I had to look after her, a new experience for me, after years of being looked after by Emily. I became an expert at selecting from delicatessen counters, from Marks and Spencer's and Harrods' Food Halls. I remember the evening I was going to proposition her about the Foundation I bought oysters and lemons outside Bibendum on my way home. We ate them with some brown bread. I grilled a rack of lamb and we had broad beans from the freezer. I found a bar of black chocolate in a cupboard to have with our coffee. This seemed to me a pretty persuasive menu.

Julian was as picky as a child, worse than Cordelia, and had to be tempted by small quantities of delicious things that she liked. She was, unusually for a woman, a meat-eater, loving offal and particularly tempted by things on other people's plates. She ate the oysters with enthusiasm and, while cutting into her rack of lamb, she told me about Victor's latest problems.

'Rose wants a dog.'

'Ah. Remind me, Rose is the daughter.'

'No, that's Josie. Rose is the granddaughter. Victor simply adores her, but he doesn't want her to have a dog.'

'Ah.'

'They used to have a lovely big half-poodle cross, with a fluffy grey-white coat, called Sleepy, because it was so energetic. But something terrible happened to it and they were all so sad that he doesn't want to go through it all again.'

'Well, this is the next cliff-hanger. Will she persuade him. What kind of dog will it be. There's plenty of mileage in this.' I wanted to get through Victor quickly so that I could broach my own subject, but she was too quick for me.

'Nicholas, confess. What do you want to tell me? You've just heard that Emily wants you back? You're selling the flat? Out with it.' She did not sound worried.

'I haven't any news for you, good or bad.'

'You're up to something. You're completely transparent, you know.' Just as she was completely opaque.

'I want to ask your help.'

'Yes? To do what?'

'Some skulduggery.'

'I don't know what that means. You use such god-awful schoolboy language sometimes.' She sounded cautious. 'I don't want to have anything to do with Emily or the children, ok?'

'It's nothing to do with them. It's to do with Minna and the painting. You'll enjoy it.'

'Oh, yes?'

'I want you to be an art student and do some research for me.'

'Is that all?'

'Yes. Do you mind?'

'No. I thought you were working up to a really big deal. Of course

I'll be an art student.' She ran her fingers through her hair. 'I'll have to scruff myself up a bit.'

I told her about the e-mail message.

She said, 'But there aren't any tests.'

'As far as we know. But it's fairly extraordinary, when the Litvak is in the forefront of the application of all kinds of science to restoration. I thought that they hadn't done any because there was no need, because there was no doubt. But perhaps they did some after all.'

'And this is a message from someone on the inside. Someone who heard your lecture, or who has read about it in the papers.'

'I suppose so. Now, what I want you to do is this.'

It is appalling how quickly one works out everything that has to be done once one embarks on dishonourable behaviour, even justifiably dishonourable behaviour. It becomes just another administrative problem that has to be solved.

A couple of days later we met at a cafe in Mayfair. As we ate lunch, I instructed her on how she would register at the Foundation in order to use the library, the cover story she would use, the material she would ask for. I knew that the library permitted students into the stacks to find their own books. I was hoping the same rule applied to the archive and documentation centre.

As we left, she bent down to pick up from the pavement a single glove.

'A missing half again,' she said, as she put it on the railings of a neighbouring house to call attention to it. I watched her set off. She was wearing black jeans and a white jacket, a scarf wound around her neck against the cold and mittens on her hands. She looked vulnerable and young, easily ten years less than her real age.

I went off to the Courtauld to read about van den Bergh. I had discovered a thesis on him, available on microfilm. There was no point in waiting for Julian and, although I wanted to lurk outside the Foundation's fan-lighted front door to meet her as soon as she came out, I forced myself to sit at a desk and to make some notes for two hours before returning home by taxi. I had stretched out the

90

afternoon, thinking that in this way I would find her home before me and as soon as I arrived I would have news of what she had discovered. She was not there. As soon as I opened the door, her absence enveloped me. I waited impatiently, watching the six o'clock news. I poured myself a drink and ate some nuts, rapidly cramming them into my mouth and crunching them vigorously.

She did not come in until nine. I realised sometime between six thirty and seven that she either had another appointment, which she had not told me about, or was deliberately teasing me. I turned to the sports channel. Watching sport is, I knew from Emily, among the most provoking activities that men can engage in and it was only this thought that lent interest to the mannikins running around their falsely green rectangle.

When at last I heard her key in the lock, I did not move my eyes from the screen although surreptitiously I lowered the sound and said, 'How did you get on?'

She was removing her scarf and jacket in the hall. 'It was only quite a good film.'

'You've been to see a film?'

'Yes, I went to the Minema.'

'And the Foundation? How did you get on there?'

She came in with her arms raised as she lifted her hair to settle it over her collar. 'What?'

'The Foundation?'

I felt a tide of frustration rising within me. There was nothing I could do to make her tell me the truth. I had no hold on her at all.

She started to laugh. 'Oh, dear, I can't keep it up any longer because you're so funny, Nick.'

'What do you mean?'

'Nothing. Nothing. Cheer up, I've got everything you want.'

She produced a folder. 'I've got it all here for you.'

I was expecting a few pages of hand-written notes. The hideous realisation washed over me: she had stolen a file.

She went on. 'I found a very nice assistant who showed me how

91

the library and archives were catalogued. I pretended I was interested in the van den Bergh and I asked for the scientific data. Apparently the archives are not open. You need special letters of recommendation describing your research signed by the Archbishop of Canterbury and the Prime Minister and at least three members of the Cabinet, which have to be considered by the archivist before you are allowed access.'

'So you saw it was hopeless and beat a graceful retreat.' I was wondering how I could get the material back as quickly and secretly as possible before I was professionally ruined.

She was laughing now, squatting on the edge of the sofa with one leg up, her arms wrapped around it. From this yogic pose she looked out, her face animated with laughter and risk and success.

'Not at all. Do you think I am the kind of person who gives up at a little obstacle like that? This guy wanted to show me round. He was showing off.'

I could imagine the scene. A library assistant given Julian's attention would not want to stop at a brief account of the Foundation's eccentric cataloguing system. He would want to prolong the help he could give, show her everything, mesmerised by the iconic face.

'We were in the archives, when the phone rang. At first he ignored it. Then he felt obliged to answer it, so he went off down these corridors of filing cabinets, leaving me alone. I opened a drawer and saw it was arranged by artist. It wasn't difficult to find V for Vermeer; even I know the alphabet. I took out the whole file, which wasn't very big, like that.' She indicated a half-inch space with her finger and thumb. 'And I put it in my bag. Nicholas, don't.'

I had pulled my hand down over my eyes like a blind. What, oh, what was I doing? Sexual obsession was one order of folly. Theft was quite another.

'Don't.' She prised up my fingers. 'I'm cleverer than I look, I promise.'

She was laughing at me, at what she had done.

'Then I took out one of my own folders and a newspaper and I put them on top of the filing cabinet and moved back to *exactly* the position I had been in before he left me. When he came back, he showed me how the system worked. We went into another section of the archives and he was pulling open the drawers and explaining that these were the materials on the different paintings in the collection. I was so disappointed, I thought that what I'd got had come from the wrong place and would be completely irrelevant. But, but . . . Just you wait.

'I let him show me a whole lot more things. I was *so* patient and he was *so* boring. Then I said I would get out a book and do a little work. I sat down at a desk, you know they're like little phone booths with mahogany wings, so you can't look at your neighbour's notes. I thought I might as well go through the Vermeer file since I had gone to all the trouble of nicking it. Not great on filing, those art historians. It was a real old mess, so it took me a while to realise that what I'd got was a sort of administration file, not the stuff that researchers would be given anyway. And it was stuffed full of goodies. All these charts and figures, the lot, that obviously no one was ever meant to see, even if they had all their letters of accreditation. Then I went to the photocopying room and photocopied everything and brought it back to you,' she finished at a gallop. 'I hope you're pleased. It took hours.'

'My God, Julian, you're a natural criminal.'

'I think I must be.'

'And what did you do with the original file?' I wouldn't have been surprised to hear that she had chucked in the Serpentine on the way to the cinema.

'Oh, that. I just walked into the archives and put it back. There was no one there. But if there had been, I would have said that I had forgotten my folder. That's why I left it there. And to mark the cabinet, because they all look the same.'

She held the folder out to me. 'I hope you still want it after all that.'

She stretched herself out on the sofa, pointing her bare toes until they touched my thighs, raising her arms above her head, elongating her fingers until the bones cracked.

'What I can't understand,' she said, 'is why it matters so much to Minna. I thought you lot, intellectuals I mean, were dedicated to the service of abstract truth, that you had higher and more spiritual goals than the rest of us, who are lying or not quite lying or implying something isn't really the case, all day long.'

I put down the file. I was no longer interested in its contents.

'Scrub that last bit,' Julian was saying. 'I know you're not really like that. If people who believe in God and the eternal retribution of the afterlife can't manage to behave well, how can anyone do so for the mere love of truth and learning? But still, why does it matter?'

I stood behind her, putting my hands on her shoulders, slipping them under the neck of her sweater, feeling her skin beneath my finger tips.

'I don't think you should discount love of truth,' I said. Her upstretched arms reached behind my head, pulling it down to her. 'But it gets mixed up with other things: discovery and possession. The abstract truth you see becomes the particular truth that you yourself have found, that you have toiled over and made your own. When it is suggested that it is not a higher truth, probably not a truth at all, it is an attack on you, your labours and your possession.' Her face beneath me was upside down, giving her a new and unfamiliar appearance.

'But so much energy to protect an idea. The venom, the fury . . .'

'Who was it who said that academic disputes were so intense precisely because the stakes are so small? But they're not small at all. They're vast. The loss of a life's work, a belief, a beloved object. It's like discovering your wife is a whore, your lover unfaithful, your mother not your mother. It's like losing your most treasured object in a vile burglary.'

'Oh, come on. She's still got the painting. If it'd been stolen, then she really would have lost it. It's still as beautiful as it ever was. What's she got to complain about?'

'As might have been expected, you take the modern view, that is, every object is unique, nothing is fake, the question of authenticity is projected on it by us. It's only in our minds that it is the real thing or not. But all this takes no account of the passion and attachment we have for our ideas, chiefly because they're our own and not because they correspond with the truth. Minna will feel bereft, not of the painting, as you say, she's still got it, but of her idea, which was her way of possessing it.'

I could identify with Minna. I could not be possessive of Julian. She would not permit it and I had no status to demand any kind of loyalty. So my desire to have what I had no right to manifested itself in trying to discover her history. It was an attempt to comprehend her, hold her. If I knew about her then I might understand her. If I understood her, then I would have captured her, at least in my mind, which was a type of possession I liked. It was my truth and though, like Minna, I was commissioning research, I did not really want to find anything that contradicted my own conviction.

'That's the way we possess anything really, or anybody. We have an idea of them and when we're forced to change it, by their actions or our own, it's hard to accept we were wrong.'

12

Prisca always called me at my office when she had family business to discuss.

'Your father is going to be in London at the end of the week. He wants to meet your new companion. Indeed, so do I.'

I had made no attempt to hide Julian from my friends and family; I simply had not introduced her to any of them.

'Why did he speak to you, rather than phoning me directly?' I asked, evasively.

'Nicholas, you know your father is incapable of talking to you about anything of significance, even to fix a date for dinner. Of course he rang me first. Anyway it's time for you to come clean. I've had Emily on my back as well.'

'Emily? How did she . . .?'

'Well, since even I have had reports of you with a stunning brunette at the Festival Hall, the Wigmore Hall, Covent Garden, the River Cafe and Harvey Nichols, all of which sound fairly unlikely places for you, I can't imagine that the friends who noticed you are likely to hold back on reporting their sightings to Emily. Is this a ploy to make her jealous?'

'It isn't a ploy of any kind. And there's no question of coming clean; I'm not hiding anything.'

'Good. Then let's say Friday evening.'

'I'm not sure . . .'

'Friday evening, the two of you. I'll be in touch about where we'll eat.'

I would have to turn up and face an inquisition by Prisca and my father, but I was not sure whether I wanted Julian there. However, I was bound to pass on the invitation and she replied, without hesitation, 'Of course I'll come with you.'

Prisca phoned to say we would eat at her house in Islington.

'Are you certain, Prisca?' This sounded really bad news. She had not cooked in years, to my sure knowledge, living on the House of Lords' restaurants and invitations to dinner.

'Don't worry, you'll be fed. I've recently mastered the microwave. It occurred to me that if Emily heard of us all dining at Frederick's, she might be upset. I'll tell her anyway, but at least this way she won't get any extra reports on the evening.'

'No one to contradict your slant, you mean.'

'Oh, she'll speak to your father, so it won't be a one-sided impression.'

There was no possibility of co-ordinating a front with Julian, who knew the bare bones of my family structure, but not the sinews and tissues that bound them together. I never normally spoke about my feelings: only Prisca managed to prise out of me my wishes for the future. I hardly knew any longer what I wanted. I wanted Julian, and so Emily, the children and the life I had been driven out of had to remain on hold until I was ready for them again.

We arrived separately, converging by chance on Prisca's front door in Gibson Square at the same time. Julian was walking. I kissed her cheek and said, 'Couldn't you find a cab? Did you get lost?'

'No, it wasn't that. I just decided to take the tube. Is this it? Let's go in. I'm cold.' She hustled me up the steps and rang the bell. I was puzzled by the unusual idea of her taking the tube, and from Sloane Square to the Angel, one of the most tedious journeys on the underground.

Prisca led the way upstairs to her chaotic drawing room dominated by books. That night she had tactfully put out my father's most recent volumes, huge coffee table tomes weighing in at several kilos, adorned with ravishing photographs.

My father was already seated by the fire with his particular brand of whisky in his glass. I saw, with relief, that the evening was to be eased by the presence of my lawyer cousin Jamie, who divided his time between Brussels and London, and his sculptress wife, Sybil, who had never got on with Emily and so might be counted on to be sympathetic, at least initially. They rose to greet us. My father shook Julian's hand warmly, and still holding on to it, placed her in his favoured chair, drawing up another beside her. He was soon engaged in deep conversation, or rather deep monologue, his preferred form of social interaction. The full force of his charm was directed at her.

My relationship with my father has always been difficult. His weakness is his lack of concentration, illustrated best by his number of marriages, four at the last count. In recent years, since his retirement, we have got along better, because we rarely see one another. My latest, and longest-enduring, stepmother keeps him busy in Scotland. He continues to expand the family art collection, and he has taken up history. This is such a wide-ranging subject that when his interest in one area flags, he can always take up another. It has also been the excuse for travel for 'research' when life in Scotland gets too cold or too boring. This hobby has not been unproductive, because he has an excellent picture researcher and has published a number of glossy books with a minimum of text on various Scottish subjects. His most recent enthusiasm is the history of his branch of the Ochterlonies, which he claims is of general interest, because it illustrates the banditry of early capitalism.

Prisca fussed around finding us drinks.

'The first Angus Ochterlonie was a genius in his way, don't you agree with me, Jamie?' My father was lecturing Julian and did not wait for confirmation. 'After getting himself half-educated as a doctor, he set himself up as a pharmacist. He started with a small loan and ended up a millionaire. I believe in the early years he and his family lived more or less on porridge, because he couldn't bear to spend borrowed money on his living expenses. Things were much less controlled in those days. It seems fantastic that someone could mix up a concoction of his own and sell it to people, but that's what he did. He invented all kinds of pills and potions for application inside and out. There was one rather bad moment, early on, when he was using arsenic, for face whitening I think, and was employing it in excessive quantities. There were a few deaths, but he got through that little difficulty, because, after all, *il faut souffrir pour être belle.* Wouldn't you agree, my dear?'

I found I was suffering from the embarrassment children feel in the presence of a parent. I could not bear to listen and went down to the kitchen to watch Prisca putting containers in and out of the microwave.

'Minna Horndeane is a vengeful type, isn't she?' she remarked, pouring the soup from its cardboard box into a plastic pot and snapping the lid on it.

'What do you mean?'

'Haven't you heard about poor Patrick Jameson?'

'Don't tell me they didn't give him the job?'

'They didn't. And apparently it was Minna who absolutely refused to have him.'

'I saw him only the day before yesterday and he didn't say anything.'

'He would probably find it hard to tell you, especially as he would have to say that it was because you were one of his referees that he lost it.'

She took the pot out of the microwave and opened the lid, removing her fingers quickly from the blast of steam. 'Oh, oh. Wonderful things, these machines, once you've got the hang of them.' She stirred the soup, replaced it and shut the door.

'I can't believe it,' I said. 'He was made for that job. They can't have been so stupid to let themselves be overridden by Minna.'

However, I did not doubt that Minna would harm the career of a third person, unconnected with our quarrel, because he was identified with me. The alarm rang again on the microwave. Prisca was more cautious this time in checking the contents.

'I crossed swords with Dr Horndeane a year or so ago when she gave evidence to a Lords committee. She has a very possessive view of the truth.'

'Minna's got a rebel in her camp, which I suppose is not surprising. She doesn't get on well with her colleagues.' I told her about the e-mail messages. I had received three of them by now.

'What's the point?' Prisca, like Julian, asked. 'It's not as if it's a matter of life or death.'

'Prestige is one reason. No director wants to see the quality of his collection downgraded. But it's more than that with Minna and the Vermeer. She wrote her first monograph on the picture, so she has some sort of sentimental attachment to it. I think she's in love with it. There must be a name for a passion for a representation of reality, but I can't remember what it is.'

'Would she go as far as faking documentation?'

'I've got hold of some of the tests. Don't ask me how. There's nothing incriminating either of the painting or of Minna on the file.'

'She wouldn't leave it there. Perhaps your e-mailer knows something. Who do you think it is?'

'It must be Anthony Watendlath, her deputy. He doesn't want to put the knife in himself. It wouldn't endear him to the Board, if he hopes to succeed Minna, to have been seen ruining the previous director and undermining the value of the collection. He needs someone to do it for him, and dish Minna in the process.'

'So you're a cat's paw for Anthony Watendlath?'

'No. As far as I am concerned, Minna has nothing to do with this. It's a question of . . .' I hesitated. Why did I persist in this search? 'Oh, it's simply the quest for knowledge. What Julian calls love of abstract truth.'

'Call the family, will you? Such a funny name, Julian. So Roman. She looks rather Roman in temperament, too, as if she would fall on her sword to save what she saw as her honour. Fine, of course, if her loyalty is to you.'

She poured the soup into bowls, adding, 'Or perhaps she would make *you* fall on her sword.'

The curious evening passed without the direct challenge I had feared. My father was enchanted with Julian; Sybil invited her to her studio; Jamie was impressed. Only Prisca did not like her, though she limited her disapproval to her remarks about Romans. I was perplexed and disappointed. I could see no reason why the two women should not be friends.

At midnight we dropped my father at his club. After saying goodbye to him and seeing him inside, Julian put her hand on the driver's door.

'Do you mind if I take over?' she asked.

Although I was surprised, for I had not been driving particularly badly, I didn't mind. Emily used to complain constantly about my driving; Julian, in contrast, would sit beside me without comment on my choice of routes or slowness at junctions. We moved off in silence.

'I'm sorry about this evening.' I said. 'I'm not sure why we had to go through it.'

'Don't apologise. I enjoyed learning about the disreputable past of your respectable family. It made me think that the Mafia of today may just be the founders of eminent families like yours, Nicholas.'

She was glancing in the mirror as she spoke. There were few cars about at that time of night. We approached the traffic lights at the top of St James's as they were turning orange. Suddenly, instead of braking, she accelerated, passing through the lights on red, as if banging a door behind her. I said nothing. I did not want to be a nagging passenger like Emily or to suggest that I was worried about my car which, though it cost a fortune, was not particularly precious to me. I simply did not like being driven at such a furious pace.

Her profile with its faintly curving nose and rather abrupt, rounded chin was dark, rimmed with light from the street lamps of Piccadilly. I watched her eyes flicker from the road ahead to the rear-view mirror. She was heading, fast, for the underpass, when suddenly, at the last possible moment, she swerved in front of a taxi and drove up the slip road to Hyde Park Corner. She did slow down a little as she approached the roundabout, but did not stop, inserting herself as skilfully as a stunt driver into the traffic. I could not prevent myself from saying, protestingly, 'Julian.'

She took no notice. The lights at the top of Grosvenor Place turned red in front of us. As we drove at greater and greater speed, my brain slowed events down. On our left a taxi and lorry, which had been waiting for their turn, began slowly to move forward. They inched onwards as she accelerated through the red lights, manoeuvring the car ahead of the vehicles moving towards our predestined impact. I could see the taxi driver's face: his eyes bulged and his mouth was open. He was not cursing; he was simply waiting in horror for the expected impact, a moment away. Julian drove in snake-like fashion across the traffic stream, veering right then left, as if she were avoiding fire. The cab's black bonnet and radiator grill disappeared from view without hitting my door. She swung the car to the left again, into Grosvenor Crescent, and slowed down, leaving Hyde Park Corner echoing to the strident relief of blasting horns.

'Are you trying to kill me?' I asked. She was looking in the mirror again. In the emptiness of Belgrave Square her speed no longer seemed dangerous.

She laughed. 'Oh, darling one, were you frightened? Of course not. *I*'m not trying to kill *you*.'

As usual, she refused any further discussion of what had happened. She lay in bed asleep beside me, and I put my hand protectively on her flank. I now had a retrospective justification for my employment of Mr Colin Trevor. It was not simply a question of satisfying my gnawing desire to know; she was in danger. The mugging and the break-in were part of a campaign to terrorise her. She needed protection.

There was a pendative to that evening. Prisca rang me two or three days later. She was too subtle to ask direct questions. She was just there on the end of the line and I found that I was telling her things I did not mean to say. Prisca was like that; it was a power that she used deliberately to gain influence over people.

'She's very beautiful,' she said.

'It's not so much that she's beautiful. It's the fascination she exerts. And she is so much fun to be with. She makes me laugh. She is so extraordinarily self-contained. I never know what she is thinking or what she is feeling.'

'You never know what anyone is feeling,' Prisca commented. 'I've never known anyone less conscious of emotion, his own or anyone else's, than you.'

'This time I'm trying to understand.'

'Hm. Your father was so funny about her.'

I did not reply. It was one thing to hear Prisca's opinion, my father's quite another.

'He said to me on the phone when he rang to thank me for a delicious dinner, (*What* does she give him to eat, poor lamb, if he thinks *that* was delicious?) he said, "Nicholas was utterly morose. What do you think they talk about?" And then he said, "I don't suppose they do much talking." ' She giggled.

'Julian and I have a great deal in common,' I said humourlessly. 'We go to the theatre and concerts and the opera all the time. I never did that with Emily.'

'That's nothing. You and Em had a whole life in common. You're just going out with Julian and having sex. And you do one because of the other.'

'I've had enough of this conversation, Prisca,' I said and put the receiver down.

13

The question of how Christmas was to be spent that year took up an inordinate amount of negotiating time during November and the early part of December. I finally allowed Emily to take the children to the Dorset house and spend both Christmas and the New Year there. I hoped that some time in the future I could use this concession to win something I really wanted. Julian and I flew to the Yemen and spent a week in a country without Christmas and a winter without snow.

When we returned, I realised that Julian was in hiding. We no longer went to the little restaurants that she loved, or to the cinema or to concerts. It took a week of excuses for me to understand that this was more than dislike of the film or not feeling like Lebanese food. It was much more than the occasional nervousness that she had shown previously; it was a consistent refusal to leave the flat. Every day I looked around the square for someone watching our building, but I could see nothing out of the ordinary. I made a point of asking Victor when I came in at night if Julian was upstairs, or if she had been out. His reply was always, 'I couldn't say.' Yet if she was afraid, she did not show it in any way beyond refusing to go out. Her self-control remained rigid. She did not stride up and down, or peer out from behind the curtains. She was calm as always, never irritable.

I could only guess at why she behaved in this way. The people she feared must be Russians. Was it Anatoli, the former lover, who was persecuting her? I had only indirect allusions in her conversation to go on, references to incidents in the past in which she was unlikely to have been alone; Anatoli must have been there with her. Under the surface of the story an x-ray would reveal another figure, a pentimento, who once made part of the artist's concept of his composition, now painted out. Or did the threat come from the other man, of whom I had found no trace, the naked sleeper? Why would they want to harm her? In every interpretation of events that I tried out for myself, I only ever thought of her as an innocent victim.

She came into the kitchen one evening to drink a glass of wine and talk to me as I peered at a duck's breast I was cooking. I had just discovered that you could buy ready cooked fried potatoes so dinner was more interesting than usual.

'Julian. I want to talk to you about going out.' Her smile did not disappear; it was simply fixed, as if she was skipping this scene.

'Going out?'

'Why don't you leave the flat? What's out there? Who are you afraid of?'

'Don't be ridiculous, Nick.'

'Then why do we never go out in the evening any more? No concerts. No films.'

'Because I don't feel like it. Don't you like spending the evening at home with me?'

'Yes, but . . .'

I could not make her admit that there was anything wrong. Her self-imprisonment made my appointment at Blackfriars especially important. Colin Trevor met me in his glass booth, in which the air was stifling. Outside it was savagely cold. An Arctic high was hanging over southern England and the air was like a knife from Siberia, striking the lungs. He sat in his shirt sleeves with my file in front of him.

'I'm afraid to tell you, Professor Ochterlonie, that we have had, er, certain difficulties with this case and we haven't been as successful in accumulating as much material as I would have expected.'

'Ah.' I was reprieved. Unsuccessful spying did not count. 'Why was that?'

'I won't trouble you with all the problems we encountered, because it would sound as if I was trying to make excuses for our performance, and I don't want to do that. We pride ourselves on delivering what the client asks for. And what you wanted was very straightforward: background information on two named individuals, addresses supplied. In a case like that, there's usually a lot of sources we can access to build up a dossier but, unfortunately . . .'

'All right,' I said. 'Just tell me what you have found. What have you got on Mr Vozkresensky?'

He was visibly relieved that I was a co-operative rather than a retributive client.

'Anatoli Vozkresensky is a partner in a Russian bank. We've been able to find out a little about why Scotland Yard was making enquiries about him. It's not the Fraud Squad, as you suggested, but the Home Office, and it's not Vozkresensky himself, but one of his partners who interests them. Another of the directors of the bank is called Muzafarov and he has had a block put on his visa, because MI6 claim he was a notorious KGB operative in the old days of the Soviet Union.' He stopped speaking, nervously ruffling the top right-hand edge of the papers in the file.

I sat absorbing this information. So Anatoli was Vozkresensky. So who was АФ? The naked sleeper? Or was Muzafarov the sleeper? No, because he couldn't get a visa . . . And Trevor was wrong about Scotland Yard. Tom Naish (Fraud), as he called himself, was enquiring about Vozkresensky, not Muzafarov. It looked as if Trevor had found nothing on Anatoli, but was offering something on one of his partners as a make-weight.

'And where is Vozkresensky now? Did you manage to discover that?' Was he living around the corner in London? Or was he on the other side of the world? Did Julian still see him?

'We have to assume he's in Russia. At least, he's not here, as far as we know. Just now.' Then with a burst of frankness, 'Though we did discover that he has a multiple entry visa for the UK, valid for a year from last June. So he could be moving in and out all the time.'

'Do you know what he looks like?'

'Yes, yes, we do.' His eagerness was too much. 'We had success there very rapidly. Almost as soon as we started the investigation.'

He was turning through his papers. He handed over to me a photocopy of a press cutting. Anatoli, the same Anatoli who appeared in all Julian's holiday photos, his smile, gleaming, amiable underneath his thick moustache, was shaking hands with someone. His suit fitted him impeccably; his shirt was a bold bankers' stripe; the shot cuff of his outstretched hand showed a cuff link the size of a traffic light.

'All this must be very disappointing to you, Professor, I realise, and in the light of our failure we're going to waive all charges. Please don't mention it. It's not often we have such lack of success. Our name is made on customer recommendation.'

I could not have cared less how much they were charging. 'I said at the beginning that time was not the essential factor for me. I dare say you'll get better results next go. Perhaps the Bank . . .'

'No, Professor. I feel this is a case we're not going to be able to help with.'

I looked at him more attentively now. He stared back at me with defiant unease.

'We've not produced what you wanted, for which I apologise unreservedly. But it has enabled us to see the nature of the investigation and we have come to the conclusion that it would not be worth going any further.'

'Ah. I'm disappointed. But if you think so . . .'

'We do.' The plural pronoun gave him authority.

'I was going to ask your advice about a new development. I hope you'll let me put it to you, even though you don't intend to continue.'

His reluctance was manifest, as he said, 'By all means, I'll be glad to listen.'

'Miss Bennet. I didn't tell you before, because I hadn't realised . . . She's now nervous. She seems to be afraid of . . . an attack, say. I wondered . . .'

Colin Trevor, his aged boyish face flushed, was on his feet. 'My advice to you, Professor, is to go to the police. Much the best thing to do.' He was already at his glass door, ushering me through the whispering open-plan offices.

I took the bus back to give myself time to think about this interview. It had clouded over since I left home and the sky was threatening. I sat on the top of the number 11 and looked down at the scurrying figures in the Strand, streaming across the road at the traffic lights, pouring down the steps into the warmth of the tube.

That man was frightened, I thought. *I've never known anyone less conscious of emotion, his own or anyone else's*, Prisca had said. But I recognised fear in Colin Trevor.

The bus trudged round Parliament Square and began its journey up Victoria Street. I emerged from my thoughts when it stopped at the Strutton Ground lights. I ran down the stairs, jumping off the platform accompanied by the angry shout of the conductor. I strode down Broadway towards the sign in the middle of the pavement that proclaimed New Scotland Yard. At the desk in the entrance I asked if I could see Detective Constable Tom Naish.

'I haven't an appointment,' I explained. 'He came to see me a few weeks ago and I just wanted to go over something again with him, if he's free. Here's my card.'

He might be out, away, abroad, in a meeting. How often do you find someone in his office, drinking tea, available? But he was. I was sent high up in the building and was impressed that a mere Detective Constable, which did not sound a very powerful rank in the hierarchy, commanded a secretary and a room, albeit a small one, of his own. He met me at the door and shook hands.

'Come in, Professor Ochterlonie. I'm better briefed than I was when I came to call on you before Christmas. I know who you are this time. Tea, coffee?'

I wanted neither, but accepted tea in an attempt to ease the interview.

'The wiser choice. I'll arrange it.'

While he was gone, I looked around. A computer stood on his

desk, but this was not a paper-free office. Piles of it lay on every surface. A stream of it, like unrolled lavatory paper, had recently issued from the fax opposite me. He came back carrying two mugs with some concentration on not spilling the contents.

'I hope it was milk, no sugar. I forgot to ask.'

It was hard to tell whether the disadvantage that he felt at our last meeting was going to work to my benefit. He sat down; we both clutched our mugs of tea, and paused.

'I was hoping, Professor, that you had something to tell me about your neighbour. A sighting, perhaps.'

'No, I've not seen him. At least, I wouldn't know if I had. You haven't got a mug shot, I suppose.'

He went to his desk and spoke briefly into the intercom.

'No one's moved back in next door,' I said, to fill in time. 'It's being renovated, but no occupants.' The door opened and the secretary brought in a box file from which Naish took out a newspaper cutting and handed it over to me. It was the same one that Colin Trevor had shown me an hour earlier.

'Have you seen him before?'

'I've never seen him in the building.'

The problem was explaining Julian. I had come because I was determined to do something to protect her and I hoped that Naish might have some advice. I was also acting on Trevor's desperate words, go to the police. I put down my tea.

'You're probably well informed about all this now, so what I'm saying won't come as a surprise to you. There was another occupant of the flat opposite me, a woman called Julian Bennet. I mentioned her before.' I half-expected him to confirm his knowledge by saying something like, 'Ah, yes, the tart.' But perhaps his information was even more detailed. I waited to see if I was going to have to start from the beginning.

'Yes,' he said. 'She moved into the flat with him right from the start, I understand. And stayed on there even after he disappeared.'

'That's right. She's now living in fear, which I think is connected with her former... partner. She thinks she's being stalked. There was the wrecking of her flat. Before that she was mugged. It looks as if someone is threatening her. In fact, trying to kill her.'

His first and obvious question was whether she had told the police about her fears. I had to admit that the answer was no and that she had told me nothing either. I was hoping he would provide me with the information she would not give.

It was easy to see why Naish had joined the police force. As an interrogator he had the extractive power of a vacuum cleaner. He drew from me what I knew about Julian, her tenure of the next-door flat and her relations with Anatoli. He gave me back nothing, while maintaining the friendliest attitude.

'The best thing you can do, Professor Ochterlonie, is to persuade Ms Bennet to come to us, to tell us everything she knows and let us see what we can do to help her.'

I sighed in exasperation and he said patiently, 'We have no idea whether it's her former partner who is threatening her or someone else. We don't know what they want, whether it is revenge or intimidation. We don't know how intimately she is involved. Until we know the background, where the threat comes from, there's little we can do. But you did right to see me. Now I'm briefed, I'm ready at any time to come to your assistance.'

'You can't give me any idea whether the threat is real, serious, I mean, from your knowledge of the case?' It was my last, feeble attempt to gain information.

We were standing now. He was smiling affably. 'If you mean you came here hoping I would say that these aren't killers and all this – bother – is for show, I'm afraid I can't give you any such assurance. On the contrary, everything I know suggests they're very violent men. Our aim is to block and then eliminate their operations in this country and in Europe as a whole.'

He had been very agreeable, but the visit had not been a success. All that could be said was that I had opened my lines to the police. If I could persuade Julian to seek help, I had someone I could turn to.

14

Julian's folder of photocopies from the Litvak archives was made of laminated cardboard. It was mauve, decorated with star bursts in green and yellow, a child's folder, the kind of thing that Cordelia spent her pocket money on and filled with secret papers. I had barely glanced at it since Julian had brought it home in November, because of my unease about the way it had been obtained.

Early in January, however, Minna had written a deeply disobliging review of the Coulounieix lectures, now finished, for an Arts edition of the *Times Literary Supplement*. This goaded me into deciding I would put together my case and use the conference in Moscow in March to present my thesis. There was ample scope within my very general title, submitted months ago, to discuss the *Lady in a Pelisse*.

One day during the period of Julian's self-imprisonment, I took out the file. As it would take me all day to read, I decided to work at home and persuade her to come out to lunch with me. I ate my breakfast alone. She was still asleep when I settled down in the dressing room, where I had set up a desk large enough to lay out my papers.

I began with the early stuff, about the sale of the painting to Litvak by Schall. The seller was not mentioned by name anywhere in the correspondence, and it was made a condition of the sale that his identity should not be revealed. This could have been protection for a great family, shamed at selling off its treasures in the hard times after the First World War. Or it could have been a useful cover for the painting's lack of provenance. Litvak had relied first on Schall's name and reputation and then, after he had seen the painting for himself, on his own expertise. It was obvious that he had fallen in love with the *Lady* and had been determined to have it. Schall had made him pay for his passion. The facts that the dealer was Schall, with his record of selling fakes, and that the seller was anonymous were weights in the scale against the painting's authenticity.

At about eleven o'clock Julian emerged from the bedroom to make herself some coffee. She brought me a mug and stood beside me, looking at the papers I was working on, her arm draped over my shoulder. She was still wearing her nightshirt and her dark hair stuck up in a cockatoo's crest above her forehead.

'What are you doing at home?'

'I'm going to take you out to lunch, then we'll go to the exhibition at the Hayward this afternoon. You can't stay here all the time.'

She ignored my last comment. 'I don't know.'

'Where do you want to eat? It's starvation if we stay at home.'

'I'll think about it.'

I put my arm around her legs and kissed her waist which was at lip level. 'Go away now and come back to distract me later.'

I went methodically through the papers, which were arranged chronologically, rather than by subject. I resisted the temptation to skip these less important parts of its story, even though I knew from flicking through the file that further on were charts, the scientific tests that Minna had mentioned. The papers traced the painting's history, its purchase, first cleaning, hanging in the Litvak home in Berlin, transport to Britain, storage during the war, rehanging. There were several notes in Litvak's own hand on the file about arrangements for the picture, including one about its hanging. 'It should be placed at such a height that the eyes, which look directly at you, should reveal all the truth of the soul,' he wrote. He, clearly, thought it was real.

The temperature outside was minus five and Julian wrapped herself in her coat.

'I worry about your wearing that beast in case you are . . .' I was going to say 'attacked'. 'In case you get a can of paint slung at you.'

'I could put a notice on my back saying 'Fake'. Rather neat, don't you think, to wear the real thing and tell everyone it's false?'

When we came back Victor was already on duty. In the lift I said, 'He seems a bit off colour. Is he all right?' Julian was training me to notice other people's states of mind.

'He's worried about Rose, his granddaughter. He's frightened she might be kidnapped or something.'

'That seems a bit exaggerated. By her mother, you mean? I can't keep up with this. I thought she wanted Victor to keep her.'

'She does. No, he's a bit neurotic about it just now.' The doors opened. 'I think the mugging affected him. He sees danger in the streets. And then the burglary didn't help.'

'This is ridiculous,' I said. 'How have we managed to employ a nervous night porter?'

'He's not normally nervous. It's just his granddaughter.'

I sat down again in my dressing room. Julian was moving around for a time; the murmur of her voice on the phone came from behind the closed door of the bedroom. I had been studying her as well as living with her and I had convinced myself that she was the real thing. I had no doubt there was something very odd in her past, which was still alive and active in the present, but whatever it was she was not colluding with it. I was sure she was truthful in what she said and what she did, in her precise words and her involuntary cries. Neither was faked. What had persuaded me was what she did not say. She almost never used endearments. She never affirmed love. This logical exactitude suggested she gave what she could and no more and that I could take it for what it was and nothing else.

Now came the scientific tests. I approached them with the nervousness of someone who is going to learn the results of a medical check up. They had been done in the mid-sixties by the Foundation's own laboratories, either as a routine procedure or in response to Skaekbekker's article. The x-ray report found considerable overpainting,

115

some of which was late. A map or picture in the upper right-hand corner had been painted out to leave a blank grey-white wall, cast into shade by the fall of light from the hidden window. This was not exceptional. Vermeer not infrequently changed his mind as he worked and added to or subtracted from his composition. Nothing incriminating came out of this test, except a question mark over the signature, which was in the area of late overpainting.

It took me a long time to read the material. I only realised how long when I heard Julian in the bedroom. She was sprawled on the bed, watching a video, laughing aloud from time to time.

'It's late,' she called. 'Come and watch this with me, Nicholas.'

'What is it?'

'*Some Like It Hot.*'

'I've seen it a hundred times. And so have you, I expect.'

'I have, but it's so funny. It's so stupid and so funny.'

The pigment analysis tests were as positive as the x-ray. For each colour a history has been established, showing the chemical composition of the materials used by painters over the centuries; the pigments used by the seventeenth-century Dutch masters have been extensively studied. The tests seek anachronism. Any impurity in the paint, any substance not commonly used at that time and place cast doubt on the authenticity of the painting. The first test on the Litvak *Lady* had been done with a high-power microscope. A cross-section of paint, taken with a hypodermic needle, was mounted and polished for examination. A similar sample had been taken for microchemical tests. A minuscule quantity of lead white had been treated with nitric acid and dried. No suspicious elements had been found in the amalgam of the paint. The proportions of silver and zinc in the lead white were found to be consistent with contemporary levels, a conclusion that was confirmed by the x-ray diffraction test.

It was hard to see why Minna had not published these scientific findings that seemed so supportive of her case. However, when I came to an overview of the data I saw that, although a seventeenth-century date was confirmed, it was much less precise than Minna claimed. There was, too, the question of the overpainting and the signature.

Then I came across a second sheet of a minute (the first was missing, torn from its staple) which contained just two lines: '*in the light of the initial tests the Director has decided that no cleaning of the Vermeer should take place.*' Why would Minna decide against cleaning? The tests might have shown the painting's fabric was too fragile to withstand it, but even so there are techniques precisely to preserve works of art in such a condition. The Vermeer was a sturdy and undamaged panel. Perhaps the doubts about the signature would only be strengthened by cleaning.

Julian was moaning with laughter. She sat up and adjusted her spectacles, which were falling off the end of her nose. 'I'm sorry, am I disturbing you? Shall I close the door?' she called out.

'No, I like to see you.'

'You should see Marilyn Monroe. She's wonderful.'

'I'm not a gentleman. I prefer brunettes.'

'How can anyone fall for them? It's so absurd that anyone could think they are women. How can one laugh at it? But one does.'

Her laughter ebbed to a sigh. I heard the music of the credits cut short.

'Laughter is supposed to be good for you,' she said, getting up from the bed and smoothing the white linen duvet with which she had replaced my mother's sheets and blankets. 'Talk about suspending disbelief. You want to believe so you refuse to see.'

The reproduction of the *Lady* that Julian had bought gazed up at me from its position propped against the lamp. I looked into the pale, cold world where the light was reflected in the faintest veil of saliva which moistened the full lower lip, in the drop pearl in her ear, in the dark brown-gold silk of the jacket. She was so beautiful, she had to be real.

15

Prisca rang to ask us to come, with Jamie and Sibyl, to a concert she was sponsoring for one of her charities. I accepted without consultation, daring Julian to refuse.

At the end of the performance, which was held in a church hall on the borders of Islington and Tufnell Park, Prisca grasped my arm. 'Don't leave now,' she said. 'Let's go and eat. There's an Indian round the corner. Jamie and Sibyl are coming too. Do stay.'

Within half an hour we were sitting in front of an array of bowls with the smell of ginger and turmeric in our nostrils. Prisca was on the high that follows a successful performance, estimating how much money she had made. Julian listened, questioned with the intense focus of regard which made you believe that what you said was completely captivating.

Sibyl wanted to know about the battle for the *Lady in a Pelisse*. I had a theory, I said, but I was not ready to expose it yet. Fortunately, Sibyl was too impatient ever to allow someone else to express himself slowly, when she could do it for him quickly and much more articulately. She was a natural philosopher, moving rapidly from the specific to the general, spinning theories out of nothing, to which she played her own devil's advocate. I allowed her to take over my part in the conversation as well as her own. I helped myself to some black dal. I never knew where I was with Indian food. I liked to know what to expect, with things coming in a proper order.

'Revenge is a sort of hangover from love.' I heard Prisca saying. 'It happens when you can't step out of the past and would rather cling on and be hated than cut the link completely.' She had put small mounds of vegetables and rice on her plate and was expertly scooping them up with her right hand, using two fingers and her thumb.

'You think it's a sign that love still exists?' Julian was speaking now. She was looking steadily at Prisca, who, I noticed, darted a quick glance in my direction.

'Yes, it's self-immolation. The revenger would rather still be in the eyes and mind of the beloved, even hated, than completely forgotten.'

I thought, Prisca is aiming this at me. She thinks this is why Emily and I are fighting over the children, but she's wrong. I did not want to maintain a connexion with Emily, for I could not envisage our living together again. The break was final. I wanted justice.

Jamie was mopping up sauce with naan, leaning forward over his plate to take the dripping morsel into his mouth.

'Prisca's ideas are always upside down,' he complained. 'Revenge as an act of love, it's like saying very noisy people are basically shy. You can make it seem to be true, but it goes against common sense. We all know that shy people are quiet and retiring and revenge is done out of hatred not love.'

'Perhaps it's neither love nor hate,' Julian said, voicing my thoughts. 'It comes from a sense of justice. Where there isn't a tribunal you can appeal to, as in emotional matters, you are driven to act, because there is no other way to redress the balance.'

'The real tragedy,' said Prisca, 'is that you destroy what you love. And that's your punishment, probably the hardest of all.'

It was nearly midnight when we had finished and were saying goodbye outside the restaurant. A taxi was passing with its light on and Prisca stepped into the road to hail it, cutting short our goodbyes. Sibyl and Jamie got into their car, parked opposite, and Julian and I linked arms and walked back to where I had left mine. We were crossing a side road and Julian stepped out without looking. With a roar, a motorbike swung past us, leaning into the curve. I grabbed her arm and pulled her back towards me. I felt the air of the machine's passage, the smell of its exhaust, like the meaty breath of an animal.

'Careful, I don't want to lose you like that.'

We drove home and I put the car into its habitual place, on the first level of the underground car park. The place was empty of people, full of cars. Our footsteps echoed on the concrete, rebounding from the low ceiling. The lighting, strung along the rows of cars, was dim, just illuminating the empty alleys, leaving corners of darkness which blurred the light, taking it over.

The attack erupted out of normality with a roar. I heard the sound of an engine, of a motorbike, stopping at the barrier above us, but I only became aware of danger when two more bikes burst up the ramp from the floor below. The air vibrated with the revving of their engines. Julian was swifter to understand. She was just ahead of me and I saw her bend down to take off her high-heeled shoes. Instead of continuing their ascent, the two bikes abreast swung into the passage between the parking spaces. For a second I faced them as they rode at us in formation, charging us, fantastic beasts with thick leather skins and shiny, globular heads. They were coupled to their bikes to form a smooth-running mechanical centaur, a unit of beast and machine without any human features.

Julian, her fingers hooked into her shoes, her feet bare, was already racing towards the door that led to the lifts and stairs. I saw her glance back, to assess the threat, to check on me. Still running, she shouted, 'Run, Nicholas, run'. I could see her face contorted, her mouth moving, but I was deafened into paralysis by the engines. At last, I jumped aside into the shelter of the nearest line of parked cars and the two bikes from below swept past me, their momentum carrying them onwards, circling the parking lot. I ran across the next alley and into another line of cars. Julian had reached the doors to the lift. I knew what she would find. I watched her grab the handle, pull and push, with frantic, useless force.

The first bike, the one which had entered from above, was circling in the opposite direction from the other two. They were by now on the far side of the car park, two going anti-clockwise, one clockwise. The noise of their engines boomed around the low space, disorienting me. I reached her and took her hand.

'We'll have to use the ramp,' I said. We looked across the endless empty expanse to the ramp leading from level to level. The upward slope to the exit was narrow, with barely room for two cars to pass. It offered no cover and I couldn't see how we could reach the top before the bikes caught up with us. I changed my mind.

'We'd better go down. The door below may be open.'

Without a word, Julian nodded and ran across the roadway to the ramp. Instead of taking the slope to the level below us, she climbed the metal barrier that marked the drop and let herself down. I followed her. She moved ahead of me, running for the lift. We reached it together. It was locked. These men, whoever they were, who had frightened Colin Trevor into rejecting my commission, were professionals. They had locked all the doors, not just the one on our floor.

Above us they were regrouping. The single biker who had seen where we had gone, led the way down the ramp, followed seconds later by the other two, still in formation. Julian was crouched behind a car, between its bumper and the wall. She dragged me with her.

'We can't keep on going down,' she said. 'All the doors will be locked. We've got to go up the car ramp.'

I was silent. I still could not see how we could run up two floors without being caught by the bikes. And then what? Even when we reached the open air, which seemed like freedom from down here, what would we face? What were they trying to do, kill, maim, terrify? My lack of understanding felt like a physical incapacity, as if I was lame.

'If I go down another floor, perhaps they would follow me and you could get out.'

'No, no. It's no good. They'd split up. Stay with me. We've got to go up.'

The bikes were circling in the old routine, two together, one alone, one clockwise, two anti-clockwise, like a tightly choreographed ballet.

'They've lost us.'

'They know we're here somewhere. It won't take them long to find us.'

They had slowed down now, the carapaced heads swinging backwards and forwards, the black-tinted visors as blank as computer screens, as they examined the spaces between the cars. They met in front of the ramp and stopped, all three together, and the noise dropped till it felt like silence. They did not speak, but redirected one another by swift gestures. The engines revved and they went back to combing the alleys.

'Let them look for a bit,' I said. 'If they think we've gone lower still, we'll have a better chance of getting out.'

She nodded, not looking at me. She had gathered up her coat, so that it did not drag on the ground. Below its hem I could see her feet, the toe nails, painted dark red, poking through her torn tights.

We were in luck. After making another circuit at a still slower speed, the pair swooped down the ramp to the next level, while the single bike continued its trawling. As it worked its way to the far end, Julian said, 'When he gets to the top, we'll go.'

'You first.'

'Come right behind. It's our only chance.'

She squirmed out of the space between the bumper of the car and the wall in which we had been pressed. We both bent double to conceal ourselves behind the lines of cars. But when we reached the ramp we were exposed to view. I could tell he had seen us by the violent revving of the engine and the acceleration down the alley towards the ramp. I allowed Julian to keep ahead of me. I could have overtaken her, but only with an effort, for she ran fast. Fear must have been pumping adrenalin into her, to give her a feline burst of speed.

We reached the first level and continued to run, making for the next rise. The bike was immediately behind us. I ran straight on into the car park, not turning for the ramp, hoping to offer a distraction. Ignoring me, the biker pulled his machine round after Julian. I stopped and waited for the impact. Julian ran on, not looking back. She judged when to swerve by the noise of the approaching machine.

I could not see if the bike hit her, or if she had thrown herself to the ground, face first, her arms outstretched. Just when she seemed most vulnerable, the biker lost his appearance of invincibility. He overshot and could not turn fast enough to come back to her. In attempting to do so, he scraped clumsily on the rear end of a car and had to put his foot to the ground, awkwardly kicking himself round, his engine screaming.

Julian had already picked herself up and was once again running for the ramp to the exit. I was racing after her. The two bikers from below were roaring up to join their colleague. I was between them and her, but I could see that the single bike, for all its momentary clumsiness, was going to reach the ramp before I did.

Amid the booming and echoing of the bikes, we did not hear the approach of the quietest car in the world. I saw Julian draw into the side of the tunnel before the magnificent dark green bonnet of the descending car came into my view. It was too sudden for the speeding biker. He hit the Rolls full on and the centaur split. The man rose in the air, his body describing an arc over the bonnet, striking the roof, sliding over the boot and crashing to the ground. His machine recoiled and slithered back down the slope on its side, its wheels still revolving. As I ran past them, I saw the aghast face of the driver, a chauffeur on the evidence of his peaked cap, getting out on the opposite side. Julian was ahead of me and I only caught up with her at the barrier. She was panting; her breath grating in her chest; her mouth and eyes like ragged black stains on a white cloth.

We slowed to a walk. Julian sank down onto a doorstep, putting her head on her knees.

'Are you all right? Can you make it?'

She looked up and said, 'Oh dear, you've torn your trousers.'

'*I've* torn my trousers. You mean *they've* torn them, whoever *they* are.' Then my fury evaporated in fear for her. 'What about you?'

I reached down to unwrap her coat and revealed blood streaming from horizontal gashes on her thighs and knees. She made no sound, though my movement had lifted a flap of skin and revealed the flesh beneath. A new surge of blood was released, liquefying the surface in front of our eyes. With one hand she delicately replaced the lump of flesh, still attached by skin on one side, and held it in place as the blood ran through her fingers.

'Oh, God, Julian.' I got out my handkerchief and blotted the blood from the cuts. 'You need stitches.'

'No. Don't say anything to Victor. He gets so upset.'

Once in the flat I changed from my torn trousers, while she cleaned herself up in the bathroom. When she emerged, she lay on our bed with her legs outstretched and I applied dressings to the cuts. She was fine, she insisted, and in no need of any medical treatment at all. She lay propped up against the huge square pillows with which she had transformed my mother's chaste bed, looking extraordinarily sexy, naked, apart from a pair of horn-rimmed spectacles that she always wore when she had removed her contact lenses, holding a glass of brandy. I sat at the end of the bed holding one of her feet in my hands. It was red and swollen, the sole cut from running in bare feet. I flexed the joints of ankle and toe and they moved easily, without resistance.

'Julian,' I said. 'After this evening, don't you think you could tell me what's going on? Who's trying to kill you?'

'No one is trying to kill me.' Her face had resumed her impenetrable look.

'Julian.' There was silence. 'Julian.' I rotated her ankle, persuasively.

'No one is trying to kill me,' she repeated. She put down her empty glass and rolled onto her stomach, leaning on her elbows, her head lowered so that her forehead rested on her hands. She spoke with exasperation, as if she did not want to have to explain something that was so self-evident. 'If they'd wanted to kill me, I'd be dead.'

I lined her feet up side by side and stroked the damaged insteps like a pair of cats.

'They don't make mistakes about killing people,' she said.

'So what's going on?' From my view at the end of the bed I could see the dark hair falling forward on either side of her neck to reveal her spine. It was raised and vulnerable, waiting for the executioner's axe.

'I don't know any more than you,' she said.

'But you must have some idea. I don't even know who these people are.' I thought of the sleeping figure, face down on her bed. 'Are they threatening you? What do they want?'

'No, no.' Again she sounded angry that I needed everything spelled out. 'Listen. I really don't know. But think about it. Work it out. That's what I've had to do. If you wanted to frighten someone, what would you do?'

'Beat them up,' I said vaguely.

'No, no. Use your imagination,' she was saying. 'If I wanted to put pressure on you, what would I do?'

'Kidnap the children. Attack you. Ah. I see.' I realigned my thoughts. I remembered what Minna had done to Patrick Jameson, damaging a third person to punish me.

'If they wanted me dead, I'd be dead. You've seen what they can do.'

'So they think that frightening you is putting pressure elsewhere.'

'Yes.' Pressure on Anatoli.

'Is it working?' I asked eventually.

Her shoulder blades were raised like wings, the crest of her spine sank into a narrow channel between two ridges of muscle. I reached out to run my hand down her back to her waist and up the reverse curve.

Her reaction to my question was horrible. She turned over to face me. The stillness of her face, with its control and determination, was broken. Her mouth contorted.

'I don't know. I don't know. I don't know.'

16

Julian slept later than usual the following morning. I worked at home and as I sat at my desk, I considered what to do. I must persuade her to go to the police; Tom Naish was the obvious person to turn to. She must be given protection.

The next day I was due to go to Paris where I had a long-arranged meeting. I was a trustee of a charitable foundation set up by an old friend, an Indian art collector, to give bursaries to students in developing countries to enable them to come to Europe to study art. I was the only British trustee and I was reluctant to cancel my visit. Equally, I could not bear to leave Julian alone for a day and a half. I concluded that the only solution was to take her with me. I rang to book another seat on the train, to change mine so that we sat together, without consulting her. She accepted the fait accompli with unexpected meekness.

The next morning she restrapped her torn knees, and we set off together to catch the first train to Paris. Victor was just going off duty and, as our taxi was delayed, he gave us a lift to Waterloo in his Rover.

'What have you done to yourself, Julian?' he asked as he lifted her cabin bag out of the boot, noticing the plasters on her legs. 'No one's been having a go at you again, have they?' He sounded anxious.

'It's nothing,' Julian said firmly. 'I fell over and scraped my knees. I must've been drunk.' He still looked concerned. 'Joke, joke, Victor. Don't worry about me. I'm fine. Thank you. You look after yourself.'

'Very smart car,' I said, as he drove off. I didn't add, for a night porter, but that's what I meant.

'It's new,' Julian said. 'He only changed it in August. Before that he had a Volvo.'

'Expensive tastes.'

In Paris, we drove to the hotel together, then I went off to lunch with my fellow trustees, telling her that I would be back for a late dinner with her at a restaurant nearby.

'What will you do until then?' I asked.

'Don't worry about me. It's not difficult to amuse yourself in Paris.'

I watched her set off down the little street, heading for the Boulevard St Germain, limping, liberated from prison.

The meeting I attended was meant to agree the nominations for the year to come. As usually happened, a great deal of passionate debate went into each selection and only the necessity of eating dinner eventually brought the session to an end. When I found her waiting for me at our hotel in the evening, one glance showed me that she had enjoyed her day. I wondered if she had friends here, if her mysterious life extended into other cities apart from London.

When we left the hotel Julian took my arm. 'No, not there,' she said, turning me away from the restaurant I had booked. 'I've now oriented myself. Let me take you somewhere I know.'

We walked for about ten minutes and she led me with confidence through the little streets. We had crossed the Boulevard St Germain and were moving parallel with the river, but not actually on the Quai.

'Here it is,' she said. 'La Belle Pelletière.' We were seated on the ground floor at the back in what appeared to be a covered courtyard.

'Another of your student haunts,' I said as we sat down.

'No, Nicholas. You have the most ridiculous ideas. Students can't afford to eat in places like this, except the sort of student you were, so rich you hardly knew what real life was. Anyhow, I was never a student in Paris.'

As I looked around I could see I had been misled by the dimness of the room. The tables were well separated by pots containing bay trees and were lit only by candles. The sound of conversation did not reach from one table to another and, above the hushed hubbub, came the sound of a piano being played at the end furthest from us. I saw now it was indeed not a student haunt, but a rendezvous of another kind, allowing French men and women to combine two passions with discretion.

Julian was unfolding her napkin. 'It's good for you, Nicholas, to have a change from the pompous places you normally go to. Where did you have lunch?'

It was true that the committee had lunched, at the trust's expense, at a pompous place. Brilliantly lit, voices as reverent as in a church, silent, constant service, widely spaced tables, it had been like eating on a stage.

'I knew it. At that sort of place people go to look at other people eating and to be seen themselves. It's a public performance, not a meal.'

'Whereas this place is for another sort of drama altogether, which I much prefer. It's a very good choice.'

I could guess how she knew this place. She would have come here with her former lovers, with the Russian, perhaps others before him. The thought did not trouble me. I was with her now, not he. The past and the future were in abeyance for us both. And she felt the same, of that I was convinced at the time. She had chosen it because she wanted to be there with me. On our table were two candles and she faced me, disembodied by the glow, between two nimbuses.

She chose the sort of food she liked, a whole veal kidney, while I ate my way through a plate of cassoulet. We had reached the pudding, which she had refused, though she was stealing spoonfuls of my marquise au chocolat, when I asked her what she had been doing.

'I had a very good day,' she said, 'considering I don't like Paris.'

'I didn't know there was anyone who disliked Paris.'

'I only came to be with you.' And not in London. 'Bad things always happen to me here.'

'What happened? Did anyone follow you? Was there . . .?'

'No, no, nothing. I just went to some places I used to go. I had lunch in a brasserie in Place St Germain and saw the same old waiter I used to know. And then I went to some decoration and antique shops around there, where I've bought things in the past, just to get ideas. They have such wonderful things here, Nick, which we could use for redoing your mother's flat.'

I ordered coffee for us both. She was nibbling at the petits fours that had been placed between us. I was content. The combination of a good day's work completed, a delicious meal and Julian's company wiped out all thoughts of Minna or Anatoli or Emily. I slipped my fingers under the cuff of her blouse and around the sharp wrist bone to feel the skin of the underside of her arm. She ducked her head forward to take another petit four. I could see the tip of her tongue curling within her mouth, as she opened her lips to receive it.

At the far end of the room the piano had fallen silent some minutes ago. Now the pianist, or rather a pianist, was sitting down to applause. I had thought that the original performer had been a man and this was a woman, whom I saw briefly in the second before she seated herself on the stool and disappeared from my view. She was playing Chopin and confirmed the change: this was a classical pianist. I closed my eyes, concentrating on my pleasure. Tone deaf, I only recognise the most obvious music and this was one of my favourite piano pieces. It seemed cornily appropriate to hear it with Julian's wrist under my fingers. I felt her pulse leap and thought that the power of music to move and to convey emotion was greater than any other art.

I opened my eyes to see that Julian was looking beyond me into the mirror that hung behind us.

'This is Chopin, surely?' she asked. Her face looked startled, wary.

'They've just changed pianists,' I said.

'She should be singing. There are words for this music.' And she sang, in a low, humming tone that barely reached us. *L'ombre s'enfuit, adieu mon rêve.*

Julian said no more and we both sat in silence, I in happiness, looking at her extraordinary beauty, the chance assemblage of features in just such proportions to produce a face that was unforgettable. She had moved her attention from me and was looking at the world in the mirror. The music finished and the pianist, who had evidently played by invitation, rose and bowed to acknowledge applause from one or two tables nearby. She sat down in one of the dim corners, where she had been dining with a broad-shouldered man, whose cigar hung a faint grey canopy over them both. The first performer resumed his place.

'Shall we go?'

She removed her eyes from the mirror behind me, in which she had followed the same scene. 'Yes,' she said. 'Let's go home, to London. Horrible things always happen to me in Paris.'

'But nothing horrible has happened this time. It's been a marvellous evening. And in London . . .'

The mention of London brought back the memory of her self-imprisonment in my flat, my battle with Minna, Emily's capture of everything I used to have. There was so much to do to straighten London out.

The next morning we woke early to go to the Gare du Nord. If it had been she who had exploded with rage, her excuse might have been that it was an unnatural time for her to be functioning. But I provoked the scene, enacting it before her composed gaze. She was still in bed, awake, when I began.

The respite was over. We were going back to the same world we had left, one that was closing in on us, narrowing our range, surrounding us with fear. We had to break out, but I could do nothing without her co-operation.

'Julian.'

'Hmm?' She turned her head to signify that she was listening, but did not open her eyes.

'We've got to go to the police, you know.'

'Do you think so?' she said, indifferently, as though the idea had never occurred to her.

'You can't go on as you have done for the last few weeks, hiding yourself away, never going out. We've got to confront them, to take them on.'

'We?'

'I'm involved too. I'm not going to let these people get away with it. We've got to do something and the first thing is to get you a bodyguard.'

'No,' she said sharply. 'I don't want that.' She got out of bed and walked into the bathroom, shutting herself inside. I was knotting my tie when she re-emerged.

'Julian, what are you going to do?' I nagged. 'What's your plan if you don't like mine?'

I watched her in the mirror. She was performing the contortions that women go through every day to put on a bra. She had done it up in front, at waist level. Now she was swivelling it round so that the catch was at the back, putting her arms through the straps, manoeuvring the whole elaborate, flimsy structure into place over her breasts. Now that the wire and lace were positioned, she was psychologically armed for the day.

'I have no plan.'

I undid the knot that I had just made for the third time. We were in a parody of a bad marriage: intimacy and distance. As the comparison came into my head, I lost my temper. I had not raged at Emily throughout the weeks of our break-up, however unreasonably she behaved. I had never in my life raised hand or voice to the children. Yet, unprovoked, I was shouting in tones that could not fail to wake the sleepers on either side of us, in this expensive, well-insulated hotel.

'You're so stupid,' I shouted at her. 'You're a stupid wilful bitch you live in a fantasy world in which you seem to think that if you shut your eyes all the folly all the danger all the criminal activity that you've got yourself mixed up in won't be noticed by anyone else either you think you can use other people's time property and emotion and give back nothing and that somehow being beautiful will get you through just as it always has so far well it won't work much longer your old associates are calling in the debts and I fail to see why I bother to try to protect you against yourself you can go and sort out your own mess.'

Emotional rage is painfully childish. To listen to the appalling and illogical stuff that came pouring out of my own mouth was bad enough, worse that I felt no better for my display of resentment. There was no catharsis, for Julian did not react. She had stood perfectly still during my outburst. Once it was over, she resumed dressing. I picked up my tie, my hand shaking with shock at my unexpected fury, rolled it into a ball and put it into my pocket.

'I'm going to have some breakfast. Do you want any?'

'I'll join you for some coffee.'

We went through the rituals of breakfast and departure in an atmosphere of constraint. Our banal words were cold and sharp and were flung between us like knives pointed with unmeant significance. Once we were on the train, she put her head back and closed her eyes. We ran ahead of the dawn across northern France. I recognised the contours of the century's battlefields. Just before Arras, between the TGV line and the autoroute was a little cemetery. The crosses stood in their ranks, like a platoon which has been cut off from its company and faces annihilation. The light, when it reached us, revealed sleet spitting from a low grey sky. The gloom of having deliberately separated myself from Julian, so unreasonably and so much against my own wishes, settled over me.

I opened my briefcase to do some work and saw a pile of mail that I had picked up in haste on leaving my office on the day of the attack. I came upon a large manila envelope addressed to 'Professor O', typed onto a computer label. I tore it open incuriously and pulled out a block of photocopies. The top page was entitled, 'Dendrochronological Report on *Lady in a Pelisse*, 02/03/89.' I examined the envelope, inside and out. There was no indication of where or from whom it had come.

With a prevision of triumph, at a time when I could not have cared less, I opened the report. There was a series of preliminary memos from a curator asking for the tests and giving reasons for doing them, replies from Minna resisting. It was not clear in what circumstances they had been made, but the results were unequivocal.

The principle of dendrochronology is exactly the same as the counting of rings of the stump of a felled tree, which I remember doing on my father's estate as a child. A northern European panel painting was usually done on oak and the tree rings are clearly visible at the edge of the painting, in the thickness of the panel, as a series of parallel lines, indicating the years of growth. The width between the rings varies according to the climatic circumstances of the year and so forms a distinctive pattern, which is valid for the whole region. Fully authenticated panel paintings by a number of Netherlandish artists covering the whole of the seventeenth century have provided a standard chart of the pulses of growth for Dutch trees, against which a reading for any particular painting can be calibrated. The most important date is given by the final growth ring, which gives the date for the felling of the tree.

I looked at the chart for the second half of the seventeenth century against which the ring pattern of the Litvak panel had been placed and, for a second, I thought it was an exact match with Vermeer's life and all my efforts were wasted. Then my view cleared and I saw that the last ring showed that the tree had been cut down in 1685, ten years after Vermeer's death.

We had just passed Vimy Ridge on our left when Julian, who had not spoken since the Gare du Nord said, without opening her eyes, 'Nicholas.'

'Yes?'

'I've been thinking.'

'Yes?'

'You're right. The police, perhaps the police *are* the answer.'

'They're certainly the start.'

She hesitated. 'All right. If you want me to.'

Her head was lying back, her eyes still closed. She looked

exhausted. She put a hand up to push away hair, which had fallen forward onto her cheek. She opened her eyes and looked at me directly.

'And, Nick, I think I'd better tell you everything.'

Part 3

Russian Counterfeit

17

Julian started her story on the train journey from Paris. She added to it day by day over the next two months, sometimes returning to an episode to insert another detail that had come to her mind. This tale of a thousand and one nights replaced the saga of Victor and Mary, Rose and Josie and I listened with far greater concentration than I had ever paid to the family life of our porter. She had vivid descriptive powers and a sharp observation of people and her surroundings. She did not have to tell me what she felt about the characters she described, her attitude to each was apparent enough in the way she spoke.

At the time I assumed that what I heard was the truth, her truth. But even as I listened, I realised that she was not telling me everything. Sometimes an indirect reference would indicate more to a situation or a relationship than she was willing to say. I knew better than to cross-question her. She herself had not wanted to know certain things, and she passed on to me what she had seen, watching me to see if I read the same meanings that she had. I observed a parallel, too, between her discoveries about Anatoli and my own about her. I knew very well how you can hold two conflicting ideas in your mind, refusing to choose between them. So her story was told in shreds and I put it together in my own way to create the picture I wanted to see.

As soon as Julian Bennet met Anatoli Vozkresensky she recognised him as an outlaw. She used the archaic word to describe him several times, and when I asked what she meant, she said that he was like her, a risk-taker.

As so often with momentous meetings, it had very nearly not happened. She had been living in Battersea, an area she did not like, imposed on her by the man who had helped her with the purchase of her flat. He had chosen it because he knew no one who lived there. She was happy with the flat, if with little else in her life, and had furnished it with minimalist elegance, so that it lacked everything that made for comfort.

He had disappeared some time earlier and she now had a job, as a model, which she hated more than anything else and only ever took on when money was especially tight. She sometimes used to work for friends, or friends of friends, in art galleries, PR offices or desk-top publishing. She was welcomed because she was fiendishly efficient and supremely presentable. They begged her to stay, but she never would, because she became bored and, she said, liked the freedom to arrange her own time. She kept saying to herself, 'Why am I living like this?' She knew she was supposed to have a different sort of life. Yet she so nearly missed the moment. She arrived home about seven one evening, after a day spent being photographed in underwear of a warming rather than glamorous kind, to find a voice on the answering machine.

'Are you free? I mean, hi, hi, Jules, long time and all that. Look, are you free this evening? I'm having this little dinner and we wondered if you could come to make up the numbers. I've got this Russian guy coming who's suddenly announced he's bringing his partners and really, you know, if you're outnumbered two to one by Russians, it makes a heavy evening. At least, I imagine it does, I've never experienced it before myself. I don't even know whether they speak English, the partners I mean, and I remembered you knew Russian, so . . .'

Francesca could never say goodbye. On the answerphone she could be expected to consume the tape. Julian lowered herself into the reclining chair, whose elegant shape was the only object in the bay window, while Francesca's voice revolved with the spools. Finally, it said, 'Eight thirty to nine tonight, you know the house, number 15. See you, bye.'

She thought, oh, hell, why not?

They were all there that evening, Anatoli, the Uzbek, the Whizkid, but she paid little attention to anyone except Anatoli and later had difficulty in recalling the other faces round the oddly assorted table. Barnaby, Francesca's boyfriend, from one of the oldest banks in the City, had invited the Russians, although Julian was puzzled why he should entertain three characters so uncongenial to him. Francesca herself, Julian had known for years. She had salvaged her little house in South Kensington as the spoils of an acrimonious divorce and spent her life giving and going to parties. That she was stupid did not prevent her from being popular. She was always surrounded by laughter, some of it directed at her, which she either did not notice, or did not permit herself to mind. She was very thin and dressed as if she were twenty years younger than her real age. Her house, too, had something juvenile about it, crammed with little objects, most of them furry or lacy, that she had acquired and set down at random. She was always saying, 'Jules, you must sort me out, design me, you know. Then we could appear in *House and Garden* or *Interiors*. It would really give you a boost.'

In this dolls' house the Russians gave the impression of wearing an environment that was too small for them. It was not just their physical build: Anatoli was tall, the Uzbek bulky, the Whizkid lanky. All three of them emanated a force that suggested that they felt constrained by the diminutive country they were visiting. Julian saw them as powerful animals temporarily enclosed in a miniature zoo. At present they were moving around carefully, anxious to please, but if the desire took them, they would charge the frail barriers that hemmed them in, trample them down and escape. And it was a similar quality that she identified in Anatoli that she knew she shared with him. They both needed the edge of risk to animate them, to

141

make life worth living. And neither of them was held back from an action that seemed necessary by fear of what people thought. The recognition was mutual and instantaneous. She knew as they shook hands that he had seen her, as she had seen him.

He was a tall man, strongly built, with a fair skin, dark hair and very pale grey eyes. Only later, at much closer range, did she notice the dichotomy between the upper and lower parts of his face. The forehead, brows, eye sockets and nose were bony, sharply modelled, cerebral; the cheeks, jaw and lips under a moustache were fleshy and sensual. He sounded like an American and could have passed for one. The Uzbek, in contrast, was an old-fashioned Soviet. He was square, and the engaging smile that occasionally split his leathery face sparkled with gold teeth. He was much older than his partners, in his sixties, and still wore the standard grey suit of the Communist days. The Whiz-kid, too, was unmistakably Russian.

At dinner, Julian found herself sitting next to him. Her initial reaction was based on his appearance and produced a misjudgement that took her some time to correct. He was the youngest of the partners; she assumed him to be the junior in every sense. His name, he told her, was Igor and the abrupt sound with the stress on the first syllable, was as crude as he seemed to be. He spoke an odd, self-taught English which he filled out with demotic expressions, so she was not obliged to use the Russian that she had learned at A level.

He was wearing a grey suit, too large for him, lending him an appearance of fragility and incompetence. When she learned that he was the numbers man of the partnership, with a passion for computers, she understood that he was a Russian version of a nerd. She had long ago perfected a technique for dealing with bores which was to talk about a topic that interested her. So she chose music and gave an account of a concert by a Russian baritone. She was describing the moving sounds that issued from this gross figure, knock-kneed and splay-footed, when Igor said, reproachfully, 'He's supposed to be one of our greatest singers. You didn't know him?'

'No, I'd never heard of him before. But you're quite right. He was very good.'

'No one here knows anything about us.'

'Well that's hardly our fault. You can't be said to have been very welcoming over the last seventy years.'

'Perhaps not. But it was difficult for us. Ten years ago it was a dream to go to Europe, America, California, like going to the moon. Now, look, here I am.'

'Ten years ago? You must have still been at school.'

'No, I had already finished university. I'm older than I look, the same age as you, I should think. People have always thought I was too young.' He turned to look at her. 'You look about twenty-five, twenty-six, but I think you're thirty-two, thirty-three, the same as me.'

Julian was, for once, short of a reply.

Igor carried on, 'I was teaching in the university at Irkutsk, but I looked younger than my students. I had to show them I knew more than they did.'

'Where's Irkutsk?'

'It's in Siberia. I'm a Siberian. We're different from other Russians.' He nodded towards the others. Julian was glad of the opportunity to hear something about Anatoli.

'In what way are you different from him?'

'From Anatoli?' He laughed. 'In every way. He's a Muscovite that tells you everything.'

'But now you're partners.'

'Yeah, we're partners now. He needs me. I need him.'

'Whose need is greatest?' As they talked Julian covertly watched Anatoli in conversation with Francesca.

'Just now we, all three, hold one another together.'

'What *are* you doing? I don't really know what Barnaby does, let alone you three.'

'We have made a bank and we've just arranged for representation here with Barnaby's business. It's great for us. His is a very old organisation, very prestigious.' He was not interested in the pile of wild rice and breast of guinea fowl in a sauce, which had been placed in front of him. He moved the food around with his fork and then said, 'Is it allowed to smoke, do you think?'

Julian smiled at him said cruelly, 'No, I wouldn't try it. Francesca hates people to smoke at the table.'

'Shit, I thought so.' He sighed and drained his wine glass, which Julian refilled for him. 'And you, what do you do?'

She was used to this question. If you were a married woman no one expected you to do anything and, even if you had a high-powered career, you were probably not asked about it. But an unmarried woman had to 'do' something. She said, as she always did, 'I decorate houses'. She had not done anything in that line for at least a year, but the answer remained the same.

Igor plodded on with his research. 'You come from London?'

'I've lived in London for the last fifteen years, but originally I came from the north.'

'You're a provincial, too.'

She noted that way he was at pains to mark himself out: he was the clever boy without advantages, but with a chip. She, too, felt that she had been born an outsider, but her plan was not to emphasise the gap, but to leap over it and join the other side. She should have been one of the privileged. She was going to be. The conversation petered out and she turned to Barnaby on her other side.

She had never much liked Francesca's taste in men and Barnaby was one of her worst choices. His bland surface betrayed interest in nothing. She had tried on several occasions, by introducing more and more outrageous subjects, to elicit enthusiasm, distaste, shock, without any result.

'What does he like?' she had once asked Francesca, plaintively.

'Sex, money,' she had replied. 'What else is there?'

'He can't expect to talk about sex and money to everybody all the time. He ought to make an effort on one or two other subjects, like where he went skiing and what was the last film he saw.'

144

This time money seemed the best bet. She asked him about the Russians' bank.

'It's called the Stary Bank, which makes it sound glitzy in English, but in Russian it means old, as if it has got millions stashed away from the imperial past, respectable, rich, romantic. I don't know whether it was accident or cunning. Usually Russians are no good at PR. They tend to think that just mouthing the party line is enough to persuade the masses.' His voice dropped. 'But you can't tell with these three. They're absolutely minting it in Russia today. Don't ask me how they do it. And in financial services, for people like this,' he nodded to Igor and the Uzbek, who were talking in Russian across the table, 'the sky's the limit; it's really starry. It's like, well, it's like the early days of the industrial revolution here or America, the railway boom, or something like that. It's all new, there's no framework, so they can do as they like.'

He was happy, Julian thought, and would talk about making money for as long as she let him.

'It's a cash economy, which is about to leap into the age of electronic money. The first banks in there, are, well, they're printing it. And all this cash, hard currency, I don't mean roubles, is swilling about looking for a home. And new business, eager for capital. It's the wild west. We couldn't get involved ourselves, directly, I mean. It's unsafe, of course, and we're respectable people, but it does no harm to dip a finger in, at second hand, as it were.' He was eating at the same time as he spoke, masticating his food, as if he were absorbing dollars into his bloodstream.

'And who are they, your Russian colleagues?'

'God knows. It's amazing to me how they have sprung straight out of the Communist system. You wonder what was going on there all those years. I mean, they don't look like bankers, I agree, only Anatoli and he is the smoothest Russian I've ever seen. But it's not what they look like that matters.'

Julian hid her amazement. He had always appeared to be a man for whom appearance was all, for whom an incorrect style of tie, belt or shoe would be conclusive evidence of unacceptability.

'They're living proof that the market rules, ok. Anatoli is an absolutely up-to-date economist, knows all the western theories, understands everything. The old boy, well he's a real capitalist. It's like meeting the first Rockefeller. And as for the boy wonder. He's a Russian version of a Californian silicone chip.' He was becoming incoherent in his astonishment.

'You've fallen for Russia in a big way,' she commented, drily.

'Wonderful place, the new frontier. They've invited us to Moscow. I've already been, but I might take Chessy along for a weekend.'

When they left the table, they crammed themselves into Francesca's tiny drawing room which was shaped like an old-fashioned railway compartment. Julian sat on the minuscule sofa beside the Uzbek. Neither of them spoke. He offered her a cigarette, which she refused with a shake of her head. He was unbelievably ugly. It was hard to imagine how anyone could allow himself to become so unprepossessing, for when he was younger he must have been at least less obese, she thought. The pliability of his fleshy face had settled into thick creases around his eyes and mouth. Tufts of hair sprouted from his ears and nostrils. His eyebrows, still black in contrast to his thickly matted head, jutted over narrow Tartar eyes. He sat beside her, smoking, impervious to Francesca's distaste, as if he and she were the audience at a play.

Julian had an acute sensitivity to power. She realised this was someone who had to make no effort to please, because everyone tried to please him. It was habitual, expected. It did not date from yesterday and the foundation of the Bank. He had been used to deference for years and years. She remembered what Barnaby had been saying. Where had they come from? What had he been doing for so long under the old system that he regarded everything as his due? Stubbornly, she refused to give him what he demanded, to talk, to charm, to flatter. She watched Anatoli with a blank gaze, which could have suggested that her thoughts were elsewhere.

She was surprised when the Uzbek said in Russian, 'He is married,

146

you know. He has a wife and son in Moscow.'

She could have pretended not to understand the language. Instead, she chose not to understand what he said, looking at him directly and saying, haltingly in Russian, 'You have a wife and son in Moscow?'

'No. My wife is dead. My son is in Tashkent. I said *he* has a wife and son in Moscow.' She was about to continue with her pretence of misunderstanding him, when he added, 'You may need to know.'

She recognised his desire to inform was not well meant, and took his hostility to be directed against herself. Only later did she realise it had been a spoiling tactic, aimed at Anatoli. She made no acknowledgement.

At the end of the evening she still had not spoken to Anatoli since they were introduced and had concluded that she would have to contact Barnaby or his secretary for a phone number. But when she left, later than the rest, after congratulating Francesca on the success of her recipe for guinea fowl, she found him standing in the street finishing his cigar. He strolled towards her and they fell into step.

'You have a car?'

She held up her key ring on the end of her finger.

'I was going to walk back, but perhaps you can drive me. I want to show you where I live. I've just bought an apartment and I think I need you.'

18

Julian had always been, more or less, a kept woman. She had had no interest in a career.

'What's the point?' she said. 'Women kill themselves to work like men. They still don't get to the top and they lose everything else they ever had in the process. Who wants to live like that?'

When I commented that there was something very old-fashioned about being kept, she said it was no more old-fashioned than being a wife, and there were still plenty of those around. If I had ever given the matter any consideration, I would have thought that the mistress was an extinct species. Feminism, divorce, work and the pill had made sex easier and cheaper for men. No need to take on financial responsibility when there are attractive women, unmarried, no longer married, or still married, with careers and incomes, willing to share pleasure for nothing. Wifehood and prostitution were shrinking habitats and the landscape between had widened enormously.

'What kind of men keep women nowadays?' I asked, thinking old, fat, ugly men.

'All kinds of men,' she replied. 'Men like you.'

I rejected the comparison with indignation, for I was not keeping her. She had moved in with me of her own accord. I had not even invited her. I made no financial contribution to her upkeep. Her attitude to money was, in my view, seriously odd. She insisted on paying for herself. She always carried huge sums in cash and paid for taxis and film tickets before I could get out my wallet. At the same time she had a running joke about the approach of bankruptcy, and if she lost a five-pound note, or could not account for fifty quid there was a major drama.

'Ruin, ruin,' she would say as she signed a cheque. 'I'll have to find some more clients.'

Her first year with Anatoli was an explosion, golden stars raining from the skies. She was Danae to his Jove. He was a dazzling comet, arriving every two weeks from Moscow, working eighteen hours a day in London, making dashes to New York or Paris or Geneva. I imagined her watching this fireworks display with her customary inscrutability, impressed in spite of herself. He was, like a comet, a natural force. His charm did not lie in subtlety or wit, but in power, of personality, of emotion and of action. Part of his power was the money that seemed to flow from his fingertips.

When they met, he had come to London to take over the flat he had just bought. It was here that he installed her, with instructions and money to furnish it. Julian, who was more sentimental about places than people, always loved that first apartment, even though it was to be nothing more than a beginning, a place to stay, while the duplex opposite my mother's flat was constructed. When she had first entered it, the night of Francesca's dinner, it had been almost empty, uncurtained, uncarpeted, occupied only by a mattress and a few suitcases. They had walked around the echoing space, their footsteps resounding from the naked walls. Anatoli had opened the stiff metal casements to let in the hum of city noise and the chill night air and they had looked out over the brilliant darkness of the London night.

'To be here like this means nothing to you. You have been here all your life. You can't imagine what it feels like.'

She said nothing, judging shrewdly that he had been far more privileged under his system than she had under hers. He was leaning out now, Julian standing behind him, watching his back. She did not like heights.

'But this is just the start. We want much more than this.' He spread his fingers, as if to grasp the view by handfuls.

'What do you want? Land? Property?'

'Land? No. What would we want land for? Land is for peasants. And property? Yes, but that's not the essential. No, you have to have what you can't see. The invisible, the intangible, that's what's important.'

'And what is it, the intangible?'

'Knowledge, money, power. In Russia we got stuck. We thought that when we had caught up with railways and airplanes and space flights and combine harvesters, we had everything. We didn't realise that while we were ruining ourselves to get these things, the world was moving into computers, telecommunications, star wars.'

'This is a new focus for Russian mysticism,' Julian said, folding her arms around herself, in her characteristic, self-embracing gesture. 'The all-knowing, immanent power of the chip.'

They slept that night in the uncurtained room and she woke in the early hours when he turned on all the lights to dress. Sleepily, she watched him shrugging on his jacket.

'What's the time?'

'Six. I'm going to Moscow.'

'Now?'

'Yes, this morning, the nine thirty flight. I'll be back in two weeks.' He squatted on the floor by his brief case and threw a brown envelope onto the sheet beside her, where he had lain. 'See what you can do by then.'

She was already out of bed. 'I'm coming to the airport with you.'

So she did not open the envelope until she returned in mid-morning, opening the door timidly like a new tenant, looking round the place in daylight, as if for the first time. In the centre of the bedroom, on the mattress heaped with bedclothes, lay the manila envelope.

She lowered herself to floor level and picked it up, reflecting on what she knew of him. He was married. This, according to her theories, was inevitable. *There Are No Unmarried Men in the World,* was one of her axioms. He was forty-six years old, married for seventeen years, with a sixteen-year-old son. Formerly a civil servant ('Everyone was a civil servant in the Soviet Union.'), he was now a banker.

She lay on the unmade bed and sniffed the pillows, then rolled onto her back and held the envelope over her head. She knew what it must contain: its neat, brick shape betrayed it. She tore open the flap. Two sheaves slid out, each secured with a coarse rubber band. Each block was about five centimetres thick. She flexed the edges of both packs: one-hundred-dollar bills, one thousand in each, say. She put them down on her stomach, feeling their weight. The insulting connection was so simple and direct, sex, money, money, sex.

When Anatoli returned, two weeks later, as he had promised, she had made a start; an office in one of the bedrooms was equipped with all the apparatus of communications, computer, fax, phones. She threw the two packs of dollars back at him.

'What am I supposed to do with these? This isn't stone age Moscow, you know. You can't pay cash here, at least for the sort of things I'm thinking of.'

He was unconcerned. 'Sorry. I was in a hurry, remember. I thought you might need something to be going on with, while I was away. For food, you know.'

'*Food*?'

'Ok, ok. You've got a bank account? I'll transfer something to your bank account. No, even better, we'll make you a company. You're an interior designer, aren't you? You'd better make yourself into a design company. Better for everything, trade discounts, VAT, the lot. I'll get my lawyers to do something about it while I'm away.'

When she was with him everything was a game that she took very seriously. She spent tracts of time planning what to wear, what to offer him to eat, whom to invite, where to go. He liked companionship, laughter, long meals, even longer discussions, music, stories. She collected anecdotes with which to amuse him, about the famous, the infamous and the unknown. She arranged his free time, concerts and dinners, expeditions and weekends away, as she arranged his first flat and then the next, with a concentration that came from total engagement in the project. He never said what he wanted or what he liked. She had to create by instinct and terror. For she was sure that if she were ever wrong in judging his taste, it would be like a quarrel, in which unforgivable words are spoken.

Did she ever wonder where it came from, all this money? In the first year she asked no questions. She was never again physically confronted with it after the first morning. He did not reclaim those two bricks of dollars and she put them away in a drawer. Occasionally, her fingertips scratched the surface of the envelope as she scrabbled for a scarf. She sometimes paused, thinking it was madness to keep cash in the house, but she could not bear to part with it. To hand the two blocks back to Anatoli was, symbolically, impossible, and to turn them into figures on a bank statement would also deny them their totemic status. She would think of ways she could conceal them in case of a burglary; but she had heard that burglars studied psychology nowadays and knew the instinctive hiding places that women use to conceal their jewellery, inside saucepans, wrapped in underwear, under the mattress.

This money, excessive in the form of notes, was nothing to the sums that were expended in invisible form on redesigning and furnishing the new flat, on buying property in London, in Paris, in Cyprus. She did not let herself think about it, signing cheques without adding up the total. Her accounts, opened for her by Anatoli in her new corporate persona, swelled. In the past, she had never had enough money, even for food and clothes. Her desires, her standards of perfection, had always outstripped her means, even in the few periods when she had been relatively flush. She had never permitted herself to fall into debt. Control of spending was just another form of control, which she practised rigorously to allow herself the freedom from doing what other people did, from the drudgeries of work and marriage. Now that she had lost control of her emotions, she spent without counting the cost, without asking the price; but only ever for Anatoli.

She gave him everything that she bought with his money, paying for it herself with her obsessive care in choosing. Every object that she acquired was invested with significance. He enjoyed her explanations of why a certain chair, bust, painting had been bought, not just because the object was beautiful in itself or fitted into the arrangement she was making, but because it had reference to him, his life and interests. Everything involved him, from the little Hepworth sculpture that she saw in a Christie's catalogue and knew he had to have, to the Armani suit she bought in Sloane Street to wear for him. She collected and mounted photographs of him in great leather-bound albums. She began with the pictures of his London life. He found her recording of his doings, the creation of his life into a story, amusing and flattering, and brought more photos from Moscow, of himself when young, with eminent figures from the Soviet past, at Harvard, on his missions abroad, shaking hands with great men.

He gave her everything and nothing. He would bring her tokens from his travels: Swiss chocolates, pots of caviar, bottles of brandy, all the things he liked himself, opening them for her with enthusiasm to consume within hours of his return, as part of the celebration of reunion. The blocks of dollars that she kept had a complex meaning for her; but even she, with her capacity for mythologising, could hardly turn them into gifts of love. So the sable coat had a significance quite apart from its value.

It was in their second year together. They had already moved into the new apartment, had a well-established pattern of meetings and pleasures. He had arrived from Moscow unusually heavily laden, with a long rigid cardboard box, like a truncated coffin, sealed and bound with leather straps. He let her undo it, seated by the fire, watching her kneeling on the floor. She patiently worked at each layer of wrapping, expecting to find something for the apartment. She exaggerated her interest, because she could see that he was excited by what he had brought. She had no need, however, to simulate her astonishment when the final layer of paper was folded back to reveal the pelt, dark brown gleaming with gold, that lay

154

beneath her fingers. She lifted it and it seemed to spring upwards into her arms, so that it was like holding a live, wild animal, whose silky coat trembled with nervous preparation to leap, to bite, to flee.

He leaned back in his chair with satisfaction. 'That'll keep you warm in your cold English summers.'

She remembered then the incident that must have given him the impulse to make the present. Earlier in the year they had been invited to a grand wedding in the country. It was one to which Em and I had been asked, an invitation we had accepted and had had to cancel. Sholto had fallen out of a tree in the garden in Dorset and we had to take him to casualty to have his collarbone set. I brooded on how Julian and I had failed to meet then, what would have happened if we had.

Anatoli called such invitations 'seeing the natives' and enjoyed his powers of attraction as an exotic Russian. For her, the day had been marked by the experience of going as a couple, an illegitimate one, to a smart wedding, by the ironies of listening to vows of fidelity and participating in a social rite of which she was the ultimate denial.

It was early June and bitterly cold. As they stood outside the church for the ritual of the photographs, Anatoli had held her arm above the elbow and felt her shaking invisibly.

'Why does no one dress properly in this climate? You should have put on something warm.'

'What people usually wear in places like this is trousers, woolly socks and layers of sweaters all year round, but you can't dress like that for a wedding.' Julian hated the country and only ventured into it for social occasions of high ornamental value.

She did not know what had made the episode so memorable for him and produced that extraordinary present. Perhaps his social success, or her own, as undeniably the most beautiful and best dressed woman, unconventional in black, like a raven among the vegetation of straw hats, floral prints and pale blue tussore silk. He loved the sensation she created by her elegance, and the sable coat was a way of ensuring a shiver of English outrage wherever they went. Or perhaps he had decided, with none of the significance that she invested in things, to give her the coat, quite simply, to keep her warm.

These stories about the blocks of dollars and the fur coat were typical of the way that Julian approached Anatoli's money, in their first year together. There were, apparently, no questions in her mind, at first, about its sources or uses. Money and goods were not objective commodities, but signs of subjective states, communicating the flows of emotion. Their moral role was entirely affective and for her they had no other ethical base. I found this point of view terrifying and said so. We were walking in the park one afternoon when she told me about the money and the coat. She had lost a glove and I held her bare hand in mine, caressing it inside my coat pocket. She walked with her head down, watching her feet in their shining mahogany-brown boots.

'I just assumed that everything was legal. After all, I met Anatoli through Barnaby, who is as respectable as a British banker can be. All the labels were correct. There was no reason to think they were not what they appeared. And I wanted to believe everything was as it should be. When your prejudices and your desires combine, you don't go looking for what you don't want to see. Isn't that what you always say?'

'Is he dead?' I asked, brutally. It would explain a lot; it would ease a lot.

'No.' She took in her breath sharply. 'No, he's still alive. I've seen him, but not spoken to him. You still don't understand, do you, why I'm telling you this? But you will.'

19

She wanted to know Anatoli, just as I wanted to know her. She made my task hard, for she was deliberately secretive. Anatoli was open, but unreflective. He did not like to discuss emotions, he lived and acted and that was enough. She had to understand his states of mind by watching his behaviour. He was not going to explain what he was feeling, for he did not examine his feelings for himself, still less talk about them to someone else.

For interpretation she found help in Igor, who used to come to London too, though on a routine quite distinct from Anatoli's. He would stay in a scruffy hotel in Bayswater and arrange to meet her at one of the small, noisy restaurants that she liked. He always carried a parcel from Anatoli to give an excuse for the meeting. She always mentioned seeing him, but she never revealed how long they spent together. It was from Igor that she gained her first insights into the relationships of the partners of the bank, and later of what they did. Even at this earliest stage, tensions lay between Anatoli and the Uzbek.

'Tolya and Dyadya,' Igor would say, holding his hand out palm down and tilting it to suggest instability. 'Things are a bit nervous now. They don't always understand one another. Old rivalries, you see.'

'No, I don't.'

'If you were Russian you'd understand. It's a question of class. Our Anatoli now, your Anatoli you would say, he comes from a group which is not the same as the clan from which Dyadya comes.'

'Where does Anatoli come from?'

'He doesn't come from anywhere. He's there, on top, always has been. Even before the Revolution.'

'His family were aristocrats? How could they have survived?'

'No, not aristocrats. They were priests; you can tell by his surname. So they were never workers or peasants. His grandfather was a crony of Stalin's. Vozkresensky is a famous name in Russia from the time of the war. It doesn't have quite the stink of Beria or Yezhov, you'll be glad to know. He was a sort of court joker, which helped him to survive, and survive he did, right through to the 'sixties. His father was a candidate member of the Politburo. So he's had everything, all his life: big flats, cars with drivers, dachas near Moscow, trips abroad. He went to Harvard; that's where he got his accent.'

Igor never ate much. He preferred to smoke and drink. His arms formed a triangle over his untouched plate while he talked almost to himself. Julian, at the time, did not consider why Igor, too, was so interested in the personalities and social status of his two partners. She was too engrossed in learning what she could about Anatoli.

'To live well here in the west, it takes serious money, you know that. In Russia, Anatoli got everything free, provided by the Communist party, one way or another. You didn't need money if you belonged to the high nomenklatura, it all came to you by right. Anatoli's family weren't aristocrats before the Revolution. They were aristocrats afterwards.'

'And Dyadya wasn't?'

'No, God, no. Dyadya's hard to explain to anyone who didn't live under the old system. He wasn't high up in anything. I can't remember what his position was supposed to be, an official in the Uzbek Trade Ministry, or it might have been Transport, but he never appeared in his office.'

'Eat, Igor. I've finished.'

Igor stubbed out his cigarette and picked up his knife and fork. He cut carefully into his steak, pierced it with his fork and laid it down on the plate. 'This was how Dyadya earned his dough.'

'What? Meat?'

'A lot of it was food, but anything in short supply and that was everything. He was a fixer, on the big scale for the big guys. He could build you a private dacha with everything in it. You want a marble bathroom? You can have a marble bathroom. You want a jacuzzi? You can have a jacuzzi. He could get railway wagons full of building materials and have the rail schedule for the whole Soviet Union changed, if he wanted something.'

'So why does all this mean that Dyadya and Anatoli are . . .' She rocked her hand as Igor had done.

'It's the worker and the boss's son to start with. Anatoli got where he is without trying and Dyadya worked his guts out.'

'What's it like, Anatoli's flat in Moscow?' She had to imagine people in their surroundings. Without their background they could not exist.

'The flat. Yeah, well, I remember the first time I saw that flat, unbelievable. It's right in the centre, near the Conservatoire, in a fucking palace. Each room is huge, bigger than an ordinary apartment. We had dinner, I remember, in a dining room. What's so great about a dining room. Well, for a start, dining rooms don't exist in Russia. You live and eat and watch TV and sleep and fuck in the same room. This dining room had a table for a board meeting; twenty people could sit around it, no problem. There was a tiled stove in the corner with blue and white faience and the cutlery was all silver. There was a maid, too, so she hadn't cooked it. His wife, I mean.' He exhaled and looked at her through the smoke. 'You knew he was married?'

'Were you hoping to cause trouble? Of course I knew. What's that got to do with anything?'

Igor ground out his cigarette and picked up his fork. This time he ate one mouthful, masticating with Gladstonian thoroughness.

Julian said eventually, 'What's she like?'

With satisfaction, Igor put down his fork and took up the packet of cigarettes. He lit another before saying, 'Don't kid yourself that

159

Yelena Nikolaevna is a fat Russian babushka. She's not beautiful, like you, but she's smart.'

'Smart, clever? Smart, attractive?'

'Both. She's blond; not a real one, a Russian blond. She's clever. She used to work for one of the institutes, the Institute of Indian Studies, I think. They were more or less rest homes for the wives of the nomenklatura. But she was respected for what she did. She wasn't lazy.'

'Not lazy.' Julian laughed. 'Well, that's the sort of compliment I love to receive. And attractive? Sexy?'

'That depends on your taste. Attractive? Yes, why not? She always dressed smartly. Sexy? Not for me. She was the correct wife for a rising official. She was one of the same bunch, from exactly the same sort of background as Anatoli. They have a room in their flat, full of photos of the great ones of the old days: Mikoyan and Brezhnev out hunting at Zavidovo; Ustinov and Andropov at tea parties at the dacha in their shirt sleeves; Yelena Nikolaevna as a baby on Gromyko's knee. Ah, those were the days. Yes, take it.'

This was to the waiter who had come to remove their plates, Igor's barely touched. He allowed Julian to choose crème brulée for him and ordered another bottle of wine.

'It always helps to marry the right person. I once heard a story about Anatoli when young. He almost crashed, but his good sense put him right. He made the correct decision in the end.'

Julian was often unsure of his tone as he talked about his partners. Did he accept the reasoning that he attributed to Anatoli and the Uzbek? Sometimes his phrasing was ambiguous. She could not judge whether what he said, the way he used the word 'correct', was the remnants of Soviet-speak or ironic commentary on it.

'I heard this story from an official in the Finance Ministry who moved to work at the bank. He told me that when Anatoli was just back from Harvard, (bad influences, you see) he got involved with a musician. She was Jewish – bad news – and she had a whole crowd of friends who were not correct. Not in the sense that Dyadya was not correct, you understand. Dyadya subverted the system in order to make it work, everyone knew that. After all, we all need food and houses, caviar and dachas, don't we? No, this girl, she was called Sveta, Sveta and her friends were much more dangerous. They listened to western music; that was bad enough. They talked about change; that was worse. Some of them applied to go to Israel, that was the end, as good as standing outside the Kremlin with a placard saying Capitalism Rules or Lenin was Wrong.'

Julian had finished what she wanted of the tarte tatin. She swapped her half-empty plate for Igor's full one. He watched without comment. 'It was only a moment's madness for him. He soon came to his senses and married Yelena Nikolaevna.'

'And the Jewish girl?'

'Her madness probably lasted longer. Russian psychiatry takes time to correct these things.'

'And what was *she* like?'

'How should I know? I never saw her. Thin, dark, ugly, sexy as sin apparently.'

He reached out with the hand that was not holding the wine glass and cigarette and took her wrist. The spoon with its smooth, creamy-brown mound cleanly broken from the main mass was arrested in mid-air. 'I would've given Anatoli good advice, if I'd known him then. Just as I give him good advice now. But I didn't know him then. I was still in . . . I was in Siberia. But I could have told him: keep away from thin women. They have too much self-control. Choose a nice rounded woman who will do everything for your pleasure, suck your cock, pile your blinis with caviar and smetana.'

Julian removed her arm from his grasp, still smiling. 'And what about thin men?'

'Hungry men make good businessmen.'

'And good partners?'

'That depends on how nice the fat men are to them.'

The crème brulée at last reached her mouth and she swept it off the spoon with her upper lip, savoured it with a sucking movement and swallowed, before saying, 'Well, don't go around giving that kind of advice to Anatoli now.'

'A threat?'

'Not at all. What can I do to you? A plea for solidarity.'

'I'll drink to that.'

20

In the beginning the Uzbek came to London every month. Anatoli used to take her to see him, to amuse and placate him. She was a useful means by which he could flatter his partner with attention and at the same time avoid contact with him.

Anatoli would say, 'Use your charm on him, Julian. He needs charming.'

'I can't. I haven't any.'

She was beautiful and that was more than enough for the Uzbek, Radesh Muzafarov, the grandfather, Dyadya. He liked the company of a beautiful woman, although he felt conversation was too much for the female intellect to bear, so social intercourse was confined to jokes and laughter, which was as much as Julian's Russian could take.

Whereas Anatoli had set up a second home in London and Igor thriftily chose cheap hotels, Dyadya always stayed at the Savoy. He had a fiercely sweet tooth and Anatoli often took Julian along for tea there. The Uzbek would heave himself out of his chair at their approach and, simultaneously, two men seated behind him would rise and stare attentively beyond them. When he sat down again, they sat too. Julian remarked on their mimicry.

'Who are those men with the fake Rolexes who are always there with Dyadya?' she said to Anatoli in the taxi on the way home.

'Bodyguards, of course. And the Rolexes aren't fake.'

'Why does he have them here? What harm can come to him in London?'

'None at all. It's just what he's used to. It's like staying in the Savoy: it's status. You can't be a big man in Russia without a heavy to guard you.'

At tea, the Uzbek would consume a prodigious number of cakes and Julian was popular because, unlike Anatoli, she never refused to eat with him. This was one of Dyadya's subjects of laboured joviality at his partner's expense.

'This is not like Tolya,' he said to Julian. 'Normally, he is a good companion. We've had some great times together, eh Tolya? In the banya, eating, drinking, telling stories. What's come over you? Worried about your weight, like all these westerners?' The last word was spoken with infinite contempt. Eventually, the cakes consumed, the tea drunk, Anatoli and Julian would leave, without a word of business having been spoken. When they rose, the two dark-suited men behind them stood, watching them depart.

Julian's meeting with my father, just before Christmas, had supplied her with a comparison between my great-grandfather, the freebooting, nineteenth-century Scottish chemist and Dyadya, the Russian capitalist. She found it as amusing to link the greedy dynamism of my forebear with the gross energy of the Uzbek.

After the first year of her life with Anatoli, when she had met both Dyadya and Igor in London quite frequently, the Uzbek ceased to appear. She observed to Anatoli that they hadn't had tea at the Savoy for some time and he had said nothing more than, 'Dyadya'll be here again next month and you'll have all the jokes and cakes you can take, I promise you.' But a month passed and still no Uzbek.

At one of their dinners together Igor said, in passing, '. . . and now Dyadya can't get out, either Anatoli or I will come more often.'

Later she asked Anatoli why the Uzbek couldn't get away. For once he was willing to talk. He was unpacking from a trip to Geneva, dropping shirts onto the floor.

'He hasn't been able to get a visa recently.'

'An exit visa?'

'No, no, there's no problem there. No, a visa for Britain, the US, France.'

'Why's that?'

He shrugged. 'Who knows. No one'll ever tell you. Russians have always had a bad name in the west. Somebody puts a black mark against you and that's it.'

'So he's shut in Russia?'

'Yuh.' He was taking off his trousers now, flinging them over the back of a chair. Then, as if the removal of layers of clothing was a stimulus to confidences, he said, 'The problem is that he thinks I've done it.'

'You? How could you?'

'Dyadya's an anti-bureaucrat. His whole life had been spent circumventing a bureaucratic system. He hates it as much in the west as at home. He thinks that somehow, as an ex-functionary, I can tip off an opposite number, someone I used to know in the State Department or the Quai or the Foreign Office and get his entry visa cancelled.'

He had stripped down to his shorts now, but instead of going into the bathroom, as he had obviously intended, he sat down and put his briefcase on his knee, turning over the edges of the papers and print-outs within.

'And could you?'

'Of course not, Julian, what do you think I am? Dyadya is un-reasonable. He doesn't understand how the world works in the west. He thinks everything is done by knowing people and by having influence, like it used to be at home; well, as it still is.'

'Isn't it here as well?'

He didn't reply to her question, frowning irritably. 'I want him to be able to travel as much as he does himself. I have more work now. More risk. And I have to cope with his congenital suspiciousness. He thinks I am cheating him, manipulating the London end for my own benefit. He won't trust the documentation I take him. He's convinced that I've cut him out from a whole track, which I now have under my control in the west.' He closed the briefcase and put it down beside him, wiping his hands across his face. 'What he means is that's what he would do if he had half a chance, so he thinks I must be doing it to him.'

'But why won't they let him in?' Julian persisted, lying on the bed with her arms thrown above her head. 'Perhaps it's temporary, or a random error.'

'No. Once, perhaps. But he's applied three times now. Someone must have whispered the word "KGB" to one of the security services and they alerted all the others. We'll have to hope it's that.'

'Hope? Was he KGB? Is there something worse?'

'The Americans aren't worried about the KGB anymore. It's drugs that make them paranoid. Anyway, Dyadya wasn't KGB. He cornered a few of their enterprises in central Asia when the Union went down the can, privatised them you could say, but he wasn't straight KGB. That's not how it was. He's a fixer. These capitalist countries ought to give him a medal. There he was, a businessman operating under a command economy. He's living proof that the market can provide when central planning can't.'

'Dyadya isn't dangerous?' She sat up, taking no notice of Anatoli's own line of thought. 'Is he?'

'Not to me. I can keep him pacified when I'm back in Moscow. It's a question of soothing him. But he's as suspicious as . . . suspicious as Stalin.'

He wouldn't say more, but he had revealed enough to frighten Julian. 'Take care. Do take care, seriously. Do you have a bodyguard in Moscow?'

'Yes, I'm well looked after. Don't worry about me.'

'Is he armed? Dyadya comes to England with bodyguards. You have nobody.'

'I trust to your excellent British police. I haven't got enemies like he has, so I don't need bodyguards here. Don't fuss, Julian. Anyway, that's what I come to London for, to get away from all that.'

Anatoli's attempts to calm her fears, by ignoring them, were counteracted by Igor, who was amused to heighten them. He called her early one evening the following week to say that he was in London for two nights. They went to the Lebanese restaurant that she liked and Julian tried to question him. Normally she avoided any reference to the Bank. It was an area which she did not know about and which she did not want to be involved in. Only now, when it was a matter of Anatoli's safety, did she raise the subject.

'Of course there's risk,' he said, scornfully. 'That's what you like, isn't it? What do you expect? Don't you ever ask yourself what we do, Anatoli and Dyadya and I? Don't you ever ask yourself, how do they make so much money? How do they make so much money so quick?' He was clicking his lighter, then threw it down on the table in exasperation when it refused to work. 'It doesn't come free, you know.'

'Eat something now, don't smoke. I shall buy you a good lighter, Igor. A really expensive one, that doesn't run out after a week.'

'Don't bother. I'm giving up tomorrow. And I'm not a man for expensive lighters.'

It was true. Igor had not changed at all in the time she had known him. He still wore his light grey suits and crepe-soled shoes. She could not think of any item of conspicuous or even inconspicuous consumption that he had bought for himself.

'We're not just bankers. We have fingers in many pies.'

There was tension between them. Igor was irritated that she affected to know nothing, that she was above the money-making. He wanted to claim her complicity. She was taking spoonfuls of hors d'oeuvres from the half dozen or so dishes in front of them.

'And what sort of pies?' She put some food on his plate; he reluctantly picked up his fork.

'Metals trading, for example, construction materials. That grew out of Dyadya's old business, but now, instead of flogging it to the nomenklatura for their villas, he exports it. He buys the aluminium from the alu plants in the Ukraine and he puts it into wagons and trains and bribes it through all the new borders to Riga and ships it out of the Baltic. He can do it faster now than it was ever done in the time of the centralised economy.'

She found his account of the Uzbek's trading reassuring, innocent. He was a valiant exporter, propping up the Russian economy.

'And what does Anatoli do?' she asked, pouring him some more wine.

'Anatoli's our front man with the west; that's obvious. Joint ventures, new capital, funding from the EU, the Know-How Fund, the World Bank. They trust him. He seems respectable, one of them. Appearance is the thing. You've only got to look the part and they'll believe you. Dress a Russian up as a banker and he's a banker. Give him an American accent and a year at Harvard and he's an American banker. Hang a label round his neck and they'll read it. They never look beyond the packaging.'

'And what about you? What does your label say?'

'Mine says computers. I told you that when we met, didn't I? You know how I got alongside Anatoli?' He was laughing to himself. 'I showed him how I could hack into an account in a western bank, sitting in Moscow. Don't look so shocked. I'm not doing that now. We're here for the long term. I keep the books and make sure we can explain away those nasty little suspicions that lurk in western minds: fraud, extortion, the Mafia.'

The word exploded in her consciousness like a land mine planted long ago whose detonator had finally been tripped.

'What's the Mafia?' she asked baldly.

'What's the Mafia? Mafia is an American word, an Italian word, not a Russian one. In Russian we say, *vory v zakone*.'

'*Vory*, thieves . . .'

'Thieves at law. What do you call it, a self-contradicting phrase, something that contrasts with itself?'

'A paradox . . . A tautology . . . An oxymoron.' she left a long pause between each suggestion. Her brain seemed to need it. Igor did not respond for a long time. He had drunk most of the two bottles on the table, but the wine might have been water for all the effect it produced.

'Whatever. A contradiction. But what do you expect from our country, we are all contradiction.'

'But what are thieves at law?'

'They are thieves with their own law. The criminal world is a separate state, a secret society, and the thieves at law are the bosses, the ones who command.'

'Is Anatoli?'

'Anatoli? Fucking hell, Julian, don't you understand anything? He's official, straight. Straight CP member, straight KGB, straight anything you like.'

'KGB?'

He did not answer her question, leaving the acronym to fester.

'Dyadya's the other side, the reverse law. Do you know where they come from the *vory v zakone*? From the camps. It was like a mirror society ruled by the criminals. If you were in for murder, you were on top. Murder was better than economic crime or sabotage, which was better than political crime, which you'd call freedom of speech. At the bottom of the heap were the people who in your system wouldn't be in prison at all. I don't know what they got Dyadya for. Multiple murder probably. This was a long time ago, in the 'sixties. He came out as boss of the camp. He sat in judgement in the prisoners' court, punishing the narks and anyone who co-operated with the authorities.' He laughed. 'Very ironic, because he later made his fortune by going into partnership with the authorities. Whatever they wanted, he provided and they paid. And they turned the system over to him: transport, factories, farms, all put under Dyadya's control. But he was still a thief at law, one of the biggest. He began in Tashkent, king of Uzbekistan. Then he moved to Moscow, for the bigger market. If you can get your hands on the levers of power in a centralised system like Russia, you have everything. You're more powerful than the Tsar ever was. That's what the Mafia was, is, in Russia. It's not just part of the system; it *is* the system. In Brezhnev's day Dyadya was like an emperor. But things change. He had to draw back a bit under Andropov, went back to Tashkent for a while. But then came Gorbachev, and Dyadya met Anatoli. And the rest, as they say, is history. Now they're a bank. Capitalism is wonderful. I love it.'

'How do you know all this? Are you one of them, the *vory v zakone*?'

Igor's eyes were glazed, with a drunken brilliance fixed on her face. It was impossible to tell if he had heard or understood. She kicked him gently under the table with the tip of her shoe. 'Igor, how do you know?'

'I know, I know, I promise you. I was a camp child.'

21

For almost a year she managed to avoid what she did not want to know, refusing to understand the stories that Igor forced on her. Listening to her account, interpreting her words, I had no doubt that Igor was in love with her and that his attempts to shock her with information were a kind of sexual attention-seeking. I wondered whether Julian's extraordinary face, its secretive blankness, incited him to take greater and greater risks of frankness. Julian did not betray to him how far he affected her; nonetheless, his efforts to teach her had their impact, however much she tried to suppress her knowledge.

One night Igor made her understand. She only ever mentioned it in fleeting references, which by their obliqueness and frequency suggested the importance of this turning point.

In London unexpectedly, he called her to say he had a present from Anatoli; would she like to come and collect it. She went round to his hotel just off Queensway and climbed the four flights of stairs to his room.

On his bed was a plastic bag containing four large pots of caviar that he had, as usual, smuggled through the Russian customs. He delighted in his skill in doing this, exasperating Julian.

'Why don't you just pay?' she would say. 'It's not even your money you're saving. Anatoli would pay.'

'It's the risk, you must understand that. It's the principle of cheating. I have to do it. Anyway, what's his is mine; we're partners. So I'm saving my money.'

'What if you were caught?' She understood very well what made him do it, but she was too intelligent to take small risks.

'If they found them, I would pay up; a bribe not a fine. But I'm too clever for them.'

This time, she saw, he had been taking big risks, too. Lying beside the casually presented parcel was a moulded briefcase, cheap, nondescript, in keeping with Igor's own style. Turning from opening the door of his room to her, Igor saw that its lid was raised. He flipped it down with the palm of his hand as he reached over it for her present, but not quickly enough to deny Julian a view of what it contained. Her two bricks of dollars, still stacked in her drawer at home, gave her a standard by which to assess the value of its contents. She could not believe what she had seen.

Igor put the plastic bag into her hands. 'Sorry it's not well wrapped,' he said. 'Anatoli always tells me to buy some boxes and ribbon to make a nice presentation to you and I always tell him I did it. So I hope you won't betray me.'

She dropped the caviar on the bed and slowly lifted the lid of the briefcase. 'Igor, what is this? You're meant to be a computer man and a banker. What are you doing with a briefcase full of cash.'

He pretended to look shamefaced. 'A bit primitive, I agree. I'm not usually involved in this side of things, but we had some courier problems and Anatoli didn't feel there was anyone else. He couldn't come himself, because you know how things are between him and Dyadya just now. So I took over. I thought I'd like to see you. We can go out for a meal, or I know, even better, let's get drunk.'

At the time, she thought he was evading her. Afterwards she became convinced that he had stage-managed everything.

'Never mind that. What sort of banker flies from one country to another with suitcases full of cash? What are you doing?'

He firmly removed her hand, closed the briefcase lid and spun the lock. 'All right. I'll put it in the night safe at the bank. Then we'll eat.'

'You're mad. We'll be mugged.'

'Don't worry. I'll hand over your jewellery like a lamb. They might be willing to take you, too. I'm safe.'

They flagged down a taxi on the Bayswater Road and took it to the City. When they drew up at a heavy, old-fashioned wooden door in a narrow side street, Igor got out and rang the bell. He spoke into the intercom and was let in by a security guard. Julian leaned over to identify where she was. *Banque de* was all she could read, inscribed on the frosted glass windows above the marble dado. When Igor returned he was in high spirits.

'Liberation,' he said. 'Let's find something to eat. We'll go to the Chinese tonight.' He gave directions to the taxi driver and leaned back, humming under his breath.

'Now I'll explain it to you,' he said, when he had let her pay for the taxi. 'It's all legit. I have all the papers I need to show what this money is. We're a bank, so we change money. Russia is a cash economy, so everything is done in cash. But eventually with a money-changing business you need to turn the cash into paper. And that's what I'm doing.'

She saw that he was teasing her, showing her something to rouse her suspicions and then explaining away her questions. It was as if he wanted her to know, was inviting her, tempting her to knowledge and then denying that he had meant what he had said. The sight of stacks of cash inside the briefcase had looked, quite simply, criminal. No one needed to carry cash around in quantities like that. Then he immediately denied the suspicions he had aroused; like a conjurer making bank notes disappear from within his folded fingers.

'It's not the kind of thing that the Big Five banks involve themselves in, it's true. But in London you can always find someone to do business with you. We found an idle private bank, delighted to handle our cash and take our commission. And all legal, too. Our courier was stopped at Heathrow last month with over a million dollars in cash, but he had all the papers necessary to prove he was legal and he went on his way like a good citizen.'

They had arrived in front of the restaurant and hesitated outside.

Elizabeth Ironside

'You don't want to eat, do you?' Igor said. 'Food's shit, eating's for kids. Let's buy some vodka and take it back to your place.'

This was Julian's first experience of a Russian drinking session, which begins with the desire to be drunk. She herself had only occasionally had too much to drink, for her love of control revolted against the abandonment that went with it. She had never before seen someone soberly set out to be drunk, tackling it like work.

Afterwards, it was never clear to her – nothing was clear about the rest of that night – whether she could only remember gobbets of Igor's conversation because of his drunkenness or hers. She had only had one glass and had been immediately in the region of raised consciousness which precedes a blackout. Igor had drunk steadily, smoked continuously, talked.

He had talked about his childhood in Siberia, about the autumn when the forests of larch turned gold around Lake Baikal, about the late spring when the snow had barely disappeared and the wild flowers sprang up overnight.

She was lying full length on a sofa in the drawing room. The fire was lit, otherwise the room was in shadow.

'What about your parents, your brothers and sisters? What did you do as a child?'

'I didn't have brothers and sisters. I didn't have parents.'

He lurched to his feet, stumbling against the coffee table, disappearing in the direction of the bathroom. She watched the shadows on the ceiling, realising she was drunk because of the terrifying feeling of freedom and omnipotence. The reckoning would come later, as it did for any kind of abandonment, whether emotional or financial. This knowledge came from deep down, embedded in the foundations of her personality, in her bigoted petit bourgeois home in Nottingham, whose much-prized ugliness had aroused her hatred as early as she could remember.

She had long ago rejected her parents, but their sense of the structure of life, of how things had to be, sometimes reasserted itself. The wicked flourished like the green bay tree, of that they had had

174

no doubt, and it was proof of their righteousness that they had seen worldly success pass them by. Their only child had reversed the premiss: in order to flourish, you had to be wicked. They had expected their ultimate triumph in the next world, when all those of whom they disapproved (blacks, Labour politicians, foreigners, snobs, in fact, anyone who didn't know their place) would be proved wrong and punished for their errors. Her father had been a policeman, who had believed in discipline for his daughter and for everybody else. Longer prison sentences and the death penalty would sort out most of the problems of society. He had died when she was still at university and had not seen her wilful flourishing. She had deliberately wiped him and her childhood out of her mind. She was a changeling, misdirected to a wrong destiny at birth, which she was altering by her own will. Yet her father's blows in swift and violent punishment, echoing in her head, had marked her expectations. The balance was being drawn up and retribution always came. An eye for an eye was the final account.

When Igor came back she said argumentatively, 'You must have had parents. Everyone has parents. You didn't spring fully formed from someone's head. Even in a camp you must have had parents.'

Igor lay down on the floor with his head propped against the sofa. 'What the hell do you know about the camps?'

'You told me once you were a camp child.' He did not reply. He seemed to have fallen asleep. She could see his eyes were closed. 'You were drunk,' she offered in explanation.

'I must have been. I don't talk about the camps usually.'

'You're drunk now.'

'My mother was a political, that's the lowest of the low. My father? Who knows? If she'd had any sense she'd have got off with the most violent murderer in the camp, who would have protected her, given her some bread. She died when I was about five, I suppose. I don't remember her. After that I was a camp child, like a camp cat, fed by everyone, kicked by everyone. That's how I know Dyadya.'

'He was in the same camp as you?'

'He was the ruler of the camp. You despise Dyadya because he's an old man with gold teeth who doesn't speak good English, or good Russian for that matter. He's not your idea of a powerful man. That's Anatoli, who's got all the elements that you respect. But you're wrong. Dyadya's been a great man all his life. He's led men and imposed his will in circumstances you can't imagine. I've seen it. That's why I know Anatoli must be careful.'

She struggled up to open one of the French windows onto the balcony to let in the night cold. Anatoli's name was throbbing in her head. He hated cigarette smoke in the apartment. His nostrils would tremble like an animal's, tasting the air when he entered. He liked the scent of lilies, her perfume, leather. Cigars he smoked in the open air, standing on the balcony, contemplating London. He would smell Igor's smoke when he returned; it would never be erased. She leaned out, gulping the fresh air, clutching the iron rim of the balcony. Igor was standing behind her. He put his hands on her shoulders, holding on gently, as though she were a piece of furniture helping him to remain upright.

His voice was abstracted, whispering directly into her ear. 'Dyadya was a knife man. A knife stolen from the camp kitchen, sharpened on a stone, a blade like a razor, a point like a needle.' One hand dropped to her waist. 'You aim here. A quick blow and out. The victim doesn't know it's happened, no blood, externally; nothing to show. The spleen is pierced, the body cavity fills up with blood. Quick, clean, invisible.'

She leaned further forward, looking directly down now, four storeys. Fifty feet below she could make out the foreshortened spikes of the railings, the squared stones of the pavement.

'It's the Judas jab. I've seen Dyadya embrace a man and leave. Ten minutes later he fell down and was dead within half an hour. The wound was in his side, just there, like a mouth, little red lips, that's all.'

She had always suffered from vertigo and rarely opened the windows or stood on the balcony. The drop was too great and too attractive. She could feel the desire for the ground in her feet, the

176

almost irresistible sensation of gravity calling her downward.

'Or you can throw it; straight between the shoulder blades of a woman trying to escape.' His arm came around her neck, jerking her painfully backwards.

'You're drunk,' he said. 'Come away from there.' He forced her to step back, the crook of his elbow pressing on her trachea. She took his hand and slowly removed it from her neck, still standing with her back to him, her other hand caressing her throat.

'Is Dyadya dangerous?'

Igor had poured himself another drink. 'We need herring,' he said. 'Caviar, smoked fish.' He strode off through the hall, towards the kitchen. When she reached him, she found the fridge door was open and by its icy light he was prising up the lid of one of the pots of caviar that Anatoli had sent. He tipped its contents onto a plate, scooping out the last reluctant, slippery grains with his finger tip.

'Black bread? You have black bread?'

She opened a cupboard. Her kitchen contained certain basics for Anatoli's unexpected arrival and black bread was one of them, but Igor would not wait. He had already taken a teaspoon to the caviar.

'In the good old days of Stalin and Brezhnev little Russian children of the nomenklatura had a spoonful of caviar everyday to help them grow healthy. And look how big and strong they grew. Look at Anatoli.' He took another spoonful. 'And then look at me. You can see the difference. He has a body women like. I'm a piece of string.'

She took no notice of his self-pity. 'Igor, stop. Leave some for me. Eat it properly.'

He opened the freezer and took out another bottle of vodka.

'Is Dyadya dangerous?'

She was lying down again when she heard Igor repeat her question. Was it on her bed that time? Now she was horizontal the world no longer swung with the rolling motion of a great ship in a storm. Instead, the words themselves seemed embodied and to fly like birds through the darkened air above her eyelids.

'No, not yet. They haven't reached that point yet. But he could be.

And when it happens, we'll have to decide which way to jump, you and I.'

He stopped talking. His head was on her thighs and she could tell he had fallen asleep, the vodka felling him from loquaciousness to silence with a blow as violent as one from the Uzbek's hitmen.

She woke feverishly thirsty, alone. Igor had gone, leaving empty vodka bottles in the drawing room, a greasy jar of caviar in the kitchen and the odour of his cigarettes everywhere. She cleaned her teeth and got back into bed and slept for another ten hours. When she woke again the amnesia of alcohol failed her. She remembered every word he had said. It had to be replaced with determination to forget everything she had learned. Igor was not to be trusted. She did not have to believe him.

22

After that drunken night information jumped at her from every side, forcing itself upon her.

She had gone to collect Anatoli's shoes which were being resoled at a little repair shop nearby. There was a queue, but she could not avoid waiting, because he was due back that night and might want them the next day. The radio chattered in the background and the blur of senseless conversation sharpened into meaning.

'... and what exactly does money laundering consist of?'

'Well, as you can imagine, it's a system of taking black money, that is money that has been made illegally in any way, but usually if we are talking about big money laundering operations, it's drugs money, and turning it into white, legal money that can be moved around the world's financial markets and invested legally in property or stocks and shares or anything you like...'

The man at the head of the queue was complaining about the unsatisfactory job that had been done on the seam of his brogue. The girl was arguing that the problem was that his foot was too big.

'... it's not literally put through the wash, ha, ha. The legitimate financial world is an immensely complex place and growing ever more so and the criminals' activities simply mirror what is going on above board. You can set up a series of shell companies, for example, which do nothing, have virtually no life, so that the movements of money between them have nothing to do with business or profit that has been generated.

They are simply ways of getting illegal money into the banking system.'

Julian shifted from foot to foot, wanting to escape, held in her place.

'. . . the sensitive point is where black money is transferred from cash to paper. Paper is traceable in a way that cash is not, so the method the law enforcers are using to attack money laundering is to watch deposits. Where do they come from and why are they in cash? You've got to have a very good story to explain why . . .'

At last she was at the head of the line and impatiently put down her ticket. The girl consulted the number and began to examine every one of the fifty or so brown paper packets stacked on the shelves behind her.

'. . . this is where the best hope lies of tracing all those narco-dollars, the profits of the cartels . . .'

She laid a ten-pound note on the counter, swept up her change. A month ago she would not have heard, however long she had had to stand there. Now it was as if she had developed an acute sensitivity, like an allergic reaction, to any mention of Russia and Russian crime and could detect any reference to it in her environment. She rationalised her fears with a lack of rigour that even she recognised. Igor had been teasing her. He liked to terrify her. He had explained the suitcases of cash: they were money-changers.

She sat opposite Barnaby at one of Francesca's dinners.

'We were in St Petersburg again last weekend,' he shouted at her. 'Have you been there yet?'

She shook her head. She would never go to Russia.

'You should. So beautiful, but in a terrible state. We went to a gala dinner at the Winter Palace to raise money to preserve the city. Everyone was there, Romanovs, the lot. You should have seen the diamonds, just like the old days, before the Revolution.'

She watched him steadily, all attention.

'It's all so changed. We were among the first in there after the coup in '91 and it was quite different then.' She remembered his excited comments on the wild west and early capitalism.

'It's all rather out of control now. Crime has taken over and the levels of extortion are terrible.'

'Extortion? Taxes?'

'No, no, at least that's legal extortion. No, protection rackets, and I don't mean petty, street-level stuff. All the big companies have to pay up. If they don't . . . A German firm refused, and they were fire-bombed. Three dead. Only Russians, but still. What does Anatoli say about it all? Pretty sickened, I imagine.'

She could never seek reassurance from Anatoli or ask him to contradict the fears planted in her mind by Igor. The unspoken rules by which they lived demanded that she knew nothing, had no worries. Her role was to smile and make him smile.

They came in late from a dinner at the Dorchester where they had been entertaining some business associates from Indonesia (there seemed to be no country in the world with which he did not do business). He turned on the television and stood in front of it, slowly pulling off his tie and rolling it around his hand, as he waited for the news headlines. She had thrown herself down on the sofa, closing her eyes. When she reopened them it was to see a shot which might have come from old footage of the last war, except that it was in colour.

Old women dressed in black, with headscarves pulled forward like blinkers, stood in a long line in the idly falling snow. Each one was tendering a pair of broken shoes, a cup and saucer, a jam jar of home-made pickles, her pathetic goods held in her hands or placed in the snow at her feet. She found herself looking at the image of her parents' ultimate terror, her only inheritance, their fear of losing their mean little house and ugly possessions, of falling into the humiliation of destitution.

She thought it must be a film, a fantasy of degradation, until her ear seized the words, '. . . *a market on the outskirts of Moscow . . .*' from the commentary. The camera focused on the face of one old woman, who stared back pitilessly at the viewer. The lax skin hanging from her high cheek-bones suggested that she had once been heavily fleshed. Her eyes were dark, shadowed and drooping, expressing neither resentment, nor accusation, simply shameless poverty.

'Anatoli, is that . . .?'

He abruptly changed channels. 'That's seventy years of Communism for you.'

Or a year of capitalism. That settled it for her. For the blade of terror that struck her when she heard one of these stories had nothing to do with a horror of wrong-doing. It was fear of what might happen to Anatoli if anything went wrong, fear that the whole edifice of his life and hers, divided between Moscow and London, might founder.

Oddly, the other subject with which Igor would try to tease her had no power whatsoever to disturb her. He liked to tell her about Anatoli's wife, who had now abandoned her institute of learning in Moscow and found herself a job in a Russian-German joint venture.

'I saw Yelena Nikolaevna on CNN last night, shaking hands with Chancellor Kohl,' he would say. 'She was part of a delegation in Bonn to sign a new trade agreement.' His stories of the power of Anatoli's wife, her enormous income, the influence she wielded on Russian politics, raised no anxiety and after a time he dropped them. She had no desire to change the status quo. Anatoli never indicated any intention of abandoning his wife or his home in Moscow. He wanted a double life, not a replacement one. She accepted this and, apparently, felt no rivalry with the powerful Yelena Nikolaevna.

When she told me this, I challenged her. The subject was interesting, too, as it reflected on my position, telling me what she might want, what I might expect. It seemed to me far more natural, given her whole-hearted commitment to Anatoli, that she would have put pressure on him, in direct or subtle ways, to leave his wife.

'Didn't you ever try to get him to marry you? You lived the life of a couple when he was in London. He set up house with you, you went around together, you were invited together, why shouldn't he marry you?'

We were sitting by the fire and the lamps were off. We never went out in the evening any more. She talked, with long pauses in which she recalled, or decided what she would tell me.

'I liked the illicitness. I mean, we didn't live in a secretive way or anything. But it was not orthodox. So I felt free. I thought, at the beginning, for quite a long time, I could just walk away and so could he. Of course, I didn't want to and I was terrified he would, but I liked the idea that it was a balance that was perfectly maintained. If it tipped, one way or the other, that would be it.' She was frowning faintly, trying to be honest. 'That was the theory. In fact, I knew he wouldn't marry me in any case. If he wanted something, he said so and he got it. If he didn't suggest it, it was because he didn't want to change things. So there was no point in my wanting it.'

Anatoli's wishes were the ultimate authority. He dealt with her fears about what the Bank did, which had been implanted by Igor. She had come across an article on the Russian Mafia in a colour supplement and had read its account anxiously, looking for parallels with what she knew of the Bank's operations. The magazine had been left, folded open at the headline *Mafia in a Fur Hat* over a picture of a broad-faced Russian in a shapka. Anatoli must have been attracted by the illustration. As he picked it up to glance at it, Julian made a movement, immediately cancelled, to prevent him. He saw it and recognised her intention. His eyes moved back to what she had not wanted him to see. He skimmed the pictures and their captions, glancing at the article as he went.

She turned to leave the room when he called her back. He was wearing a harsh expression, one she had never seen in all their time together. His tone was usually light, his air humorous. The only seriousness that ever entered their relationship was that of her desire to please.

'Julian,' he repeated. With one gesture he tore the whole supplement across its width. 'It doesn't exist. Don't read stuff like this. Don't even look at it. Don't think about it. It does not exist.'

183

23

Anatoli's denial of the Mafia broke down a psychological barrier, reversing his purpose. To name it, even in negation, was to admit it. Whatever the connexion, it was immediately after this incident, Julian said, that he began to make use of her. More cynical, I dismissed the explanation based on the psychology of personal relations. It was far more likely, to my mind, that Anatoli had decided she must be initiated and so implicated in whatever it was the Bank was doing.

The next day he asked her to arrange a dinner for a business associate.

'At home,' he said. 'The best of everything.' Then, seeing Julian's horrified expression, he roared with laughter. 'Don't worry. Did you think I wanted you to be like Francesca, running out of the kitchen with some delicious dish created by your own hands? She drives me mad telling me of the superiority of her cheese, the special way she treats her vegetables.'

'Since I don't cook, I don't see how I could. Anyhow, you shouldn't laugh at Francesca. You enjoy her food.'

'I do. "Anatoli, I have made this extra-especially for you." ' He wickedly pulled his mouth into the earnest expression that Francesca used, imitating her tone of voice. 'We'll just be the three of us. You and me and him. And can you organise it that service stops with coffee? I'll look after brandy and liqueurs. We don't want to be disturbed if we're talking business, as I hope we shall by then. You'll stay of course.'

185

'If you like.'

Later, the dinners she arranged for Anatoli blurred. The only way she could distinguish them was by her own part in them: the flowers she had chosen, the amusing table centre she had bought at a certain shop, the witty menu she had devised with the caterers. Only this one, for her first guest, stood out in every detail.

She expended enormous efforts on the preparations and waited to meet their guest with high anticipation. He was tall and fleshy, with a striking olive-skinned face and melancholy eyes and mouth too large for their frame, overscored with heavy black eyebrows and moustache. His loose-jointed, awkward body was contained in an impeccably expensive suit. Julian did not learn who he was that evening. When she shook his soft hand, his name was not mentioned and, for all the notice he took of her, she might as well not have been there. But Anatoli wanted it, so she was.

The atmosphere between the two men was at first cautious, revealed in exaggerated laughter at one another's anecdotes. Their guest refused the Krug and the Ducru Beaucaillou '81 she had ordered, and they all drank orange juice. They ate the feuilleté and the lamb, the vacherin and the salad, the tarte aux fruits de la passion with appreciation. Once they settled down to business and the maid left them, they drank coffee and ate petits fours. The little pile of sweet things was devoured in ten minutes. Their guest ate with the eagerness of the addict, his lips snapping on them, sucking at the melting texture like a baby at a teat. This was someone, like Dyadya, who adored sugar and she went quickly to the reserves of presents she had received. She arranged more chocolates and pate de fruits on a plate and sat down again with them beside the fire. She was attentive to their needs for more coffee, more chocolates, clean ashtrays. She paid no attention to what they talked about. She watched their guest smoke incessantly, as he listened to what Anatoli was saying. Neither of them made notes or consulted papers. Finally, he rose, forgetting to shake her hand or thank her as he left, ushered out solicitously by Anatoli at three in the morning.

Anatoli was jubilant. It had gone very well, he said. She did not ask what 'it' was.

Now, she became a parody of a wife, spending her time in arranging the house and entertaining guests. Yet as a hostess she was closer to the professional than the social variety, for she presided over meals to which other women were never invited and at which she was herself almost invisible. Hours of thought as well as money went on producing the perfect meal for guests whose only purpose was business. They did not notice that the huge mass of acid yellow flowers, punctured with orange lilies, exactly matched the colours of the new painting she had just bought, nor that the menu had been composed with the guest of honour's passion for golf in mind. No detail was too small for her attention, but she did nothing herself. As she had always known, as long as you have money, anything is possible, and at once.

By undertaking all this with her fanatical thoroughness, it was easy for her to ignore the subjects that were discussed and the goods that were bargained for at her table. The guests were usually anonymous. Sometimes, with surprise, she recognised an opposition politician, or a junior minister, a businessman or a lawyer whose influence Anatoli needed to cultivate and she looked with curiosity at a face made familiar by television.

The first evening set a pattern for those that followed. The purpose of the meeting was not social, but politeness and caution forbade that the real subject should be mentioned until the end. The conversation, until the important topic was reached, was so standardised, she sometimes thought dreamily, that they could just hum and it would make no difference at all. There could be different notes for different stages of the meal. There would be something rapid and light for the half hour in which they assembled, standing in the drawing room in front of the fire, sipping their champagne or whisky, moving round to be introduced, and talking about the decoration of the room, the paintings, her latest acquisition for Anatoli. The conversation always became more concentrated once they had sat down in the Chinese yellow dining room: golf, Wimbledon, racing, football, which Anatoli followed with learned passion, depending on the national taste of the guests. Julian, who had no interest in any sport, would listen to her neighbour with her rapt expression of boredom.

With the main course came the serious stuff, politics and economics, and the discussion would range across the world's war zones and stock markets with the dispassionate, wheeling flight of a bird of prey. After cheese had been served and removed and the dessert was in front of them they had reached the sweet centre of the evening. She could always tell what sort of negotiation it was to be by the rise or lowering of tension at this stage. If she felt excitement in the air, she knew there was hard bargaining to be done and she might well still be sitting pouring coffee, or herb tea, or brandy in the early hours. If there was a relaxation, she knew that it was all agreed and it was simply a question of talking over the details.

When Igor was next in London, he said, 'I heard you sat in on the arms negotiations.'

'Arms?' Julian said vaguely.

'Don't tell me you didn't understand what they were talking about, because I won't believe you. For an intelligent person, you are sometimes unbelievably fucking stupid.'

She continued to gaze at him blankly. They were sitting in her drawing room. He was lying on the sofa with his feet propped on the coffee table, inserted between the huge volumes on the paintings of the Hermitage and the Louvre, smoking. She had given up trying to prevent him and had bought a machine to clean the air of his tainting presence. Beside him was an overflowing ashtray which he would not permit her to replace, and on the other side, on a small table, a vodka bottle and glass. He had discarded his suit jacket and tie and his physical presence was represented by his voice and the hollow looseness of his white shirt and grey trousers, which seemed to suggest that he was not there at all. There was no one within.

Julian was sitting opposite him in the wing chair by the fire, undistressed by his abuse.

'But I am fucking-stupid, Igor. That's why I'm here now. That's why I was there then. I must say, your English has come on a long way. When we first met, I don't think you would have got the intonation right on the unbel*iev*ably-fucking-stupid.'

'Ok, ok. You can be as fucking-stupid as you like with Anatoli, but cut it out with me. This guy Iman is a big arms dealer and we've been working on him for some time to convince him that we've got access to more than cases of Kalashnikov machine guns and clapped out, standard-issue Red Army pistols, which is the usual menu on offer from Russia nowadays.' He wasn't actually smoking his cigarette. It hung between his etiolated fingers, the smoke shimmering upwards to make a veil in the air between them. Julian's gaze was fixed on the loose hand, the chain of smoke.

'It was Dyadya,' Igor was saying. 'Even though he can't get out, he can still see where we should be going. He's unbelievable. He's opened up our sources in Russia. He spotted Iman.' Igor talked on. The Uzbek had obtained access to the output of one of the most sophisticated arms factories of the former Soviet Union, one whose production was still in demand among Russian generals. The idea was to sell arms abroad in order to finance the Russian Army's needs and Dyadya was the chosen agent for these dealings.

Julian made no response to the story. She sat holding her wine glass in both hands, her elbows lodged on the arms of her chair. Igor collapsed onto the floor. The tension that maintained his body, fakir-like, horizontal, gave way. He was crawling towards her. When he reached her, Julian, startled, had already put down her glass. Approaching her from below, he reached up, grabbing her chin, forcing her to look at him.

'Listen, Julian, pay attention, will you.'

'I am. I listen to everything you say.'

'I'm offering you a deal. I want you to do a little spying for me. Tell me who comes to these dinners he gives in London, what they say,

189

what they agree. And don't give me that stuff about not understanding all that boring money talk.'

'Why do you want to know?'

He ignored her question. 'You must tell me about who comes, who he sees here, what's going on in London, and I'll tell you what it means. I'll explain what Anatoli won't. You need to know, so you can worry. You think it's your worry that keeps him safe, don't you? So, as long as you listen to me, you'll know what you have to worry about. We'll watch his back together.'

She did not respond. The cover story, of protecting Anatoli, did not quite conceal the reality of the spying.

He dropped his hand, allowing it to run down the length of her body as he turned and leaned his back against her knees. He stretched across the coffee table for his vodka bottle and poured himself another glass, swallowing it with a single sharp toss of his head.

'I'm not sure.' She looked down on the top of his head. He had fine straight hair thinning on the crown so that she could see the eggshell gleam of his skull through its mesh.

'Why does he need someone to watch his back?' she asked. 'Is it Dyadya?'

'Julian, are you stupid or what? If you knew why your back needed watching, you wouldn't need to watch your back, you'd turn to face it. Yes, it could be Dyadya, though that seems to have settled down now. But it could be anyone, anything. That's the point.' There was silence. She leaned over to touch the CD player and fill the room with music.

'And why do you want to protect him?' She put out a hand and stroked his hair, so that the filaments were no longer criss-crossed, but lay smoothly in parallel.

Igor always spoke with a suppressed violence when he had been drinking, as if only with the loosening of inhibition could his exasperation with her reveal itself. 'I've told you, we're partners. What's his is mine.'

He reached for her hand, putting it to his lips. He took her index finger into his mouth, working it with his tongue. With sudden viciousness he bit it so deeply that Julian shrieked. She pulled it away from him, nursing it to her chest, examining the bleeding punctures. Igor did not move.

'And, Julian, it's not just for Anatoli. You need me, too.'

24

Later I looked back on this secondary relationship, the one with Igor, with more attention. Even at the time she was telling me about him, I could see that, however strong her obsession with Anatoli, she had an equally powerful connexion with his partner. It was hard to judge on what it was based. One of its pleasures was its secrecy. She enjoyed a hidden life, even an innocent one. Innocent? The impression she gave was that they just talked. She liked evenings in restaurants, discussing the parties she gave, the atmosphere, the relationships between the guests. At the time, although I noted her love of the illicit, the sexual element in her friendship with Igor, I failed to draw conclusions for my own case. I wrote him down as an alcoholic, perhaps impotent, in love with her, content with power over her. This derived in part from the secrecy: he could always betray her to Anatoli. But he needed the information she supplied about Anatoli's dealings in London, just as she needed what he told her about Moscow, about the men who gathered around her table, and most of all his reassurance. She needed to know that all was well; Anatoli was safe; it was not yet time to abandon ship.

One evening they went out to an Italian restaurant. It was crowded and so noisy that even though the tables were closely packed there was little danger of anyone overhearing two consecutive sentences amid the surging waves of conversation. They settled into their familiar attitudes at the table, like a long married couple. Julian sat with her forearms resting on the cloth, leaning forward, his arms were raised to his face, a cigarette in his fingers.

'So who came on Friday night?'

'Two, no three. One came after dinner, for brandy. The first two I'd never seen before. They're Americans, Latinos, very smoothy, with long, thick, black oiled hair and big belt buckles. I don't think Anatoli knew them. They were all very tentative.'

'No, he wouldn't have met them before. It was all set up in a complicated way through third parties. They're not principals in any case.'

'I could tell. They talked about anything. They tried cars; that was all right for half an hour, but there is a limit. Then they did sport: football. That kept them going through two courses. Every football team in the world: Marseilles, Munich, Moscow, Olympic, Dynamo, Ajax. They were so enthusiastic that they ate. At first they were just picking at their food, rather nervously, but when they started on goal-scoring averages they shovelled it in. I wondered whether I had allowed enough.'

'And what were they like, the two who came for dinner. Not what did they look like, what were they like?'

'But what they look like is what they're like. They were very similar, not twins, but as if they had been put in the same mould and come out not quite matching. Late thirties, early forties. The smaller one was older and the leader; the other looked at him all the time, to assess his reaction. Little sideways glances.'

'They're cousins,' Igor stated. 'From Colombia. They always do business together. They work for an uncle and he's developed them as very efficient aides. They are both loyal to him and a check on one another. They work as a team, but he handles them separately, so they're never tempted to be independent.'

'They wanted to be pleased. And they had the same physique as Anatoli, square and muscled, and I always think people like people who look like them. So they were instinctively prejudiced in his favour.'

'What about the Chinese?'

'You know everything already. Why do you bother to ask me?'

'You thought I'd be surprised?'

'*I* was surprised. I wasn't expecting him. He really is Chinese?'

'Of course.'

'Well, he didn't look like any Chinese I've ever met before. He was tall and thin, like you. You see, you'd have got on with him, according to my theory. He didn't have one of those round jolly Buddha faces. It was a long, flat oval, like a mask with slits cut for his eyes, and the ridge of his nose barely rose from his face, but it was sharp and curving, not flat and squashy.'

'You're obsessed with appearance, Julian. How did he behave?'

'But don't you get a sense of him from what I say? I'm trying to give you an impression.'

'Ok, go on. Not a cheerful type. Sinister. I've got all that. Like me.'

'Yes, so far you've understood. He was a groper too, a knee-squeezer and within five minutes of sitting at the table.'

Igor was caught by this detail. 'And what do you do with a knee-squeezer? Do you slap his face in the traditional way of outraged virtue?'

'No, I move my knees.'

'Do you tell Anatoli?' He was genuinely interested, distracted from his main purpose, as if he was not sure what her answer would be.

'No, I tell you.'

'Ok, go on.'

'Oh, the Chinese. He arrived when dinner was almost finished and they stopped laughing at once. No more football. He had a brandy, but he didn't eat anything. No pudding, no fruit, no petits fours. You see, just like you. Then they moved to sit by the fire. They were all drinking brandies, huge glasses, but they sobered up, the more they drank. They didn't do business, whatever it is. It was all testing. Talks about talks. There was a lot of travel chat. You know, have you been to . . . Do you know . . . The best time of the year . . . Fabulous hotel . . . Even better. So they're going to meet again somewhere in the Far East, the Mandarin, the Raffles.'

'And how was Anatoli that evening?'

'What do you mean, how was he? He hasn't been ill has he?'

'Forget it. There was obviously nothing wrong if you noticed nothing.'

'Can Dyadya travel east to Singapore and Hong Kong?'

'It depends. Hong Kong, no. Singapore, Bali, Phuket, perhaps. Anatoli should take you. You'd enjoy some sunshine. It only ever rains here.'

'Why the Far East?' Julian asked. Every change she probed to discover what it meant for Anatoli and for herself.

'New routes. Russia doesn't just face west; it faces east as well. Vladivostok is another world. It's a long way from Moscow there. Dyadya has some let's call them colleagues there and he's interested in all kinds of possibilities. In the east they look to Japan, to Hong Kong, to the west coast of America. Cars, for example. In Moscow you only see European cars, but in the east it's Japanese ones. It's natural. Not that they buy them. They have the same stolen car scam with Japan that they have in European Russia. You know about it? You've got something wrong with your car and you can't afford to have it fixed, so you make an arrangement to have it stolen. The car disappears to Vladivostok, you claim on your insurance. Everyone's happy. The system's so finely developed in Russia that you can order the make, model, colour of your car and they'll get it for you.' He was laughing at the classical efficiency of the criminal market and then saw Julian's face.

'Don't worry. This isn't our business. I promise you, Dyadya is a big man and we only do big things. We don't get involved with car scams, prostitution, protection. Nothing so innocent.'

Did she know what business was being done between Anatoli and the Latinos and the mask-faced Chinese? She must have known, but refused to understand. She conveyed this to me in the half-stated terms of the stories of her conversations with Igor, of the dinners she gave for Anatoli, which had no point, except for what wasn't said. She was not supposed to know about what was traded, always referred to as 'goods', whether it was aluminium or arms. Even Igor, who explained about the aluminium works, the transport systems, the arms factories that had fallen under Dyadya's control, did not make explicit what was being negotiated here. But it was clear that her refusal to acknowledge what Anatoli did, was profoundly irritating to him, an irritation that finally burst out one weekend when he was in London.

They went for a walk in Richmond Park, about as far towards the countryside that Julian was prepared to go. The day was fine; they had had an amusing lunch and she began the walk through the park cheerfully, linking her arm in his. So it was all the more strange that things went badly wrong between them so quickly.

Igor, relaxed by a day with Julian entirely to himself, was unguarded enough to make some criticism of Anatoli.

'Anatoli plays at being the gentleman banker, like the others here. They take on the manners of the aristocrats they're not.'

'Give it a rest, Igor. Go back to Moscow and join the Communist party. Why shouldn't he enjoy the money he's earned in any way he likes and in any company he likes. You don't have to spend your time here if you don't want to.'

Igor seized her arm. 'I don't mind how Anatoli spends his time, his money, his life. I just don't like him to kid himself, or you, that he gets his money like anyone else.'

'He works for it, like anyone else.'

She turned away from him to end the conversation, to continue the walk, but she was held back by Igor's thin hand gripping her upper arm so tightly that his thumb nail seemed to pierce the muscle through her soft jacket.

'Anatoli isn't one of these people; he's busy corrupting them. You should know what he is doing. He is pretending to be one of them, ok, but he fools himself and you, too, when all the time . . .'

Julian pulled away and raced down the hill. Soon she was out of control, slithering on the soft earth, with Igor pounding behind her.

'Stop, Julian. You'll break an ankle.' As she reached the turn in the track, Igor caught up with her. He grabbed her hair, holding it in a tail at the nape of her neck, so that her chin jerked up.

'Who do you think they are, the business associates that Anatoli brings to your dinner table? Do you ever ask yourself about our Latin American friends? Do you think they're exporters of baby food via Vladivostok?'

If Julian wanted to know and not to know, Igor wanted to tell and not to tell. He had worked himself sufficiently into a rage to speak and then caution got the better of him. He released her hair and gave her a little push. Without looking back at him, she walked ahead down the path. She could see a dog, a black English cocker, foolishly chasing some birds; a child threw a stick for it. When Igor rejoined her, she knew nothing more would be said that day.

25

In only one case did Julian admit to more intimate knowledge of the workings of the Bank. This involved a trip she made with Anatoli and Igor to Istanbul.

The week before, Anatoli was in London for the weekend, eating breakfast, devouring ham and cold meats with the vigour of someone about to go and play golf who needed to be fortified in advance against the cold and the wind. Julian watched him over the rim of her coffee cup as he put down his fork and wiped his lips under his thick brown moustache.

'Have you ever been to Turkey?' he asked.

'Turkey? No.' She had, in fact, hardly travelled at all. She had never liked discomfort, so she had not backpacked as a student. Since then France, Italy or America had been the limit of her journeys, usually for a weekend in a grand hotel.

'I'm going to Istanbul and I thought you might like to come.'

'I should love to. How long for?'

'I'm not sure, a few days. We leave on Tuesday.'

She knew that whatever the purpose of the visit, it would not be tourism. Anatoli hated sightseeing and could barely be persuaded to glance at St Paul's from a taxi window. She was his holiday and when he went elsewhere it was only for business. The fact that he had invited her on this trip suggested that he needed some kind of amusement while he was there.

She looked forward to the visit, but, as Anatoli had no enthusiasm for the project, she guessed that it must be an expedition ordered by the Uzbek, one that Anatoli did not like but could not avoid. Her assessment was confirmed when they arrived at their hotel in the early evening to find Igor sitting in the foyer playing chess on his pocket computer.

Anatoli was making his way purposefully towards the reception counter.

'There's Igor, Anatoli. You didn't say he was coming too.' As she said Igor's name she caught sight of Anatoli's look of surprise, fury and even fear. It was so fleeting that she could convince herself she had not seen it.

'Didn't I? I must have forgotten to mention it.' He continued on his way, only raising his hand causally to Igor, as if he had been expecting him.

Leaving Anatoli to check in, she walked over to Igor. He did not lift his eyes from the little screen.

'Who's winning?' she asked. She realised her tone was ingratiating. She had been frightened by Anatoli's fear.

'I am, of course.'

'Because you handicap the programme.' She spoke more scornfully this time, to compensate.

'That's the rule: make sure your opponent can't win. Then you can't lose.'

'Put it away, Igor. What are you doing here?'

'I've always wanted to see a harem and the finest is to be found at the Topkapi Palace, apparently. Interesting to see how the sultans kept all those women. Polygamy has always seemed to me a rather demanding system for men, quite apart from its unfairness to women. But some people say that women like it. What do you think, Julian?'

They left him to go to their room. Anatoli was soon busy with the telephone and Julian sat on the sofa with her heels propped on the coffee table, pretending to read her book, trying to work out what was happening. Anatoli had been reluctant to come; he had not expected Igor to be here. Igor must have been sent by the Uzbek to watch Anatoli. The lack of trust between them was nothing new, but Igor's role was. He had never sided with Dyadya before.

That night they were joined for dinner by a Russian couple. Igor was not with them. The next morning, however, he made his way through the dining room at breakfast time and came to sit at their table. He carried a guide book which he opened and read at he drank his coffee.

'Santa Sophia, I think, to begin with, don't you? It seems the obvious place.' To her astonishment Anatoli made no protest and they set off together.

Igor and Anatoli had been unanimous in rejecting a guide, and they wandered around the mosque's emptiness disconsolately. They obediently raised and lowered their eyes, directing their glances to whatever Julian pointed out to them, as she read from the guide book. They were tourists of form, not even very convincing ones, making the visit because this is what every foreigner in Istanbul must do. Only when she was reading a section on the Orthodox Church did Anatoli's attention sharpen into interest.

'Whatever it is fashionable to say now,' he commented, 'the Soviet empire worked well in binding people together with one language and one culture. The Russians united central Asia and freed people from all this . . .' He looked disdainfully at the Muslim decoration which overlaid the Christian structure. Igor's hands were joined behind his back, as if to stop them from involuntarily twitching from nicotine deprivation, or from punching Anatoli.

'Anatoli, don't give me that nationalistic crap. We brought them all the benefits of civilisation and look how grateful they are.'

Anatoli faced his partner. 'Russian rule was a force for good. It gave order and structure and protection. It's now fashionable to take up western ideas and say it was colonialist exploitation and all that, but people will soon see what the removal of Russian control will mean. They'll fall apart, all those new states, in political chaos and social backwardness.'

'You're an old apparatchik, Anatoli.' He did not speak affectionately.

'You continue to mouth the same old excuses, as if no one had shown you the camps and the corruption.' He stopped himself, as if there were no point in even beginning the list of the iniquities of the old system. 'It's a new world out here. You can't sit around and regret your lost glories like the old émigrés after the Revolution. You've got to adapt.'

Anatoli did not seem particularly annoyed by this outburst. 'I think I've adapted. What about you?'

There was no further discord that morning, but Julian expected Igor to break away from them as soon as he could. However, he returned with them to the hotel where they had decided to lunch. The meal passed without incident and plans were made to continue their sight-seeing with a visit to the Topkapi Museum that afternoon.

'The museum?' she said in dismay, looking at Anatoli. He ignored her appeal.

'We thought the museum would be interesting. Then we'll go to the souk.' Igor was nodding, as if the programme, pre-set, had been correctly memorised by Anatoli.

Towards the end of the afternoon they sat down in a cafe to drink cups of sandy, sweet Turkish coffee. Julian unwrapped several little objects she had bought, laying them out on the table for admiration. She caught a glance passing between Igor and Anatoli. Igor's head barely moved, as he glanced at the backs of two men in leather jackets, sauntering down the alley of the bazaar. This was it, she thought. This explained their uncharacteristic desire to see Santa Sophia and the museum and the bazaar. They were waiting for someone to make contact.

They waited. Returning, the leather jackets swerved into the cafe, drawing up two more chairs to their table. Julian wondered what the signal had been, and then realised that she was, in all probability, the identifier: a girl in a fur. For it was clear that the men had never met one another before. They shook hands across the table in the awkward fashion of large men in cramped spaces, staring at one another in an assessing manner.

They had long, lugubrious faces and thick dark moustaches, a seriously projected masculinity. She had time to make this judgement in the disconcerted pause in which no one spoke. Then the older of the two men said in Russian, 'Let's go.' The other stood up and said to his companion, 'The girl?'

Anatoli was on his feet by now. 'She comes with us,' he said.

They led the way out of the cafe, walking some distance to a side street where they unlocked an elderly Mercedes, untidily tipped on the narrow pavement over the gutter. Julian was placed in the back between Anatoli and Igor so she could see the road in front of them, the endless traffic, the clouds of diesel exhaust. They drove their way to nightfall and she fell asleep. When she woke they were talking quietly in Russian. She kept her eyes closed and concentrated on picking up what was said. She soon realised it was only football. The car slowed, turned and finally halted and when they emerged numbly into the darkness, the air had a sharpness that suggested they were near the sea.

They were led up the steps of a large house with a Grecian portico and into an entrance hall of a villa of some grandeur. They were expected, a man was waiting for them at the foot of the stairs. He shook hands with Anatoli and Igor and, seeing Julian, shouted over his shoulder, making no effort to greet her. A woman came out of the door behind them and shepherded Julian out of the men's way.

She was tall and strongly built, wearing a tightly gathered skirt, reaching to mid-calf, a broad red cummerbund around her waist and on her head a black silk scarf which hid her hair. She held open the door of the room and said, 'Please, go ahead,' with the unmistakable accent of Boston. Julian obeyed.

The room they entered was a curious combination of western and eastern, as if a family of nomads had abandoned their tents and installed themselves in an empty house. The structure was western, but the floor was covered with overlapping rugs, which were also draped over a divan and a chest, the only furniture, pulled up close to the warmth of the logs burning in the fire place. Julian took in her surroundings before looking once again at the woman who had invited her in. She could now see that the clothes were not a traditional costume but more like fancy dress, and had been put together for effect, political as much as aesthetic.

'I'm Meira. Would you like some coffee?' When Julian did not reply at once, she said, 'Do you speak English? *Gavaritie po Ruski?*'

'English,' Julian found her voice. 'I speak English.'

'Good, then we can talk to one another. My Russian is pretty lousy and my Chechen is non-existent. What about the coffee?'

'Would tea be possible?' Julian felt that she might wither up if she drank any more of that desert drink, the driest liquid she had ever tasted.

'You not only speak English, you are English. I can do tea, but it'll be Russian tea, no milk, if you can take that.'

When Julian told me this story, one word told me everything. Once it had been spoken I knew why they were there, what Anatoli and Igor must have been doing. But when Julian made this trip, early in 1994, Grozny was a town unknown in Europe and the Chechens an unheard of people.

Meira returned after an absence of twenty minutes with two glass cups in metal holders, filled with golden brown tea in which floated sprigs of mint. She perched the brass tray on the kelim-covered trunk and seated herself on the cushions by the fire, spreading out her wide skirts over her crossed legs. It was not long before she was pouring out her history. She spoke like one who loved to talk and was starved of opportunity. Julian listened with a horrified fascination. There were many differences between them and one fundamental similarity which she recognised at once: a life lived entirely for a man.

Meira's story of easily diverted passions, abortions, disappointments and optimism was a tale from hell for Julian, who could not bring herself to contribute her own history and instead made herself into a good listener. She was born in Boston where she grew up, at some stage she had married and moved to New York. Chronology was not her strong point and events were coupled in her narrative by an internal logic unrelated to time. Her husband disappeared from the scene. With the fall of the Soviet Union she came to Europe to visit her family's homeland in Georgia. Here, she had encountered Mansurkhan Ibrahimov, her current lover, and committed herself to his cause. He was a Chechen, one of a warlike people who had declared themselves independent of Russia in 1991, soon after the August coup.

'Now it's a question of arming ourselves,' Meira said. 'All Chechens have guns. It's a kind of tribal society in which a man has to have a gun and a car to be validated as a man. But you need more than a rifle to take on Russian tanks and they're the enemy.'

'And that's why we're here?'

'Yes, you guys can get us mortars and rockets which are the very least of what we need. We want jeeps, tanks, planes. It's to protect ourselves you understand. If you've lived for centuries under the pressure of a ruthless great power on your northern border, you know that when you've grabbed your independence, you're going to have to preserve it.' She opened the French windows, letting in icy air. 'Do you want something to eat? Shall we see what we can find?'

The kitchen was as spartan as the rest of the house. A scarred white butler's sink was piled with dirty dishes and below it a lidless dustbin was filled with leftovers. Under the table a large tabby cat sat, with one back leg raised in the air so it could comfortably clean its belly fur. Meira was turning the contents of some blackened saucepans.

'What'll you have?' she asked. 'It looks like rice. This is lamb. It's very good, I can tell you. One of the bodyguards makes it.'

Julian was drawn to the door into the dining room where the men were sitting amid the debris of a meal. Some plates were stacked at the end of the table, others had been pushed to one side by the diners, in favour of coffee cups, wine glasses or what looked, in Igor's case, like vodka or plum brandy. The squalor struck Julian before she observed the people.

Mansurkhan was obviously the leader. He was a big man in his fifties with dark hair and a grey beard, the two zones strikingly demarcated, with grey stripes running up his sideburns to his temples. The curling hair that escaped from the neck of his open shirt was grey too. He was leaning on his forearms, his black-nailed hands spread out in front of him. Igor was smoking, as usual, leaning back in his chair listening to Mansurkhan. The atmosphere was one of debate, but not of hostility. The only discordant note was struck by Anatoli, who was taking no part in the conversation. He had drawn his chair away from the table and was sitting sideways with his arm along the back.

In the car returning to Istanbul she dozed uneasily between Anatoli and Igor, feeling the tension in their silence. When they reached their hotel, Anatoli said in Russian, 'Igor, come to our suite, will you? I want to talk about this.' Julian had by now woken up and when he continued, 'Julian, do you want to go to bed?' she looked at her watch, saw it was two thirty and said, 'No, I don't think so. I'll have a night-cap with you two.'

She had never wilfully misunderstood him before and he looked as if he might strike her. Julian turned her back on him and sat down.

'Now,' she said, as if oblivious of his unexpressed fury. 'Let's have something to eat. I hope you two are not going to be ill. I saw the kitchen and couldn't eat a thing, so I'm starving.'

She leaned over to take the phone and called room service for sandwiches and a bottle of wine. She then prowled round the room, nibbling dates from the dish of fruit on the table.

Anatoli sat down heavily and said to Igor, 'We're not going on with this.'

Igor was standing with his back to him, looking at the night view of the city. 'We're committed. You've just committed us.'

'I'm going to uncommit us.'

'You're going back to tell Mansurkhan that you're not going to deliver everything we've just promised?'

'I'm not going to do it now. But it is going to become impossible for us to fulfil the order.'

'You can't do it. If we don't deliver, all of us in Moscow will be in the shit. No question.'

The Art of Deception

'We shouldn't be doing it. We're arming them to fight Russians.'

'A bit late to worry about that sort of thing. I don't remember any problems about dealing with our friend Iman, or the Latinos. If we don't sell these guys the stuff, someone else will. Anyway, we can't get out of it now.'

The knock of room service silenced them both. The waiter fussed around with plates and napkins and wine glasses, while unresolved anger thickened the air. When he had gone, the silence continued, as if they knew that there was no reconciliation of their positions.

'Who are the Chechens?' Julian asked.

'They're the thieves and murderers of the empire,' Anatoli said.

'They're an independent republic in the northern Caucasus which needs to protect itself. Quite reasonable.' This was Igor. Then he added, 'Anatoli's right. They have a powerful underground network in Moscow and have had for years. They're hitmen. So I can't see that we'd survive long if we went back on our word.' He had let out the information to frighten her. It worked.

'Anatoli.' He ignored her.

'Dyadya has his own reasons for this. As far as I am concerned it's good business. The Chechens want what we've got. They've money to pay. And even more important, they've got oil. It seems to be late in the day to say we shouldn't arm them. He'll do business with Colombia and Hong Kong and Iraq and now he makes a fuss about Mansurkhan and the Chechens. You can't work by making promises and not keeping them. If we go back on it, we'll find ourselves dead on the street.'

Anatoli had been furiously eating sandwiches. 'It's no good. I'm not going to go ahead with this.'

Igor shrugged. He had ignored the food and lit a cigarette. He turned his head to eject a stream of smoke with a force that belied the careless movement of his shoulders.

'And,' Anatoli went on, 'I find this fear of the Chechens in Moscow ridiculous.'

Julian watched the row develop, making no effort to intervene.

She crouched in her chair, her terror growing. For once she thought Anatoli was wrong.

The words they used had no meaning, because they simply reiterated their positions in different ways without changing the sense. Anatoli shouted. His face was suffused with rage, his fists clenched. Igor was pale. On the surface he appeared calmer, but she sensed that his anger was even more powerful than Anatoli's. Even though Anatoli now dominated the room with his large figure and his noisy rage, the arithmetic was against him. If Igor and the Uzbek wanted something, they would get it and the fact that he had opposed it, fruitlessly, would count doubly against him. It was no good having a row with Igor. He had to be persuaded that the deal was impractical, or it was not worth it, or it was not in his interest. Somehow, too many other things had got mixed up in this very simple matter: Anatoli and Dyadya, Anatoli and Igor, Russian and Uzbek, nomenklatura and outsider.

Russians never gave up. They could go on all night, making things worse every time they circled over the old ground. She stiffly released her knees, uncoiling her legs which she had drawn up to her chin, and rose from her chair. They took no notice of her. Anatoli was leaning forward, his chin jutting at Igor who was lounging back as if held in his place by the force of Anatoli's fury.

She put her hand on Anatoli's shoulder. 'Anatoli.' He ignored her, continuing his flow of Russian rhetoric. 'Anatoli, this is enough. We'll get nowhere like this. Leave Igor alone. You'll have to sort it out calmly in London or Moscow.'

He stopped speaking abruptly. She was standing over the two of them, dominating them. The silence stretched between them, thinner and thinner. She was waiting for it to rip open and expose what had happened. This was when things went wrong. She had chosen Igor, to save Anatoli, and Anatoli would never forgive her for it.

26

Once the Chechen war broke out, Anatoli spent more time in the west, most of it in London, as if he found life in Moscow intolerable. His visits were longer, but did not have the predictability of the past, so Julian lived in a state of expectation, always hoping to find him at home when she returned, or a message on the answerphone to say when his plane was due in. The sight of his coat slung over a chair in the hall, the sound of his voice, 'Julian, it's Anatoli,' never failed to produce a halt in her breathing, a falling sensation in the gut. The physical symptoms of obsession were always there.

'I always knew it would end, that is, I always feared it was too good to last, which is why I worried so much, why I tried to learn from Igor where the danger was, to arm myself. I meant to prevent it, to outwit fate.'

We were sitting in the dark; she held a brandy glass in her palm. She spoke to herself as much as to me. I thought how much of what she told me about her feelings for Anatoli applied to mine for her. I never drew the analogy to her attention.

'When the end came I had been expecting it, fighting it for years. But I didn't see it when it came. I imagined shootings in Moscow, arrests in the west. I had never dreamed of this.'

'Weren't you ever frightened for yourself?' I asked. 'Not for Anatoli.'

'Not at first, but after Istanbul, yes, I understood how dangerous it was. I remember, just before Anatoli disappeared, we were in Paris. You know how I hate Paris. Bad things always happen to me there.'

Both Anatoli and Igor were there for several days 'on business'. Julian and Anatoli were staying at the Crillon and Igor in one of his little hotels on the other side of the river in the sixth. Julian had come to join them to see Anatoli and to finish furnishing an apartment for the Uzbek. He had bought a block of flats in the eighth arrondissement and had taken the two top floors for himself. Although he was still unable to leave Russia, he continued to invest in property in the west. Julian had on several occasions flown to Cyprus to make arrangements for the purchase of property there, to see lawyers and architects and builders, to carry out the designs she had made for the house by the sea. Anatoli did not like her being so actively involved with the Uzbek, but she reasoned that she was helping him in his difficult relations with his partner. She did not hide from him what she was doing; on the other hand, she never went into the details of her visits.

She breakfasted with Anatoli on the day after his arrival. She knew from experience they would have little time together. He would disappear during the day and at night they would dine with Igor and other Russians. They arranged to snatch lunch together in the Place St Germain.

It was unseasonably mild. The sun shone as she walked along the Rue Napoleon looking in the antique shops for furniture that would please the Uzbek. She had chosen several samples of fabrics for the curtains in the drawing room and almost decided on a set of heavy gilt Louis-Philippe chairs which were of a size and grandeur to suit him, if he were ever able to come to France again to sit in them.

She arrived first at the brasserie and the waiter, an old friend, placed her at her favourite table in the warmth of the sunshine through the glass, to look out over the square to the church tower. After some time she saw Igor striding across the cobbles, his grey raincoat flapping around his long legs. He made straight for the entrance to the restaurant and came to join her at her table.

'I don't think Anatoli's going to make it. Did he call you? No, you don't have one of these things.' He took a phone from his pocket with his cigarettes and said, 'No alcohol for me in the middle of the day. I'll just have a bottle of wine. Will you share it?'

'No, thanks. I'm going to have a steak.'

'Ah, you're a carnivore, truly a Latin, not a central European. Latins need meat. Look at them.' Around them Frenchmen sat eating steack frites or the plat du jour which was faisan pommes dauphinoises, according to the blackboard. 'Northerners need sugar to keep them warm, to stop them getting depressed.'

'And what are you going to have?'

'Nothing. I don't eat lunch. You know me. I keep going on nicotine.'

His phone rang, calling disapproving glances from those around them engaged in the serious business of eating. He answered in Russian. His glance at one point darted at Julian and he seemed to hesitate. When he closed the phone, leaving it lying beside his plate, like an extra knife, he said, 'One of Dyadya's people is coming to speak to me. I've told him to join us here. You don't mind.' It was a statement, not a question.

About twenty minutes later she saw, over Igor's shoulder, a powerfully built man making his way towards them. He was middle-aged, his face etched with lines, his eyes narrow slits beneath jutting eyebrows. He bowed and smiled and sat down between them, speaking rapidly to Igor. Julian's Russian had advanced since that first evening when she had been invited to Francesca's, but she understood nothing of the patois in which the newcomer and Igor conversed. She ate her steak and tried to judge by their gestures what the relationship was between them. The older man was deferential to Igor, leaning forward in his chair, his hands between his thighs. Igor smoked and asked a few questions, interrupted once or twice. At one point the new arrival reached into the breast pocket of the jacket he wore under his grey and black anorak, and drew out a paper. He placed it in front of Igor, smoothing out the folds.

As he did so, Julian saw that three fingers of his right hand had been severed at different points. The index finger was missing altogether, the middle finger had been cut off at the first joint from

211

the knuckle, the ring finger lacked only the top section, so that it was the same length as the little finger, the only one, along with the thumb, that was whole.

When their visitor had gone, Igor drained the last of the bottle of wine into his glass. 'Sorry about that,' he said. 'I must go now. Where do we meet this evening?'

'We're going to some Russians who live on Avenue Foch. Are you coming?'

'Yes, there'll be caviar and they know how to count the vodka, Russian-fashion: a bottle a head.'

'And will he be there, your fingerless friend?'

'Him? No, not his scene, man. He's an aide of Dyadya's. You know how his hand got like that? The punishment of the court.'

'Of the court? They don't . . .'

'Not the Soviet court, though their punishments could mean much the same thing in the end. No, this was the thieves' court, with the thieves at law sitting in judgement. It's not an anarchic world. It has its rules and its punishments.'

'Was he in the same camp as you?'

'He wasn't in the camps. He came to Dyadya as an enforcer. He was a sportsman, a javelin thrower, I believe, but not absolutely the best. What becomes of those people when they get old, at twenty-five or thirty? They've been trained for one thing since they were ten years old, then they're no use any more. They're strong, fit and used to the best of everything. So they get recruited as bodyguards. He was picked up by Dyadya. But at the beginning – I didn't know him then, this was years ago, when Dyadya was a boss in Tashkent – this guy was very arrogant and he made some mistakes. And that was his punishment.'

He held up his own hand, palm inwards, the fingers clumsily folded down to mimic the javelin thrower's injuries. 'Pretty, isn't it?'

She did not permit herself to show any reaction, but she felt the sudden sickness of vertigo, when you look down and the earth far below spins in space, independent, unattached.

'But what did he do, exactly? And why is he still working for Dyadya?' She had concealed her emotion, but was betraying herself by asking too many questions.

Igor became vague and dismissive. 'Don't ask me. He disobeyed the rules; that's enough. And why does he still work for Dyadya? What else could he do? Who else will protect him? You can't escape. And he's a reformed character, one of Dyadya's most trusted men. He has seen power and knows it works and he is a living witness and warning to everyone else. He holds up his hand and we're all reminded.' He rose. 'See you tonight then.' He bent towards her. 'You look pale. I'll call for another coffee.'

She finished the bitter cup, draining its last drop onto her tongue, then walked slowly to the hairdresser, to have her hair washed, her nails painted, in preparation for the evening. She sat with her fingers splayed on the towelling cushion while dark red lacquer was applied.

What would happen to her if she tried to get out? Hitherto, she had only thought of the horror of Anatoli's leaving her, preparing for the pain of the knife, severing the link, on which she felt her existence depended. Now, she considered the reverse. As the manicurist bent over her nails, painting each one with meticulous care, she thought of the javelin thrower's hand smoothing the paper. Had it been held down, as hers was now, for the punishment to be performed? She imagined the butcher's hatchet blow, chopping through the joints, leaving the strings of the tendons and the splintered bone.

She shuddered and her hand jerked slightly. The manicurist tutted and, with the delicacy of a surgeon, applied a pencil to eradicate the slip she had made.

When you had cut off the digits, did you immediately call a doctor to staunch the blood, or was the victim left to deal by himself with the results of the crime and the punishment, she wondered. The stumps had looked strangely natural, rounded off, like shortened, nailless fingers. Perhaps his crime was that he had simply wanted to get out. They had cut off the fingers that had scrabbled to find an exit.

213

Could she escape? Could she leave this hairdresser's shop, take a taxi to the airport and fly . . . Where? She never felt that she had any hold on Anatoli. He came and went of his own will. But when she thought of escape for herself, she saw that she was so closely entangled with him that she could only get away by becoming someone else, starting again. She would have to cut herself off, abruptly and brutally, chopping off the fingers of her right hand. She would leave the flat. She would never again touch her bank accounts. She would begin again with nothing. She would need a new name, a new persona, a new place. It was impossible. She could not face the pain.

Her nails were finished. Each one formed a neat, blood-coloured oval.

27

The party that night on the Avenue Foch was not a normal Russian evening. Anatoli had left her the address and told her to arrive about nine. He would be unable to come home to accompany her, so she would have to make her own way. She had assumed it was to be a dinner of the kind she often sat through, with a group of his Russian friends, eating and talking for long hours around the table. Although her Russian was not really good enough for her to join in, and she made little effort to do so, she enjoyed these evenings. Plates of zakuski, salads, cold meats, smoked fish would be laid out in front of them. Then would come little dishes of hot mushrooms in cream, fried aubergines. Talking and sipping vodka, the guests would take a little of one thing, then of another, then return to whatever it was that had been particularly good. That would take a good hour and a half. Next would come the soup, which would be tasted and discussed like a fine wine. The main course, grilled meat, would be disposed of quite rapidly, in preparation for the final orgy of discussion, which would take place over the dessert, the bowls of fruit and plates of tarts and cheesecakes, with which they drank more wine, sweet this time, or tea. Sometimes Anatoli's Russian friends brought women with them, always ones remarkable for their beauty, with whom Julian refused to make any common cause. She would sit, faintly smiling, amid the haze of cigarette smoke and Russian conversation, watching Anatoli and waiting for the end, when they could leave together.

This evening was something quite different. The door on the tenth floor was opened by a white-coated man servant and she found herself in a reception room which, although it contained some twenty-five or thirty people, still looked empty. It was very dimly lit, with groups of candles on distant tables. She could not see Anatoli and no one came forward to greet her as she made her way down a few steps, into the room. At first she had an agreeable sensation of anonymity, then in the dimness someone waved and she realised that she had met many of the guests before at one time or another in Anatoli's company. She saw Igor standing in one corner, deep in conversation.

A tray of drinks was presented to her. The choice was a cultural one between vodka and champagne. She chose France for safety's sake. Music was playing and she moved into a previously hidden section of the room to see a grand piano in one corner. She walked slowly through the gloom, among the groups speaking in Russian, French, English, to the pillar behind the piano. A new level revealed itself here and she went up the three steps to look over the space with a professional eye. The room was almost V-shaped and the point of the V was composed of walls of glass, partly drawn back to give onto a wide terrace. There must be magnificent view. She could see a few people standing outside in spite of the cold, clearly discussing business. Anatoli still had not arrived.

Below, the golden light concentrated on the piano distracted her eye from the darkness of the rest of the room with its star-like candle-light. She watched the lyrical movement of the playing hands on the keys. She wandered back, down the steps and out onto the terrace where a strong wind was blowing. It buffeted her sharply and she thought of retreating, but, as usual, she could not resist going to the edge.

She placed her hands on the stone parapet, leaning inwards and directing her eyes straight ahead. She could see the Arc de Triomphe illuminated, perpetually encircled by moving lights. Irresistibly, she was drawn to look down at the broad ribbon of Avenue Foch with its streamers of headlights. On either side of the main avenue ran broad strips of greenery. From above, the tree-tops had the spongy, reticulated texture of brains; the paths ran across the grass like veins. Her breathing became shallow and rapid and, feeling a weakness in her legs, she leaned over the balustrade. The earth below seemed to leap towards her. She became conscious that someone was standing beside her. Igor.

Inside, the pianist was playing Chopin and had begun to sing. She had a beautiful contralto voice and was singing in French. Julian did not grasp the words, but the meaning was clear: women love, men leave, love does not die, it lives on, unreturned. The gallic combination of cynicism and sentimentality was instantly comprehensible. When Julian hummed the song to me later, I came to the conclusion that its power lay not in the words or the music, but in the emotion invested in it by Julian herself. At one moment it had been just a song, at the next its banality had become a personal truth.

She turned into the reception room and felt at her back the sharp wind, contrasting with the warm air of the apartment. Anatoli entered and stood at the top of the steps, looking over the company. He did not see her. The pianist was playing again and Julian sensed rather than saw his reaction. Only someone acutely attuned to his moods would have noticed anything. She saw that his slow movement down the stairs and across the room was full of purpose, even though he allowed himself to be halted en route. He shook hands, patted shoulders, embraced, but still drove forward throughout the song. She thought that his determination was directed at a fellow guest, someone she did not know, something to do with the ever-present rivalry with the Uzbek. Only when she realised that the object of his journey across the room was the piano did she understand.

The pianist, leaning forward over the keys, swaying back with her eyes closed, was concentrating on her words and music. Julian watched her self-absorption. It was a sort of masturbation, she thought, a self-induced ecstasy, taken while the mind created a vision of the absent lover, for whom the pleasure was intended. The pain was like a knife, worse than a knife. Later, when the mugger's weapon penetrated her, she did not realise what had happened, at first felt nothing. The pain of understanding was sharper and more immediate. She instantly read the future in that meeting.

Anatoli waited until the song had come to an end, then approached the musician. She rose to speak to him. The light shone on the keys of the piano and did not reach their faces, illuminating only their handshake. Julian could see his large palm, marked off by the abrupt white line of his cuff, enclose the leaf-like hand of the pianist.

'Thin, dark, ugly.'

She was as Igor had described her, and probably sexier than she had been twenty years ago. She now had a scrawny French elegance for which beauty was really unnecessary and carried with her a whole past of suffering and survival.

So Julian never got round to finding out whether she had the strength to quit. Anatoli went first. The end came silently, no rows. He simply left a few weeks later and did not return. He departed in the early hours to catch the morning plane to Moscow. He kissed her cheek as she lay dozing and she put up one arm to embrace his neck. She heard the door close. The finality of the sound cut through her sleep and she knew he would not return. Yet she still waited for the phone call, announcing his arrival. After three weeks she began to stay in the apartment most of the day, in order to be in when he came. Then she forced herself to go out, so that she could hope to discover him there on her return.

But there was no sign. No Anatoli. No Igor. No answer to her calls and faxes. She did not know where he was, why he had disappeared. He could have been assassinated, for all she knew. She sometimes imagined him lying in a Moscow street, at the entrance to the Bank's offices in Gorky Street, blood ebbing from the hole in his back. He could have had his visa removed, like the Uzbek. There could be any number of explanations. But in her heart, she knew what had happened.

All she could do was wait.

Part 4

Art and Perception

28

Held captive, belted to my seat, my knees jammed into the chair back, I had time to consider what I had learned about Julian in the past weeks, since our return from Paris. There is something about airplane cabins that leads to self-examination: the enforced immobility, the sense of barely moving when you are in fact flying at six hundred miles an hour, the abruptness of the transfer from one existence to another.

Julian's account of her life with Anatoli, once she had decided to give it to me, had flowed freely. It was a solace for her. She recounted incidents, apparently for no other reason than that to mention his name gave her pleasure. She refused to investigate her own suspicions, only hinting at what she feared. The effect for the listener was of a reflexion in a triple mirror. The frontal view was a laughing Anatoli, full of generosity and good humour, but the wings offered glimpses of a harder profile. Although she spoke of him in the past tense and never made explicit her feelings in the present, she had no need to. She had not changed her mind or her heart since her first meeting at Francesca's party. I felt no jealousy. Her loyalty to him, even after he had abandoned her, only made me admire her the more. Her devotion confirmed her contrast with Emily who, like Anatoli, had so arbitrarily and disloyally withdrawn her attachment.

All this was very muddled thinking and being suspended at 25,000 feet above Eastern Europe did not make things any clearer. Even then, with the false sense of detachment produced by air travel, I realised there were some unresolved elements in the picture, but I did not linger on them. Through the porthole I could see a floor of cloud suspended below us. It did not move and nor did we. It had a dense, compacted solidity that made it appear we could land on it. I only allowed myself to think of the pleasure of Julian's companionship at the conference I was about to attend and not why she wanted to come. We were on our way to Moscow.

The conference on Art and Perception had been in the planning a long time. Its dates had wavered for a time and finally been fixed for March. Why anyone should choose, years in advance, to have a conference in Moscow in March was easily explained. It had to be Russia to show solidarity with a country newly entering the world of art scholarship in a way that it had not done before; it had to be March because June, the more agreeable month originally chosen, had proved inconvenient for various important participants. So we had to put up with the cold and dark of the late winter in Russia.

Moscow had been on my programme before Julian. When she had realised where I was going, she had said, half-joking, 'You can find out if he's all right. You could give him a message.'

'I could give him a message to make sure you are not stalked and mugged and burgled any more.'

'I don't think he's the person to deal with that. He needs to be warned about what's going on. He ought to get out while he can.'

She had made her announcement while we were at a concert. The orchestra was seated attentively and just before the conductor entered she leaned over to me and said into my ear, 'I've booked my ticket. I'm coming with you to Moscow.'

Applause broke out. A tiny figure was making his way to the podium. She turned away from me, shutting her eyes, enclosed by the music and unreachable by my frowning protest. I might feel no jealously of Anatoli, but I did not relish the idea of her seeking him out. I watched the glowing golden shapes of the string section, the patterns of curves and reverse-curves cut across by the piercing lines of the bows, and hardly heard the music.

She would do whatever she wanted. I had no thought that I could persuade her to do anything else. This guided my reasoning. Perhaps she was right after all, reaching Anatoli to tell him of what she had experienced might put an end to the risks she was facing in London. It would also be an opportunity for her to draw a line. If she could say goodbye, she might be able to put the idea of him aside and concentrate on me.

The first half of the concert allowed me to work myself round to her point of view, one that I would have to accept in any event. In the interval I took her arm and led her out of the hall.

'Is it sensible?' I asked her. 'What good can it do, for you or for him?' We did not walk towards the bar, but to a corner of the foyer where the stream of the audience moved past us, leaving us isolated.

'It could save him,' she said. Her face turned full on me, illuminated with feeling, unlike her normal, unrevealing expression. 'He must get out. He often talked about when to quit. The money that was stashed away in off-shore accounts and in property around the world wasn't just in case politics in Russia went bad. He always knew there might be a time when things went wrong in other ways and he would have to go. And he must see that it's now.'

'This is crazy, Julian. He leaves you to face attacks here in London and now you must go to Moscow to save him.'

I pointed out to her that Moscow was not the safest place for her. She brushed this aside as irrelevant. If you can be stabbed outside your own front door in London, she said, why worry about what could happen to you in Moscow? And selfishly, I felt happier that, if she was at risk in either city, she was with me rather than left behind. I felt a deep unease, but was forced to accept her plan.

It was a long time since I had visited Russia. The chief thing I remembered from that visit, apart from the Serovs, which I had gone to see, was the lack of advertising. It had made me realise how visually important in western cities are the images, the colour, the wit of advertisements. Moscow then had only huge hoardings or giant frescoes painted on the sides of buildings with long exhortations read out to me by my voluptuously attractive guide. The workers and peasants depicted were heroic versions of her, with sturdy legs and shoulders and deep chests. The slogans were puzzling. '*Electrification is the Dialectic of the Masses*,' my guide had translated for me.

'But what does it mean?' I had asked.

She had looked at me as though trying to discover the motive for my wilful stupidity. 'It means electrification is the dialectic of the masses.'

This time there were no superhuman heads of Lenin dominating the street corners. More brilliant, even more cryptic in their own way, were the illuminated signs in Latin script, *Rothmans, Marlboro, Sanyo, Daewoo*. Otherwise, things were the same as I remembered them ten years earlier: the looming buildings, somehow overscale in comparison with the trudging figures in the streets, who were not stick-like Lowry ants, but thickset and rotund as trucks. Last time I had stayed in a modern international hotel with pretensions it could not live up to. This time I had chosen an old hotel, which had recently been refurbished by western firms to great acclaim. It was in the city centre not far from the Kremlin, which I thought would be strategically more useful for Julian.

What she intended to do in Moscow I knew only in the sketchiest terms. Her plan was to see Anatoli, to persuade him to disengage himself from the Bank and to leave the country, thereby saving himself and, presumably, her. She had not told me how she was going to achieve this end and I could not see how, given that he had apparently abandoned her, anything she said could have any bearing on his decisions. However, it is no good telling people things they do not want to know. Julian would find out his reaction for herself and the experience might help to reconcile her to his loss.

The safety of Moscow in comparison with London looked doubtful as we waited to check in at the hotel. Doormen of a size remarkable even among Russians let us into a foyer of light and warmth. On a sofa sat a man, a caricature of a capitalist from a Communist propaganda sheet. Between his teeth he clenched a cigar at a priapic angle. His formidable paunch rested in front of him, gently encircled by his arms. Standing on either side of him were his bodyguards, muscular young men with longish dark hair and gold bracelets hanging over the backs of their hands. They were both dressed in dark suits and ties, but their metier as wrestlers or shot-putters could not be disguised. So much ostentatious protection made me nervous and I hustled Julian into the lift and up to our room.

'You're having dinner with someone this evening,' she said as she dropped her handbag on the bed and unwrapped herself from her sable coat.

'Yes, there's someone from the Rijks Museum I've arranged to see. I've got the name of his hotel, so I'll give him a call. He might join us here.'

'I'm not sure what I'm doing.'

'You can't expect to see Anatoli tonight, Julian.'

'No, not Anatoli. I'm going to phone Igor.'

I opened my suitcase and took out my clothes, carrying them to the wardrobe in the corridor. I closed the door on the bedroom as I heard Julian lift the receiver. I hung up my suits slowly, then unpacked my washbag. Her voice was inaudible against the whirring of the bathroom fan. When I re-emerged, she looked up from her suitcase.

'I reached Igor in the end. He's told me the name of a good restaurant for Russian food, so we can all go there, I mean with your art historians, and Igor will join us later, if he can get away. Do you mind?'

'Not at all. Do you know where it is, roughly? Is it far?'

'He said to take a taxi. I've got the address. Why don't you get your friends to meet us there?'

29

It was snowing with conviction when we left for the restaurant and the ice that accumulated on our shoes in the few steps to the car melted into little pools on the rubber mats beneath our feet. Julian sat beside me, not speaking, looking out at the sparsely lit streets. She had opened her fur coat in the powerful warmth of the car heater and her hand lay on the seat, fingers as relaxed as a sleeping cat. Since I knew that this trip, the meeting with Igor, the hope of seeing Anatoli again were supremely important to her, I wondered how she produced this semblance of indifference. It suggested exceptional powers of self-control or of concealment.

We left the city centre and were running along some kind of freeway beside the river. The water was frozen and snow lay on the surface, a glimmering silver band on our right. The taxi picked up speed, so that when we hit a rut we bounced over it with such force that my head hit the car roof a number of times. With great abruptness we stopped at a barrier and an armed guard appeared at the driver's window. Some conversation in Russian produced a demand for money. Roubles proved unsatisfactory and only when dollars were offered could we proceed.

Another few minutes and we drew up at a low building on the river front. In the entrance was the cloakroom where we left our coats, which were by no means the only items deposited there. Julian watched a couple ahead of us removing hats, gloves, scarves, fur coats, boots and galoshes. She pointed to the plastic bag the woman carried out of which she drew a pair of high-heeled shoes.

'Look,' she commented. 'That's how you cope with the snow. It's like school used to be. You have indoor shoes and outdoor shoes and a shoe bag.'

I had been more interested in the cupboard behind the cloakroom attendant, which he had been closing as we entered. It contained rows of guns in their holsters.

Henrik had already arrived. We found him installed at a table with three companions. He stood up and waved to us and even in the darkness I could see that his normally pale Dutch complexion was flushed. Conferences are well-known inhibition-suppressers, and I suspected that vodka had also been playing its part. We shook hands.

'This is some place your friend has recommended, Nicholas. I brought along a few colleagues who I found in my hotel. I'm sure you've met Brian Simpkins, Kennedy Zankowitz.' My extended hand was passed across the table from one to the other, each of them only appearing as a face, lit with striking chiaroscuro effects by the little candles on the table.

'. . . and Dr Horndeane, you certainly know.'

Minna was the last in my circuit. She did not proffer her hand, simply nodding at me curtly. I withdrew mine. I wondered what she was doing there. It was most unlike her to take part in jolly group outings in the margins of a conference. She was more likely to receive personal invitations to visit private collections inaccessible to anyone else, or to dinners with local politicians or celebrities. She smiled coldly, showing her tobacco-stained, crooked teeth and her eyes moved on to Julian.

'Come and sit down,' she said to her. 'Why don't you? I didn't catch your name.'

Henrik placed his hand on the back of the neighbouring chair in a proprietory way. 'Yes,' he said approvingly. 'You sit there. And Nicholas over there.'

In my memory the next few hours appear only moderately bad, because so much worse was to follow. At the time they seemed an endless purgatory. I was sitting between Kennedy, a fierce female academic from Ann Arbor, and Brian, a Yorkshireman from Edinburgh University. For the last thirty years he had maintained the role of working-class-boy-made-good, having to concentrate with ever greater determination on his accent and life style in the face of the indifference of the young, whose lives had developed beyond the categories he had known in his youth. Marxist art history had now fallen out of fashion, at least in the form he had practised it in the 'sixties. Indomitable, he now worked on technical analysis. Science would, he hoped, prove more certain than economics as a basis for interpreting works of art. I rather liked him.

Conversation with either of them was impossible, because of the noise of the band. We were close to the dance floor, but even had we been placed much further away, in one of the remoter corners, we would have been little better off. Both Henrik and Minna, I noticed, made an effort to defeat the noise and talk to Julian. One or other of them was whispering or shouting into her ear most of the time. I smiled apologetically at my neighbours and watched the other diners.

Next to us was a Mafia family party, two older women and several younger ones as well as the men. Elsewhere there was a preponderance of males and most of the women were very high-grade tarts, judging by their beauty and the elaborate frottage of their dancing. It seemed to me an odd place for Igor to have recommended to Julian to dine: a cross between a Mafia joint and a trap for foreign businessmen. Minna, Julian and Henrik had their backs to the performance that succeeded the dancing and so missed almost everything. With admirable masks of detached, academic interest Brian and Kennedy were watching the three tumblers whose erotic acrobatics were eliciting continuous applause. When they had finished, the diners showed their approval in an even more positive fashion, throwing folded paper onto the stage, while the clapping became rhythmical.

'Good God, it's money,' Brian said, to no one in particular. This was presumably a Yorkshireman's idea of madness. Then, after watching even more closely, 'They're dollars.'

The applause lasted five minutes, until the tumblers finally withdrew. The band continued to play while an assistant hunkered round the floor, carefully gathering up the money. A girl, dressed in an imaginative version of Georgian costume, was circulating from table to table. She wore a long skirt and a tight, embroidered corset embracing her midriff and supporting a generous bust, which was covered, just, by a white blouse. She nursed a basket beneath this voluptuous shelf of flesh and it was as much as to admire her fine breasts as to examine what else she was offering that so many men acknowledged her approach and bought a rose or a packet of cigarettes from her. I watched her nudge Henrik, who at first took no notice. He turned his head to find her swelling mammaries at eye level. His expression was comic. Seduced by his own surprise, he admired a number of items from the basket. Finally, he selected a knife, with a slender blade and sharply pointed end. Once the beautiful vendor had departed he seemed at a loss with what he had done. I saw him present his purchase to a bemused Julian.

The audience renewed its attention to the food. This consisted of small plates of smoked fish, tomatoes, caviar, parsley, Russian salad, pickled cucumbers. From time to time a waiter would remove one of the dishes and replace it with another. Out of boredom I helped myself to more herring. Julian, I noticed, had piled her plate with caviar, which she had not yet touched.

My head was giving warnings of an imminent migraine; the familiar squeezing sensation pulsed at the back of my neck. I could not leave without Julian and she would not go without seeing Igor. I felt in my inner pocket for my tablets, as the dancers took to the floor again. Henrik leapt up and bowed to Julian. The rest of the evening was a kaleidoscope of flashing lights and violent, inharmonious noise, which could have been inside or outside my head. I made no attempt, after the onset of the migraine, to turn my neck to speak to my neighbours. All I could see was Julian's pale face in front of me, with

Minna's turned towards her. Beyond her, I recall a beautiful prostitute, tall and blond, caressing her own body as she danced around her client.

At some point another troupe of performers took the stage, men in Cossack tunics and boots and women in a Disneyland version of Russian costume which ended at the waist, below which a G string and some shreds of gauze substituted for traditional petticoats and aprons. There was a great deal of stamping during this performance which confused me further, so that I did not see the arrival of the Uzbek until he was well into the room. He crossed the dance floor, escorted by the maitre d'hotel and several bodyguards. Halfway to his table he noticed Julian. He did not stop to greet her, but sat down alone, immediately next to the dance floor, with his bodyguards behind him. Without a word from him, food and drink were placed speedily on his table, and with the deliberation of the greedy, he put a selection of zakuski on his plate. Not until he had tossed back two glasses of vodka and started on his meal did he send over to Julian.

She looked around in surprise, for she had not seen him come in, then went over to sit with him. I was in a dream-like state in which people can materialise without explanation, so I accepted that this gross figure must be the Uzbek. Who else could he be? I was struck by the relationship between them. I had assumed that he would show a patronising, avuncular attitude, encouraged by Julian's submissive behaviour. I saw that she had lost the remote expression she had worn most of the evening; her face was expressive and lively. She was listening to him, not looking at him directly. He spoke rapidly, without pauses, gesturing with his hands on the table. She raised her eyes to his face, regarding him directly. Her reply was as long as his speech. She answered authoritatively; there was no subservience. They looked more like partners than patron and client.

Eventually, she rose and came back to us, leaning across to me, saying, 'Shall we go, Nick? You look dead beat. Igor won't be coming.'

30

'I'll be back before dinner,' I said, to the pile of hair on the pillow, when I left the following morning for the start of the conference. 'I'll see you then.'

The meetings evolved in the way of all conferences, with a special post-Soviet, Slavic tone. A Russian academic made a long opening speech. There was a break for coffee, which gave one a chance to compare the list of invitees with those who had actually turned up. The count was quite good. Curiosity had triumphed over the fear of crime and the Russian climate and there were enough eminent academics for them all to feel that they were at an event of appropriate importance, and enough of the scholarly masses to make the thing well attended. The organisers were satisfied, which is more than can be said of those participants who had economically booked themselves into the cheaper hotels. However, this sort of discomfort is part of the conference experience and grumbling about it leads to bonding over the coffee cups and much more besides.

I saw Henrik, red around the lower eyelids. I could not have looked much better, though the migraine was over.

'I thought vodka was supposed to be hangover-free,' he said, as we stood together in front of the coffee urn.

'Perhaps it was the combination with the Georgian wine,' I suggested.

'Possibly. However, before the effect hit me, it produced some remarkable insights to add to my paper for this afternoon. I was working on it at three this morning. You got a copy? Be sure to come to listen to my new ideas.'

'I'll be there.'

I took the cafeteria-style lunch which was arranged for us, attended Henrik's reading of his paper on Rubens and Marie dei Medici and, after the tea break, dropped into the session for the scientific specialists. I often thought of Julian and wondered what she was doing. When I returned to the hotel, I found a note for me in our room.

I'm out this evening. Enjoy your dinner. See you when you get back. J.

She must have spent the day trying to get in touch with Anatoli. Perhaps she had achieved this already. I imagined the effect of their meeting on him. The demands of a woman you have fallen out of love with are profoundly irritating, as I knew from my negotiations with Emily. But perhaps Anatoli had not fallen out of love with her. His absence might have been compelled, not voluntary. According to Julian's story, Anatoli had left her to return to Sveta, whom he had encountered by chance in Paris. As I thought over what she had told me, I realised it was an entirely subjective account. She had seen someone she took to be Sveta, and had interpreted Anatoli's reaction to her in the light of what she knew. His disappearance from her life had not followed immediately on that incident and might very well have no connexion with it at all.

I imagined now, not the irritation of facing a past companion, but the joy of being reunited with a lost lover. His gain would be my loss, his joy my pain. I was forced to imagine life without Julian. I set off to my conference dinner in a bad mood.

You can imagine the worst and still not think it will happen. So I had done nothing by my anticipation to protect myself from the alarm I felt when I returned from dinner, pushed the card into the door of our room to find it unlit. I examined the room carefully for a sign that she had returned while I was out. In the bathroom her jars of face creams were marshalled in neat rows. In the wardrobe her clothes hung, emanating only the faintest trace of her scent. Beside her bed

234

lay a magazine and her spectacles. Nothing had changed.

She must have left.

I put on more lights.

I switched the television on to CNN for two minutes, then, unable to concentrate, I turned it off again.

I emptied my briefcase on to the desk and sorted through the papers I had accumulated in the course of the conference.

I studied the following day's programme, which included a special meeting with the curators of paintings at the Hermitage.

I looked at my watch. Eleven thirty. Late for the end of a conference dinner; such evenings were usually over by ten or half past. I had lingered, deliberately drawing the evening out, afraid of what I would find, or not find, on my return.

At length I undressed, showered, sat down again with a paper on my knee, simulating the act of reading by passing my eyes along the lines of typescript. I managed not to glance at my watch for five minutes at a stretch. It was uncanny how the desire to look at it became overriding at exactly the same interval. So I watched the minute hand pass the seven, the eight, the nine, and all the way round to twelve thirty. I promised myself to go to bed at one o'clock. It was five to one when the door opened.

She came in exhausted, dragging her coat behind her like a dead creature. She tossed it onto the bed and said, 'Oh, Nicholas,' as if she had forgotten my existence. All the husbandly instincts, of reproach, concern, indignation, to which I had no right, rose in my throat and died away. I could not afford them.

'Ah, Julian,' I said in a professorial way, as if I had only just recalled that she might return to share my room and bed. 'How was Anatoli?'

All her usual vivacity had evaporated; I had never seen her so cast down. She sank on to the end of her bed gracelessly, her knees apart.

'He won't see me.' She was talking to herself as much as to me. 'I tried all morning on a private number that Igor gave me. I went to his office. I'm sure he knows I'm here. I just want to speak to him face to face for five minutes.'

235

I felt enormous pity for her and for myself too. I stood up and gently rubbed her bowed neck.

'Oh, dear. Poor you.' I could see her face in the mirror opposite us. Even though it was drawn with misery, she had not lost her startling looks. If anything, she looked more beautiful than ever. No tears, she never lost control. 'Perhaps you have to give up, Julian. He doesn't need you. He'll have to look after himself. And we'll tackle looking after you in a different way.'

She looked up, pushing back her dark hair. 'I need your help, Nick.'

For a second I thought this was an appeal for emotional support.

'You've got to see Anatoli for me.'

I sat down again. 'No, no. Be reasonable. How can I possibly do that?' I did not point out to her that it was as if I sent her to plead with Emily to come back to me. It was not just that I was reluctant to do it, though I was, it would be ineffectual.

'But you must. Don't you see? He won't meet me, but he won't be expecting you. You can take him by surprise. You can explain to him.'

'No, Julian.'

'Yes, yes, yes. Listen. Igor has a meeting with him. He set it up for me. Not in his office because I can never get beyond the secretaries and security men, but in a bar. So you can just go up to him, sit down beside him and talk to him.'

'So could you.'

'No. He wouldn't listen to me. He wouldn't even let me sit down. If I came in, he would walk out. I realise that now. I think I still hoped, when we arrived in Moscow, that I would be able to talk to him. I can see, after today, that it's hopeless. But I still want to warn him.'

I was searching for other ways out. 'What did you say to the Uzbek last night? You seemed very matey, the two of you. Couldn't you just tell him to leave you alone. And to lay off Anatoli too for that matter.'

'For heaven's sake, Nicholas, this isn't a game.' She lifted her head and her tone altered. 'Naturally I told Dyadya that Anatoli wasn't with me any more. But that isn't the point. He needs warning. You *must* see go and see him.'

'But what on earth do you want me to say? Just think about it, Julian. The situation is ludicrous.'

I knew at that point I had agreed to do whatever she wanted and that nothing I could say would make her see the absurdity of it. She was obsessed. I misinterpreted the nature of her obsession, but I recognised the state of mind.

'You must tell him that it's time to leave Moscow. His life is in danger here. You can tell him what has happened to me, to us. You can speak with first-hand experience. Here in Russia they solve these questions with a gun. Hundreds of bankers have been shot in the last two or three years. He must get out. He must come to London. He has plenty of money and property there. He doesn't have to live here to make money. He knows all this. He's planned for it for years. He must understand that now is the time to do it.' She stopped speaking for a moment; then she finished, 'You can tell him he doesn't need to see me. I'm not expecting him back.'

I did not reply. She stood up and undressed, as if the matter were settled. I watched her hang up her coat, her jacket and trousers, strip off her underwear. She disappeared into the bathroom and the soft sound of running water filled the room.

'It's tomorrow evening about six.' She had put her head round the door for a moment. Ten minutes later she was in bed. She put out the light and said, 'It won't even interrupt your conference.'

Sleep came to her at once. I felt the involuntary jerk of her limbs as she fell into oblivion. I lay awake, reflecting on her need to warn Anatoli, to protect him, even when she said she had no hope of seeing him again. I could not match her selflessness. I would go on supporting Emily and the children, but that was easy for me. The money cost me nothing. I could not maintain the constant thought for Emily's good as Julian did for Anatoli. I knew, too, that I could not carry out her instructions in the way that she wished. But I would do what I could and the chances were that the moment Anatoli met me and understood what my bizarre mission was, he would tell me to mind my own business and leave. Then I would have done all I could.

My reason for agreeing to intervene lay with Julian. Anatoli must be the judge of his own risks. I wanted to say that he had a responsibility to see that Julian was no longer threatened. There were presumably ways he could tell his partner the Uzbek, or whoever was threatening him, that he could see Julian dead with equanimity and it was, therefore, a waste of effort to apply pressure on her.

31

The next day I was chairing one of the sessions of the conference, an office I had been asked to undertake because I was neither French nor American and so was expected to hold the chief debaters apart and probably to be torn to pieces in the process. This diplomatic or sporting task occupied me for the bulk of the afternoon. At the end of the day's business I met Julian and we walked back to our hotel together on the rough, ice-covered pavements. The snow had stopped the night before and the temperature had fallen further. The air was clear and sharp and stung my nostrils and ears. She had acquired a fur hat to match her coat. It had a pointed leather crown with a broad circle of sable all around it, sitting on her eyebrows, so that she looked like a fierce Tartar horseman.

She gave me my instructions and sent me off in a taxi. The place, when I was delivered there, appeared to be a restaurant not yet serving, though in the process of preparing for, the evening's meal. The cloakroom had no attendant to take my coat and, after I had waited for a time for someone to come, I simply hung it over my arm. A bear-like figure, presumably a bouncer, watched me with the indifference normal in Moscow. I looked around the hall and could see a larger room beyond, in which several waiters were laying out cutlery with considerable clashing of knives. The bouncer, seeing my indecision, pointed to a stairway behind the cloakroom, which descended to a basement. Here, the room was furnished in a shabby dark red, filled with heavy armchairs and small tables. A bar in the far corner was lit; the rest was in shadow.

At the foot of the stairs I allowed my eyes to become accustomed to the gloom. It had the appearance of a night-time place, used only by favoured regulars during the early evening. One group of them was seated at the far end by the bar, five or six bulky men in grey suits, leaning forward to talk to one another, paying no attention to anyone else. They were at ease, with no wariness about them.

Then I recognised Anatoli, sitting by himself, his bodyguard some way away from him. He was equally secure, immersed in his work. His briefcase was open on the low table in front of him and papers were piled on his lap and on the floor. If he was waiting for someone, he was not expecting him soon. I wondered exactly what arrangement had been made to entice him here. Igor had set it up. A query formed in my mind about Igor, then I dismissed it; it was too late to question the circumstances now. When it became apparent to Anatoli that someone had betrayed where he was, for I could not have come here by chance, it would be Igor's problem not mine. I very nearly turned and walked back up the staircase. I knew what I had to say; I had no idea how I was going to say it.

My hesitation was ended by the thought that I could not go back to Julian and admit I had seen him and said nothing, and by the sound of people entering above. This minute, irrelevant factor was enough to swing the balance and propel me forward. I sat down in the chair opposite his. He looked up and I saw his expression change to surprise.

'Mr Vozkresensky?'

'Yes?' He sounded puzzled, wary, but not afraid. He spoke with an American accent. The bodyguard got up and came round behind me.

'My name is Nicholas Ochterlonie . . .'

He was gathering his papers, stacking them efficiently and piling them into his briefcase. 'Yes?'

'I've come to see you on behalf of Julian, Julian Bennet.'

He closed the case, depressing the catches with powerful, blunt-ended thumbs. 'Oh, yes? Why's that? You're a lawyer?' He gestured to the guard to sit down again.

'No, no, not at all.'

'A pity. I've some business to do with her, for which she needs good legal advice. I suppose it's about that money.'

'Money? No. I know nothing about the financial arrangements between you.'

He was settling back in his chair. 'So what have you come about?'

'You know she's been trying to contact you . . .'

'Has she? Is she in Moscow?' He lied convincingly. I could have sworn that this was the first he knew of her presence in the city.

The people I had heard entering a few minutes earlier were now coming down into the bar. There were four of them. Their heavy, rubber-soled boots came into view through the open treads and sides of the staircase. The cloakroom attendant was evidently still not there, for they had not taken off their outdoor clothes, not even their shapkas, the flapped Russian fur hat. Their only concession to the overheated interior was to have opened their coats. They clearly did not intend to stay long.

'She is indeed. She's very anxious to speak to you. It's because she failed to reach you yesterday that I'm here now.'

'Who are you?'

The new arrivals were moving about in a lumbering way, two of them passing awkwardly behind Anatoli. They stopped on either side of him and one said, 'Anatoli Feodorovich.'

Anatoli turned from me, and it was in his reaction that I first saw danger. I made to rise and the newcomers clearly thought I was the guard. Immediately, my arms were taken from behind by one of the men, while another frisked me with the speed of long practice. The bodyguard reached inside his jacket. One of the men holding me saw the guard's movement and, faster than he could act, shot him. The bullet entered his chest on the left side just below his shoulder. He crashed backwards to the floor, knocking aside the chair in which he had been sitting. Blood and flesh from the exit wound hit the wall behind him. Even while all this was going on, I remember thinking, AF–AФ. So it *was* Anatoli's cuff link.

241

The barman had disappeared. The conversation among the group at the far end of the room was frozen, like a Dutch genre scene. Our glances, fixed on the weapon, seemed to stretch over endless time and space. My eyes shifted uneasily back to the bodyguard, towards whom I had made an involuntary movement of aid. He was lying on his back, his mouth and eyes open. Blood was seeping out from under his body. I was tugged backwards. I did not resist, for there was nothing I could do. Blood would continue to drain out of the hole in his back; there would be a lot of it to clear up.

Anatoli, too, was being held and searched. He was speaking angrily, but with control, not shouting. None of the men replied. The one who had spoken his name took his hand out of his pocket, moving his gloved thumb into his palm. Running smoothly from beneath his fingers, the silver triangle of a double-sided blade appeared. He turned his hand over and we all looked at the knife.

Then, with co-ordinated speed, the four men seized us by the arms, gathering up Anatoli's briefcase. Ahead of me, Anatoli was led up the stairs. It was a tight fit for three large Russians in all their outdoor kit, but they mounted at speed. I was forced to follow. Hands behind me propelled me upwards. My feet moved; I was not being dragged, yet I went against my will. Force, moral and physical, projected us both out of the building into two cars. I saw Anatoli thrust into the first one just before I was pushed into the back of another with my two companions on either side of me. In the front seats were two more men. I was still clutching my overcoat, which I had had no opportunity to put on. Now as I was pushed into the car, my head was covered with a jacket, which was pulled under my chin and secured by twisting the sleeves together at the back of my neck. This cut me off from everything. I was filled with frustration and rage.

I had not been in someone else's physical power since I was a child. When I was about eight or nine my class at prep school had been ruled by a man on the brink of insanity, perhaps driven so by years of association with wild and unreasoning eight-year-olds. He

242

enjoyed both physical and psychological cruelty and the most terrifying aspect of his personality was its unpredictability. Blows would erupt without warning and we lived in a state of terrified bewilderment. Later, I often wondered why we did not complain to our parents, or band together to rise up in revolt against his tyranny. I recalled that sense of powerlessness now that my resistance was enfeebled by my knowledge that my captors were numerous, ruthless and, furthermore, did not understand a word I said.

I was held in position by the men on either side of me, my nostrils filled with the sweat and cigarette smoke that permeated the coat wrapping my head, trying to reason myself out of the impulse to unreasonable action. I did not speak Russian; I did not know where I was or where I was going; the climate was inhospitable and to escape into the night outside was to invite death by hypothermia. These were all reasons to submit to violence and to hope for the best: that they would realise their mistake in taking me and would let me go of their own accord. Futile resistance lacks dignity as well as purpose and invites pain. But I did not want to submit, to wait patiently until they came to their senses and let me go or decided to correct their error with a bullet. Better to make an attempt to escape, but best to do so with Anatoli, who would at least provide language and local knowledge, some understanding of what all this was about. So I persuaded myself that I must bide my time in unheroic inaction, until a real opportunity presented itself.

I remembered an incident from that period of bullying in my childhood, that I had suppressed so effectively it had never come to my mind before. I was alone and late, running guiltily up the stone steps of the cloakroom entrance, when the tyrant appeared in the doorway, shouted at me, lunging out with his arm to cuff my head as I passed him.

A surge of hatred and a sudden irrational impulse to act roared up, pounding in my head, blocking caution. With the agility of a child whose spare time is spent in kicking a football around, I lashed out at his grey shins, catching him off balance, between one step and the

243

next. He staggered backwards, crashed to the ground, his head striking the blue bricks of a downpipe drain. I knew I had killed him and ran on without verifying that terrible and wonderful certainty. Of course, I had done no such thing; I had only inflicted concussion and amnesia. My erasure of the memory must have been out of sympathetic fear that he would recall who had been responsible for his injuries. The memory of that irrational violence comforted me now.

The drive seemed to last for hours. Eventually we came to a halt and doors opened, letting cold air into the tight fug of the interior. Russian voices shouted to one another. I was led with my hood still in place across the snow, up some steps into a wooden-floored house. Resentfully, blindly, I had to rely on my bear leaders to find my way. I was pushed roughly through a doorway, banging my shoulder on the jamb. I stood, waiting, wary. I heard the door close and the lock double turn.

32

In my muffled darkness, I waited for a voice, a blow. It took me several seconds to realise I was alone. I was not bound, so I pulled off my head covering, but it improved matters only marginally as the room was unlit. I inched my way back towards the door, fumbling for a light switch. I could not find one; it was evidently placed outside. So I explored my prison by touch.

The room was small, and its arrangement and furniture so odd it was hard to imagine what its purpose was, apart from housing unwilling guests. There was a second door opposite the one by which I had entered. Along the two other walls ran hard benches covered with leather. There were two easy chairs with cotton antimacassars and a table covered with a lace-edged cloth, on which was a bottle. I opened it and sniffed. It was water, an unlikely drink for Russia. Next to the entrance was an empty wardrobe, a few wire hangers clashing disconsolately as I opened the door. I made out all these petit-bourgeois details with my hands, but I could not put them together into any coherent whole. The oddest aspect was the lack of a window. It did not make sense to me.

I smoothed my palms across the table's surface and discovered a telephone, one of the old bakelite kind with a revolving dial on the front. I picked up the receiver and heard the dialling tone; I replaced it rapidly. I had not reached the stage of laughing aloud on my own, but I was near it. I had a phone in the darkness, but I could not speak. The only phone numbers I could remember were those of my mother's flat and the house in Holland Park. Could I phone Emily to tell her I was in Russia and had been kidnapped? What could she do about it? There was a violent carelessness about these criminals, who were protected by the helplessness of their victim. In the end I could think of no one apart from Emily that I could call. I had not memorised the number of the hotel, and had no other numbers on me. I picked up the receiver again, imagining the bizarreness of the conversation I was about to undertake. I was frustrated at once. I had dialled two zeros when a voice cut in. 'Da? Da?'

After rolling up my own coat with the jacket that had formed my blindfold and placing it beneath my head, I lay down on the bench and considered my future. Although it was clear I could do nothing, I could feel frustration building up, the desire to do something, even if it was only to shout at the darkness, to kick the unfeeling wooden panels of the door, to act against the arbitrariness of events.

I lay and thought about what, who, had brought me here: Julian. Blind in the darkness, I pictured her, her striking physical presence and her equally determined personality, her extraordinary obsession with Anatoli whom she forgave everything. She had not recoiled from evidence of money-laundering, drugs-running, arms-dealing. Even after he had rejected her, she still wished only his good.

Thoughts of Julian, although absorbing, could not provide me with any explanation of why I was here. The very brief glimpse that I had had of our captors, their heavy forms descending the stairs, the black-head studded nose of the man who had frisked me, gave me very little to go on in guessing who they were or why they had attacked Anatoli. Julian's assumption was always that the danger came from the Uzbek, but her tales of the Latinos, of the Chechens, of the Middle-Easterners who had frequented her flat suggested that there were many people who, if they fell out with him, might use violence against him. Or perhaps it was a random kidnapping, for ransom, one event among many in the general lawlessness of the place. I had no means of choosing between the various possibilities that came into my mind.

I drifted from consideration of these alternatives into an uneasy doze in which state I must have passed some hours. I was brought back to consciousness by the sound of the door being unlocked. In the opening I saw a group of figures outlined in the lighted space, two men were propping up a third. They threw him into the room. The door closed and we were left again in darkness.

He groaned, and I heard him turn his body as if to settle himself more comfortably. Then he just lay on the floor, unmoving. I could hear his breathing, stertorous, irregular. It was the respiration of a man in pain. I moved on my bench, sitting up, to let him know I was there.

'*Kto?*' The word was a groan, rather than speech.

'It's me.' It was not much of an answer, but my language was sufficient explanation of who I was. 'Are you all right?'

He did not answer the question and I moved cautiously and crouched beside him on the floor. 'There are benches,' I said. 'You'd be more comfortable lying on one of them. He still did not speak, but he co-operated when I put my arm under him and hauled him to where I had been lying.

'What happened?' I asked. 'Are you badly hurt?'

Again he did not reply. He was moving himself into position on the bench. At last he said, 'What are you doing here?'

'I've been asking myself that question since I arrived. I can only assume it was because I was with you at the time of your . . . arrest. Are you all right?' I repeated.

'They beat me about a bit, so I'm feeling pretty rough. But there's nothing broken, unless its my nose.' There was a silence. 'Now, what *did* you come to see me about?'

I sat down in one of the chairs. On the face of it, Anatoli and I were not the most suitable cell mates, yet I felt cheered to have a companion in captivity, even an injured one. Escape seemed more rather than less likely now.

'It's a long story, but I suppose we've got time for it. First, is there anything I can do for you?'

'I don't suppose there's any water?'

I found the bottle on the desk again by touch and poured some of it onto my handkerchief. He took it, pushing aside my hand in the dark. 'No, no. I can do it myself.' He spent some time cleaning himself up, concentrating on his face. Then he held the handkerchief to his cheek without moving.

'Would you like to start by telling me why we're being held here like this?' I said.

'It's too complex to go into,' he said shortly. 'You got involved because you just happened to be there. Sorry about that.'

'I came to see you about Julian . . .'

'Julian . . . yes, you said. Well, there may be more to it then. If you're connected with Julian, perhaps it wasn't coincidence.'

This seemed to me to be a leap too far, a paranoid belief in conspiracy. 'I can't see how she had anything to do with what's happened.'

'No, you wouldn't,' he said impatiently. 'So what's the problem with Julian?'

'She was concerned that something like this might happen, or worse.'

'Oh, yes?' He was not concentrating on Julian. He had other matters to think about.

'Julian has been attacked twice in London and her flat has been completely destroyed. She's convinced that these things were done by someone who hoped to put pressure on you through her, someone who didn't know that you were no longer together.'

My rapid summary had at last caught his attention. 'She was attacked,' he repeated slowly. 'What happened to her?' I noticed that he did not ask if she was all right. Perhaps he didn't care.

'The first attack was a mugging. She was knifed. I wondered whether they meant to kill her then, but I suppose not. She says that if they had, she would be dead, that these people don't make mistakes. The other two incidents weren't life-threatening: they were simply meant to terrify.'

Seeing things freshly, from Anatoli's point of view, I realised there were certain peculiarities in the sequence of attacks. In theory, one would expect a series of threats to begin with the lesser and to culminate in the greater; instead the worst incident had been the first.

'When did they happen, these attacks?'

'The mugging was last year in September. The wrecking of her flat was in November. The last incident was a couple of months ago.'

'What happened to the flat?'

I described the destruction that had been created with artistic flair in Julian's, his, beautiful apartment. 'So you see, she felt right from the start that there had to be a connexion with you. She tried to get in touch with you, with no result. Did you ever get any of her letters or messages?'

'No.'

I didn't believe him. I could imagine him refusing to take a call, tearing up faxes and letters unread. I heard him move restlessly and stretch himself out.

'So they thought to get at me by attacking Julian,' he said ruminatively when he was settled.

'Who are "they"?' I asked. 'The Uzbek?'

'What do you know about the Uzbek?'

'Not much. What Julian has told me.'

'Nothing then. She'll only have told you what she wants you to know. Women never tell everything; they always keep something back. They believe knowledge is power because they don't have any other kind. And Julian is very imaginative in her stories about herself and her past. She didn't tell me about you, for example.'

'There was nothing to tell. She didn't know me then.'

'So who are you? What did you say your name was?'

'Nicholas Ochterlonie.'

'And what's your status? Husband, lover, legal adviser? You must be my successor. It's impossible to imagine her without a man.'

'I was coming to Russia for a conference and I agreed to carry her

249

message to you, as I thought it would be a way of ending the danger to her. If you no longer care about what happens to her, it's in no one's interest to threaten her.'

The ironies of bearing warnings to my predecessor and rival were vivid to me. Now I had done all I could to carry out Julian's commission, I wanted to know who had kidnapped us and what were we to do about it. However, Anatoli now seemed content to talk about her.

'I suppose she's right; it must have been Dyadya. He hasn't been able to get a visa for Europe for so long he has no reason to know that she was out of the picture. Poor kid, it's hard on her getting involved with someone like me.' His tone contradicted his words. He really felt that Julian was fortunate to have known him. 'She's lucky to be alive. Dyadya doesn't usually go halfway on something like this.'

'And I assume he's responsible for imprisoning us today.'

'Yes.' He was prepared to talk now that he realised that he did not have explain everything. 'I've just spent the last three hours with him, having the mother and father of rows. And we are his guests, until I do as he wants.'

'What does that mean? Indefinitely? Are you going to submit to it?'

'No, no, never.'

'And why hasn't he just shot you? Isn't that what usually happens here?'

'He needs me,' Anatoli said confidently. 'He won't kill me yet.'

I hoped he was right, because he would certainly shoot me at the same time.

'What's the quarrel about?'

'Dyadya's an old-fashioned boss, Russian style, which means an autocrat. The idea of a partner, an equal partner, is not easy for him to deal with. He suspects me of cheating him all the time and we disagree about some of the deals he's made. I'm a Russian and he's an Uzbek and there are certain things I think we shouldn't do.' I could hear anger in his voice. 'He wanted to sell arms to certain groups inside the former Soviet Union, and it wasn't difficult to see who they were going to use the weapons against. Us, the Russians, I mean. I told him at the time that it was wrong. But he used all the old arguments. If we don't sell to them, someone else will, and why should we see the profits going into our rivals' pockets.'

'And where does Igor fit into all this? Does he support one side or the other. Does he hold the balance?'

'He's irrelevant. We need him for the technical stuff. He's a financial genius, but he's basically an accountant. As long as we can get him the capital and the political cover at home and abroad to go on creating money-making schemes, he's happy. He's not involved in all this.'

'And why not leave now when the going is good?'

'It's too good. You can't believe the money you can make here, if you know your way around. And I don't like to give way to the Uzbek. Even if I took most of what we had abroad, I would be leaving him more than his share here.'

'But you'd still be alive. Better to live in London with a few millions less, surely.'

'Not in London, Julian makes my life complicated there. Let's say Paris.' He laughed. 'She's a demon, you know, Julian. You should be warned. One of the ways she tried to get me back was to siphon off a huge sum of money that was passing through an account to which she had access. It was stupid of me to have used that route, but I didn't think she was watching the numbers on every account every day, which is the only way she could have caught it. God knows what she's done with the money. But it was one reason why things got particularly bad between Dyadya and me. He regarded it as incontrovertible evidence that I was cheating him. I put it right, but the damage was done.'

Much later, I was to remember this conversation, to wonder how I managed to ignore the information about Julian that I didn't want to know.

'And has he resorted to force before? Is kidnapping you and beating you up part of his normal negotiating technique?'

251

'No, it's not. He's under particular pressure just now. The Chechens are demanding delivery of arms that he's promised them. A hell of a stupid contract. He's having trouble delivering because he also has commitments to the Russian Army. He's their agent and they are demanding a huge increase in supplies. They're not paying for it, but they're taking it. In theory, Dyadya's onto a winner, paid by both sides, double the profit; but when there are problems, you double the trouble.'

Anatoli spoke with admiration for his partner, even in the throes of their disagreement.

'When I was a boy, if we were entertaining someone at my father's dacha and we needed food, caviar, smoked sturgeon, veal, strawberries, melons, we would turn to Dyadya. I remember once he told me about an operation he was particularly proud of, in which the same trainload of construction materials was accounted for in four ways, three of which were making him money: export from Riga, a KGB-owned hotel in Frunze, a Politburo dacha near Pskov and a Ukrainian building site in the Crimea. They all thought they had had the materials and they all paid up. From the KGB he got gold, from the Politburo, dollars, from Ukrainian authorities he had permission to build his own tourist development in Odessa and from Riga all he got was gratitude for fulfilling their norms. But he will have cashed that in later.' He laughed.

'When I came home from a posting in Washington, my wife wanted to do up our flat. She'd lived with an American kitchen, marble surfaces, gadgets everywhere, and when she saw our Moscow apartment again she had a fit. I've always made it my policy to please my wife and in any case we had a stash of dollars she had earned in America as a translator, so we could pay. I went out looking for someone who could give her what she wanted and I met the Uzbek again. It was the time of the coup in August '91 and Dyadya wanted to do more than fiddle the transport system and supply the Politburo with caviar and single malt whisky. He wanted an outlet to the west and he saw me as a means to it. I must say, that for someone who began his business life in the camps Dyadya has vision.'

I saw that the question that was exercising me, of how we were to get out of our prison, was one that Anatoli could put off indefinitely, while he talked over the difficulties of his situation vis à vis the Uzbek.

'In the meantime, wouldn't it help your negotiating position if we got out of here? I've already explored the room. There's no window, but there is a telephone . . .'

'Then we can call for some food. I'm starving. It must be one in the morning and I've had nothing to eat for twelve hours. Where is it?'

This was not the reaction I had hoped for. He stumbled up from his bench and located the phone. There was a prolonged interchange in Russian and I could sense that by engaging whoever it was on the other end, Anatoli had broken through a psychological door, even if the real one remained locked. Eventually, he put the phone down. 'I think they'd forgotten about you,' he remarked.

I was reflecting on the timing of the kidnapping. 'Who knew you were in that bar?' I asked.

'The Uzbek. I was there to meet him.'

'And I was there to meet you.' Sent there by Igor. I recalled Julian saying that Igor had a meeting with Anatoli, which was how he knew he would be in that place at that time. What was going on between Igor and the Uzbek was something for Anatoli to worry about.

Voices sounded outside our door. Lights snapped on and a few minutes later a guard entered, carrying a tray. Behind him another heavy could be seen covering the doorway. At first my eyes were dazzled; then I saw Anatoli. He was a terrible sight. He must have wiped away some of the dirt and blood with the water on my handkerchief, but much of it remained on his face which was ashily pale, swollen and distorted. There was a cut below his right eye which had severed the lid. The main force of the blow had been taken on the cheek-bone itself. The skin had been split open by a blunt rather than a sharp instrument and the surrounding flesh was heavily contused. It needed cleaning and x-raying. He obviously had the constitution of an ox.

He spoke in authoritative tones as the first guard put down our meal. Neither man responded with either a word or a smile; they retreated, relocking the door. Within seconds the light had been switched off. We were again in darkness.

33

'Will Julian be looking for you?' Anatoli asked. He was lying on the bench again. 'Did she know where you were going? Unfortunately, my wife is trained never to expect me. An unwise habit for a banker these days, when you might disappear at any time, but she learned it years ago.'

We had just finished eating the herring and sour cream and black bread. The food had done us both good; my mood had improved and Anatoli had become positively cheerful. When the light had been turned off he had been already leaning over the tray with an expression of greedy anticipation on his face. There was a clash of china as he made for the door in the darkness, hammering and yelling. The door had reopened and Anatoli continued to rage. It closed once again without any reply from the guard, but the light had returned.

Anatoli had sat down again. 'Idiot, gorilla,' he shouted in English for my benefit, and applied himself to his meal.

I looked round the room, my prison for the last six hours. 'Do you know where we are?' I asked.

He leaned forward to allow drips of sour cream to fall back on his plate. 'Ach, I can't open my jaw properly. Yes. It's a place about twenty kilometres from Moscow which the Uzbek bought a few years ago from the local kolkhoz. It's a stud farm. The collective farm chairman was connected to him in some way. Perhaps he was in camp with him in the old days; perhaps he simply bribed him. I don't know. I don't ask. One way or another Dyadya got the stud farm and the old

255

house. Pre-Revolution, you can see. He was always telling Julian about it and his schemes for decorating it. He's done it now, though not quite in her style, I would say.'

It was a dacha with pretensions. Even in the odd room in which we were confined the furniture was gilt and ornate. Anatoli was leaning back now, poking pieces of black bread laden with fish into his mouth. 'I've been here a few times for the hunting. The Uzbek keeps his Turkoman horses here. He's very proud of them, trying to revive some of the old bloodlines. Come, you must be hungry. Before I eat it all. They haven't given us so much.'

I followed Anatoli's example and took some bread and herring with my fingers. Taking no risks, the guards had not put cutlery on the tray.

'It was a good idea to get food,' I said. 'But how are we going to get out of here?'

'Don't complain. We've got light, food, drink. We're much better off than when you were here alone in the dark. We've got to let time pass. The Uzbek functions at night and never sleeps until about four in the morning.'

'And then what do we do?' I was thinking aloud. 'If we call the guard, two will come, and in your current condition, I don't think we stand much chance against two professionals, armed as well. We need cunning, not force. Do you know the lay-out of the house?'

'Not well, but I recognise this room. It's part of the sauna, for sitting and drinking tea, resting between sessions. That door,' he pointed to the one that had not been used, 'leads to the hot rooms and then to the cold plunge. You know what that is? The snow and the river. There is another door at the end of the corridor which opens onto a sort of veranda with steps down into the garden, so you can roll in the snow, and a long ramp, like a jetty which goes all the way to the river. You get someone to make a hole in the ice and then you can plunge straight in. I've done it many times.'

'That'll be our way out. But I'm not sure how we'll cope with the door. It looks very solid.'

The Art of Deception

So now we were lying on our respective benches waiting for the household to sleep. I would gladly have slept myself, but Anatoli was ready to talk. I wondered what Julian was doing as she waited for me to return from my mission. I could imagine her lying on the bed wearing her horn-rimmed spectacles, calmly watching CNN.

'It's really impossible to live with all that intensity concentrated on you,' Anatoli was saying. 'In the end a wife's indifference is more, what shall I say, restful, don't you find?' He sighed. 'Poor Julian. We have a saying in Russian. When a woman has given you her heart, you can't stop her giving you the rest of her body. And when you don't want her heart, or anything else either, there's all hell to pay.'

I felt an uneasy disloyalty, listening to his views on Julian, but fascination, nonetheless. I couldn't help liking him. He had an engaging character that overrode judgement of his behaviour to his lover, his wife or his partners. He was a lighter, more humorous character than the portentousness of Julian's account had led me to believe. He had luck, that essential attribute for a happy life. He was an opportunist: if a beautiful girl presented herself, he took up her offer without thought of the complications of the future. At the same time, I felt protective of Julian whose powerful character appeared helpless in the face of his egocentricity.

'And in the end she demanded too much, you know. She wants to take over the controls.'

I raised my left arm above my head to consult my watch. 'Do you ride?' I asked. An idea had started to form in my mind, for which I needed his local knowledge.

He was taken aback by this sudden switch of subject. He would have preferred to talk about Julian indefinitely. 'A bicycle? A horse?'

'Horseback riding. Do you ride? This is a stud farm, you said. We've got to get away from here somehow.'

'Yes, I ride.' I could imagine him on a horse with the air of a slightly bombastic cavalier. We had had similar privileged backgrounds within our different societies, which had given us similar childhood activities.

'Me too, after a fashion.' I had indeed learned to ride as a child, but had hardly practised it since. I did not like riding, but if it was the only way to get out, I was willing to try it.

'And sex with Julian,' Anatoli was saying, folding his arms behind his head, 'I don't know what you find, but it can't be said to be that great. She's wonderful to be with. I mean, she's beautiful. To walk into a room with her was fantastic. Everyone would look at her and she appears unconscious of the effect she has on men. Amazing. But . . .'

Poor, poor Julian, who had given her heart and got what in return? A wrecked apartment and some Mafia money.

I rose from the bench and walked over to the door to the sauna. I turned the handle softly and patted the woodwork, feeling the construction of the door. I was hoping we could take it off its hinges, but a glance at them told me that, although they were on the room-side of the door, only a tool kit, and a well-equipped one, would do the job. I turned my attention to the lock. I had already felt it in my reconnaissance in the dark. My fingers had told me that each door had a modern lock. With my fingertips I had felt the little cleft of the keyhole set in the door handle. It had held firmly against the pressure of my wrist as I twisted it back and forth.

'But sex was never that fantastic. I mean, she'd do anything, but it was rather like being in bed with a racehorse, all nervous twitching and long thrashing limbs. Going through the motions. I often suspected her of faking it.'

I did not contribute my own reminiscences, even though I listened with an eager, almost pornographic, interest to his. My view was exactly the reverse. Causing a sensation by walking into a room with her was not what I had valued. On the contrary, it was sex which had sustained us. It was like a drug, one that I was not willing to give up.

'This isn't a very sophisticated lock,' I said. 'But it's still too strong for us to break by force. Quite apart from the question of noise.'

'If it's the lock you're thinking of, I might be able to help you.' He came over to join me, testing the handle cautiously. 'What I need

258

is . . .' He looked round the room. 'Something small, pointed, metal, like a key.'

'In the desk?' I suggested. But the drawers yielded only a grainy dust. You don't sit and write in a sauna. I remembered the coat hangers. We took a couple out of the wardrobe and Anatoli twisted the hooks, but the wire was too thick to enter the keyhole.

I patted the pockets of my jacket. I had a fountain pen, my passport and wallet, three cards summarising that afternoon's papers, held by a paper clip.

'Is this any good?'

'It may do.' He unwound it, snapping it in two. 'Do my skills surprise you?' he asked. He was showing off, childishly.

'I haven't seen them yet,' I said dryly.

'But you will. I'm not just a banker, you know I'm an ex-KGB man.'

'Are you? I thought you were a diplomat.'

'They're often the same thing. That is, not all diplomats are KGB men and not all KGB men are diplomats, but there is a substantial overlap. I was never on the operational side, but before you go abroad you have to do some basic training.' He was on his knees again, squinting at the door handle through his swollen lids. 'We spent whole days on locks and combinations. Very complex things, locks. You have to have a three-dimensional sort of mind. The technology has developed a long way, but not here, I think. A skilled thief could open this door in less than sixty seconds; it'll take me a bit longer. It was my thing. I had a theory that if you were good with women, you'd be good at locks. You have to have a sense of the whole body, you see, a feeling for the effect you're having on someone else.'

He tried the door handle again to check the way it turned and then inserted one, hooked, end of the paper clip into the bottom of the key hole, pulling it to the left. With his other hand he inserted the other half, gently pushing it to and fro.

'I thought they had now decided it was basic chemical compatibility and nothing to do with skill.'

'No, no, it's an art. But going back to Julian, you don't agree?

Cold. English. Don't you find? But you're English too. You must suit one another.' He laughed at my lack of response. I was wondering when I would ever get him to concentrate on what was important.

'The theory,' he said, 'is that you keep moving the pins with the instrument, one after the other, until they are in exactly the right position and release the cylinder, so that it will turn. You just keep at it, gently, gently, until they all fall into place.'

By now I felt that verbosity and a tendency to premature self-congratulation were the chief weaknesses of Julian's lover. However, since I was in no position to take his home-made tool from him and use it more effectively, I had to listen to him.

The opening of the door came quietly. He was still talking to himself, 'Gently, gently. Now, now, now,' and the pin in his left hand revolved clockwise. He turned the handle; the door and the jamb disengaged and I saw the line between them widen. Anatoli, with more patience than I would have expected, eased it back into place.

'We're free,' he said.

I was already up and putting on my coat. I thrust the leather jacket that had been my gag at Anatoli.

'Do you know where we're going?' I said. 'At least give me some idea of the lay out of the place.'

'The dacha is U-shaped, two storeys in the centre, single-storeyed wings. The sauna, where we are, is at the end of the right arm of the U. We're at the back of the house. Outside there's a steep slope down to the river with the jetty I mentioned. The stables are over to the left.'

'What's at the front?'

'There's a short drive, a wooden gate, two metres high, and a fence the same height all along the road. It's floodlit. There's a guard on the gate twenty-four hours a day.'

'Well, that's pretty conclusive,' I said. 'We'll have to go over the river. What about dogs?'

'They're kept in a pen near the gate, German shepherds. I don't think they run free at night when Dyadya is here. Too much risk of savaging a drunken guest who has gone out to roll in the snow after his sauna.'

'So they'll only let them loose if they realise we've got away. Ok, are you ready? I'll go first.'

I opened the door very slowly, listening acutely, then slipped out. Our shadows lay before us as the light from our prison illuminated a long corridor of dark wood, the floor covered with a cotton rug. There were several doors on the right hand and one facing us at the end. We moved off in silence towards the door. One of the rooms that we passed was open and I caught a glimpse of a tray of vodka bottles and glasses. It was probably the earlier occupants of the sauna who had left the outer door unlocked, for it yielded immediately to my hand.

The cold struck us on our exposed faces. I could feel its icy rasp on the back of my throat as I drew the fresh air into my lungs. In a few minutes ice shards had begun to form inside my nose. I licked my lips instinctively and the film of saliva froze on my skin.

In front of us a snow-covered slope led down to a broad track cutting through the landscape: the river, imprisoned by ice. The black trunks of the trees stood out clearly and their shapes were repeated in their shadows on the snow. The moon lay in the sky like a wedge of lemon on a plate, its curving rim solid, the central matter grainy, and it shone with an unnatural fierceness, its light reflecting from the snow to give a diurnal clarity. We stood, listening, and I cast my eyes around to pick up the features that Anatoli had mentioned. The wind moved the heavily laden branches of the nearest tree and they scratched against one another with a grating sound. My idea was simply to get to the stables, take a horse, ride away. It could hardly be expected to succeed.

'Let's hope the dogs are shut up,' Anatoli said. We set off on the traverse of the garden, taking a route from tree to tree, rather than plunging directly across the open snowy expanse.

I could now see our goal a hundred metres away, on other side of the garden, a group of low, utilitarian buildings well separated from the house. We arrived without seeing anyone and crept around the side of the main outbuilding, a barn made of corrugated iron. It was new and well constructed and, when we rounded the corner into a yard, I saw that to get into it was not likely to be easy. No one nowadays left a valuable stud unprotected. Great sliding metal doors closed the entrance. I tried to push them apart, revealing that they were indeed as firmly secured as they appeared to be. I leaned against the cold metal and then recoiled, as if I had been burnt.

'Is there any other way in?' I asked.

'You can usually rely on two things in Russia, inefficiency and corruption,' Anatoli replied. He led the way around the building and approached a small door. He depressed the door handle, expecting to open it with a flourish. It did not move.

'But not this time,' he said with disappointment.

'It all looks pretty efficient to me.'

'So what now?'

'We could go and lock ourselves in again.'

'I'd rather not.'

'Then we'll have to walk,' I said with determination. 'We'll cross the river to the road and find a house or a car. It can't be that far. Do you think you can make it?'

'We need more clothing,' Anatoli objected. 'It's true it's not far, but it'll take us hours. It's certainly lower than minus twenty tonight and we won't survive without hats and gloves. You've no idea how quickly you can be paralysed with cold. And we haven't even any vodka.'

He was right. I was wearing ordinary brogues and my feet were already aching, the blood retreating from the body's extremities under the assault of the cold. 'What can we do?'

'I suppose we could try the guard's lodge. If there's only one of them in there we could jump him.'

We trudged back into the farmyard and, keeping to the line of the buildings, we followed a tractor track leading up the slope towards the house. We passed the last of the sheds and saw ahead a porta-cabin ablaze with light, throwing its yellow reflections onto the snow.

The Art of Deception

At the same moment we heard the dogs barking, several of them at once. While I stopped to distinguish from exactly which direction the noise was coming, to determine whether they were loose or tied up, Anatoli moved forward rapidly towards the cabin. He reached the door, bending down so that his head would not appear above the level of the window. He did not wait to explain or consult. As I came up to him, he straightened up and opened the door.

My reaction had nothing to do with fear or self-protection. A blast of heated air swelled out to engulf us and we both instinctively entered into the warmth, closing the door behind us. There was no resistance to overcome. The only occupant of the room sat at the desk with his head on his arms. The evidence of an empty bottle of vodka and two small glasses explained why our approach had gone unremarked.

Anatoli slapped the guard on the back in gratitude. 'Some luck at last,' he said. The sleeper groaned, but did not regain consciousness. 'I told you, you can always hope for inefficiency or corruption. I should have said you can rely on vodka. I could do with some myself.' He picked up the bottle and inverted it to his lips. 'Only a drop left.'

I made him sit down on the floor so that from the outside only one figure would be seen. From the rack beside the door I handed him a huge sheepskin coat, a shapka, scarf, gloves. He looked at my leather-soles. 'You'll have to have the boots. Get them off him.'

I crawled under the table and unlaced the thick boots, crepe-soled like a caterpillar tractor, releasing an unwashed odour into the room. The guard shifted in his chair, but did not wake from his stupor. My own feet were dramatically painful as the blood crept back into them. I could hardly prevent myself from groaning as I put the guard's socks on them and pushed them into the fetid cavities of his boots.

In the meantime, Anatoli had been opening cupboards and found another hat and some more gloves. He was shrugging on the sheepskin when he noticed a tall metal door and opened it to expose racks of keys.

'Real luck now. What have we here? We want car keys, a four wheel drive would be the best. The Uzbek has a very nice Nissan

Patrol for shooting. That would take us along the river bank in comfort.' For the next few minutes he was silent, running his fingers along the display. It was soon evident from the irritable sounds he was making that there were no car keys. He picked out one ring and held it while he finished reading the rest of the labels.

'This is the best we can do. It's the stables. So we either walk or ride out of here. Walking takes longer, but is less obvious. Riding is likely to catch the attention, but it's quicker and the odds on escaping if you're seen are better.'

'So we'll ride,' I said.

Armed against the cold, our movements were now more sure. We strode back towards the stables and Anatoli tried the keys on the padlock of the sliding doors. It swung open and we levered up the iron bar. We stepped in through the small door cut into the big ones. Inside, the agreeable smell of horseflesh warmed the dark air. The vast space was divided into six lines of loose boxes by three alleys. The sound of the door produced a movement in the stalls nearest to us. There was a light snickering of greeting, or warning.

'Just make sure you don't chose a stallion,' I advised.

I had been in Anatoli's company long enough to guess that he would enjoy riding away on the Uzbek's prize Turkoman horse. He laughed, but when he led his horse out of one of the nearest loose boxes I was relieved to see that he had chosen a gelding. For myself, I found a mare. She was not large and I was too tall for her, but she looked tough enough to bear my weight and I preferred a docile mount to one with pretensions to flamboyance.

We had reached the point of overconfidence. We saddled up inside the barn with curious horses putting their heads over the doors of their stalls to see what was happening. I held both our mounts while Anatoli rolled open one of the sliding doors to let us out. The metal grated and shrieked on its rollers and the dogs began to bark again.

I was leading the horses out when I saw a man running around the corner of the barn. He was speaking into a radio. We shouted simultaneously, both of us at Anatoli, who, with his back turned, was propping the metal bar which secured the doors against the wall. Still holding the bar he swung round and one end caught the guard in the belly as he ran towards us, toppling him backwards into the snow. Without a second's hesitation, Anatoli took advantage of his accidental supremacy, smashing the bar into his forehead.

I succeeded in mounting my mare, still holding onto Anatoli's gelding, which was moving restlessly.

'Get on,' I shouted to him. 'He'd already radioed for help.' He ignored me and disappeared into the barn where I could hear him opening doors and shouting at the horses. One ambled out, snuffing the snow, standing cautiously on the threshold, followed by others.

The guard lay with outflung arms and gaping mouth; I could see cerebral matter bubbling through the crushed skull. Rivulets of blood flowed down his face, finding the shortest route to the snow.

I urged my mount forward, still holding Anatoli's horse, which was now laying its ears in an angry manner. As the two horses revolved, I saw men moving in the darkness of the front garden at the top of the slope.

'Come out, Anatoli,' I shouted. He emerged, preceded by at least a dozen horses. He moved among them, slapping their rumps, shouting at them, until he reached me.

'What have you been doing?'

He had his back to me and I only heard the word, 'Diversion . . .'

Whatever it was, he had certainly frightened the horses. From within the barn came anxious neighing and the hammering of hooves on the concrete floor. I could hear shouts of the guards in the garden and beyond them the baying of the dogs.

Fortunately, I had had time, while Anatoli was within, to settle myself on my mare, even though I was hampered by the angry, circling movements of the gelding. The stirrups of the saddle that I had put on her were too short but I did not have time to adjust them. All I had to do, I thought, was to stay on my horse. I had chosen the mare well. She was fit and the atmosphere of hysteria that Anatoli had generated gave her the will to run for freedom. I led off down the slope towards the river. This time we abandoned caution and galloped across the open central expanse of the snow-covered garden, the loose horses with us. There were three of them abreast of me, and several more just behind. I could hear their breath and the sound of their hooves on the snow, the iron shoes breaking the crusted surface. The dogs' barking had taken on a new note. The sounds were wider spread, suggesting they had been released from their cage.

For the first few minutes as we rode down the slope to the frozen river, I was chiefly concerned not to fall off. I had lost one stirrup immediately in the plunging and seething of our start. I lay along the mare's neck, groping desperately for it with my huge booted foot. Only when I had at last found it could I raise myself from clutching the mane to a more upright position just as Anatoli came up from behind to join me. We were at the river bank. The drop to the frozen water was about three feet. I saw a place where the edge was broken and urged my horse down it. Anatoli followed cautiously. Some of the loose horses behind us, unguided, leapt over the edge, slithering as they landed, only gripped by the thick layers of snow. I heard the groaning of the ice beneath us and shouted to Anatoli, 'Keep going, keep going.' A horse, galloping in front of me, crashed to the ground. Looking down as the mare, driven by terror, jumped the thrashing limbs, I realised it had been shot.

And so we streamed across the Moscow river in a herd of horses, scrambling up the bank on the other side. Their momentum was carrying them onwards and I could see them still careering ahead of us. Others recovering from the terror and mass impetus that had ejected them from the stables were trotting in a bewildered fashion up-river.

I reached the opposite bank before Anatoli and turned to look back. I could see small shapes of dogs descending the garden slope and gesticulating figures by the stables. In the centre of the scene was a little pulse of orange light.

34

I walked into the hotel at nine thirty in the morning, my suit crumpled and filthy, still wearing the guard's rubber-soled boots, unshaven. However, as sartorial standards in Moscow are not high, I did not feel particularly out of place and I was not challenged by the security men on the entrance. It was only sixteen hours since I had left. It felt like a rupture of weeks.

It was early for Julian to be awake and I half-expected to find her deeply asleep as a physical manifestation of her lack of concern. In fact, she was in her dressing-gown eating breakfast when I entered our room. She looked me over, leaning sideways to be kissed.

'From your appearance,' she said, 'I would say that you've spent the night in the sauna.'

'I have.'

'I thought that's what must have happened. I've never experienced it, but I've heard stories of the banya from Anatoli and Igor. You sit around draped in a towel, sweating like a pig, talking about sex, drinking vodka and eating herring. Then you rush outside into the snow, beating one another with birch twigs. Is that it?'

'More or less, yes. I skipped the beating.'

I had only begun to think of how much I would tell Julian of the night's events when it had become apparent that I would emerge from them alive. My instinct was not to tell the truth. We had developed a habit of reticence from the start and I did not want the pain of seeing her concern for Anatoli. I found myself censoring my

267

story, omitting all the violence and leaving only the concession I had wrung from him on the way back to Moscow.

Once we had reached the opposite bank of the river we were out of range. The loose horses had gradually fallen away from us, dropping to a walk, nosing the snow, uncertain of what to do with the freedom which had been thrust upon them. I had ridden up the steep escarpment ahead of Anatoli aiming to reach the thick wall of trees that I could see above us on the summit. Halfway up the slope we hit a rough track and after a steep climb, which slowed the horses to a walk, we came to an open clearing on the edge of the forest where a derelict church stood, surrounded by wire. Anatoli halted. His horse was breathing heavily and a scum of sweat had formed on its shoulders. He leaned forward to smooth it away and later I remembered that motion of sympathy with the beast, and set it beside the instinctive force with which he had smashed the guard's head, spattering blood and brains in the snow where he threw down the iron bar.

I used the respite to straighten myself on the mare's back, to resettle my huge boots in the stirrups and to gain a new hold on the reins. Then I looked back at the dacha to judge whether we were still being pursued directly, or whether the men had decided to take cars to cut us off by road. The little core of orange had now become a wavering red and gold flower whose perfume rose as smoke. Anatoli was already urging his horse along the track. Awkwardly, I swung my mare round to follow him, turning my head to check what I had seen.

'Is it the dacha?' I asked stupidly. 'Is it on fire?'

Anatoli stopped and looked over his shoulder. 'No, it's the stables.'

'How . . .?'

'There were some cans of fuel, didn't you see them? Inside the barn. I emptied them into some of the mangers and stalls. Then I went along putting my lighter to the lot.'

'But did you let all the horses out?'

'Of course not. There wasn't time. And there was no point. They would need to save valuable bloodstock, so to leave the horses inside would delay them. I just wanted a few with us to give us some cover.'

He nudged his horse onwards. I took a last look at the stud farm. I could imagine the ululation of the burning horses, the suffocating heat, the smell of burning flesh.

A few hundred yards down the track from the church we came to a metalled road which was evidently regularly cleared by snow ploughs, for it was only lightly covered with snow. Behind picket fences wooden houses, no more than gaily painted shacks, could be made out in the darkness. In one or two of them windows glowed and I realised that people were getting up to start the day.

'All we need,' I shouted to Anatoli ahead of me, 'is a house with a telephone.'

We unharnessed our horses, dumping the tack on the side of the road and putting the animals into an enclosure on the edge of the village. We banged on a cottage door and persuaded an elderly couple to let us come in and use their telephone, with a story about a broken-down car. They did not believe us, and they eyed Anatoli's beaten face, which, even wrapped in a scarf, was a horrific sight, with terror. It had taken another hour or so for Anatoli's car to find us, during which time our involuntary hostess had nervously placed tea and bread and home-made jam in front of us, placatory offerings to visiting gods.

Julian offered me more of the same, though in rather different form, when I emerged from the bathroom, showered, shaved, dressed. I was exhilarated. There is nothing like escaping from death; and the more I thought about it the more certain I became that to have killed us would have been the only solution possible for the Uzbek, had we not evaded our captivity.

'What luck did you have with Anatoli?' she asked, pouring me a cup of coffee. 'I hope that all this bonding in the banya led to some results.'

She still refused to acknowledge the enormity of what she had asked me to do.

'The short answer is yes,' I said. 'It's not exactly what you want, but it's the best I can do for you. He hasn't said he's going to leave Russia, but I have persuaded him to come to London next time he's in Europe. You can see him there and say anything you have to say. You will be more convincing than I can be.'

'Really? You've really got him to agree? When will he come?'

'In a couple of weeks.'

'That's brilliant. I won't ask how you persuaded him. It just shows that his refusal up to now has all been to do with me. I was quite right to ask you to do it for me.'

Even if she had set out to make me tell her, I would not have recounted my conversations with Anatoli, least of all the last one we had exchanged sitting in the back of his car on the road to Moscow. He had slumped into the corner with his eyes closed, his swollen face blackening now as the bruises developed. We made the journey in exhausted silence. Reaction was setting in. When we reached the outskirts of the city and our speed was reduced by the thick traffic, I made my final attempt to fulfil my mission for Julian.

'After what's happened tonight, don't you now think it's time to leave?'

His eyes could barely open. He was fumbling in the pocket of the borrowed sheepskin and drew out a boiled sweet wrapped in paper. He folded back its coverings and revealed a sphere of unnatural green which he inserted into his mouth between his swollen lips.

'I'm not going to.' He was mumbling the sounds. 'I shall stay and fight it out with the Uzbek. I'm not going to let him take over.'

Fighting it out was quite literally what it would mean, I thought, and the stakes were not simply control of the Bank and their business empire. His life, as that evening's episode had shown, was on the line.

'How you solve that problem is your affair,' I said. 'But what about Julian? I don't see why she should be involved in all this.'

'She is involved,' he said. 'But I think the heat is off her now. The Uzbek's dealing with me direct.' This argument might be valid, but it was not very satisfactory. Then he went on, with appalling frankness, 'In any case, you have to see it from my point of view. There's not much I can do about it, and even if I could, would I want to?'

I realised, with a chill, what he must mean. If Dyadya did not have Julian to focus on, he would look elsewhere: to Anatoli's wife, his son, Sveta. As far as Anatoli was concerned, Dyadya's misapprehension had been a useful one. I decided not to tell him that Julian had already seen the Uzbek herself.

'You could see her,' I said reproachfully. 'Next time you're in Europe, go to London, sort out the money, the flat, the whole lot. Make a clean break of it.'

His eyes opened, slitted between their puffy lids. 'That would suit you, wouldn't it?'

'It would. I'd prefer it if you could call the Uzbek off, but I can see any disclaimers on your part are likely to renew his interest, so I hope you'll settle your differences rapidly, and successfully.'

We had just passed a triumphal arch and were driving up one of the great boulevards towards the centre of the city. Anatoli said, 'We'll put you in a taxi somewhere here on Kutuzovsky, so you can make your own way to your hotel. It's better we don't turn up there together. Have you any money?'

I realised that my wallet was still in my jacket pocket; they had not even examined my passport. With luck, they would have had no idea who I was. Anatoli spoke in Russian to the driver, instructing him where to stop and then turned towards me.

'It's the last thing I'll do for her. I'll come to London next month and sort things out. Give me your card. I'll fax you when I'm coming.'

It was on this surreal note that our meeting ended, as if it had been a business affair, with an exchange of cards.

271

35

I made no attempt to join the morning session at the conference and Julian and I only turned up after lunch. In the hall we met Henrik who shook our hands with some relief.

'You weren't here this morning,' he said disapprovingly. 'He wasn't here this morning,' he repeated to Julian, as if I had escaped from both of them.

She smiled dazzlingly. 'There was no need to worry.'

'I heard that you were going to talk about the *Lady in a Pelisse*. I thought Minna might have made you nervous.'

'Not at all,' I said coldly. 'I am going to mention the Vermeer, but I don't know how anyone else would have known that.'

'Because you didn't circulate your paper, as requested by the organisers,' Henrik said, 'we surmised that you had a bombshell for us.'

'It's a trick,' Julian interjected. 'It's a way to ensure he attracts a big crowd for his paper, which is going to be stupendously dull.'

'Ah, he's going to back off.' Henrik had no sense of humour.

'No, I was joking. I know nothing about it.'

For whatever reason, or lack of one, I had been assigned to speak in the large hall where the plenary sessions were held and the room was full. Julian seated herself in the front row. I couldn't see Minna.

In the way of continental academia, Henrik introduced me, listing my interests and publications, while at the same time emphasising my lack of permanent standing in the university world. I was an outsider, a maverick from whom fireworks could be expected, which solid professors like himself would eschew.

There is no doubt that what had happened to me in the previous twenty or so hours had its effect on the delivery of my paper. The essence was as I had written it in the calm of my office a week earlier, but the style and so its impact was the result of my adventures. Escape from death puts you on a high. The flow of adrenaline through the body elates you, so you feel invincible.

In my paper I had given a sizable chunk of time to the Litvak *Lady*, as an illustration of an argument about aesthetic value and the concept of authenticity. It was the hope of hearing this that had produced such a large audience.

I began by putting a slide of the Vermeer on the screen.

'This is a detective story,' I said, 'of how I found that the *Lady in a Pelisse* is not what it seems, and not what we have taken it to be for the last seventy years. The process of decoding it was a mixture of intuition and reasoning which I shall trace for you now.'

The first stage was an examination of the painting as a work of art, pure connoisseurship. I had a series of slides, the first a view of the whole, then a number of blow-ups of the details that first aroused my unease, the clumsy hand, the odd perspective of the chair. The visual is always more convincing that the oral, and these images made a strong impression.

I went on to the historical sources for the attribution, to show how negligible they were. It was based merely on tradition, going back no further than the 1920s when the painting had been sold to Litvak by Schall.

'Here,' I said, 'I thought I had the answer. Let me remind you of three other seventeenth-century Dutch works (among others) that Schall had sold for great sums and which have subsequently been revealed as fakes.'

I flashed on the screen three paintings, a Rembrandt, a Franz Hals and a Pieter de Hooch which had disappeared, disgraced, from galleries in the post-war period. My audience could see what was coming, just as I had, so there was surprise when I said, 'But I was wrong. In this case, Schall sold a genuine seventeenth-century masterpiece. The fact that he assigned it to Vermeer, an attribution that Litvak accepted, was an error, but not fraud.'

I returned to the provenance of the *Lady* with the sale catalogue of 1696, '*A Lady in a Fur signed I MEER*'. I read out the passage from Minna's monograph; then a similar claim made for the Berlin *Lady with a Pearl Earring*. I placed on the screen blow-ups of the signatures, the Litvak J VER MEER, the Berlin I MEER.

'I think we can agree that Berlin has it,' I said. 'I hope I have now demonstrated that the Litvak painting stands before us without a history. We have no record of it before the 1920s. So here it is, without baggage, for us to appreciate and evaluate, using all the ancient skills of connoisseurship and the modern techniques of science to validate it.

'What I am going to demonstrate today is that the work is, in fact, by Pieter van den Bergh, that it was executed in deliberate imitation of Vermeer, and must have been painted around 1690. Van den Bergh was a generation younger than Vermeer. The older man lived in Delft from 1632 to 1675; van den Bergh was born in Amsterdam in 1650 and lived to a great age, dying there in 1735. Van den Bergh was a highly gifted painter, who would paint to demand in the ancient or modern style. We have a contract signed by him, dated 1685, in which he agreed to paint his sitter, an Amsterdam merchant of the Dutch East India Company, who seems to have developed pretensions, "in the style of van Dyke". Here is the result.' I put a picture onto the screen. 'It has never deceived in the way that the *Lady* has, for though it is a very skilful imitation of van Dyke, the costumes, and indeed the date, set it half a century later than the master. Van den Bergh was also responsible for the decoration of a salon in the country palace of the Princes of Orange, since lost, but which was described in admiring terms for its imitation of the Chinese style.

'It is one thing to say van den Bergh had the skill to imitate Vermeer and to paint the Litvak *Lady*, quite another to prove that he did so. But there are a number of links connecting him with the painting. The first is merely indicative. We have a very interesting entry in the diary of an English traveller who visited Delft in 1691, hoping to see some of the works of Vermeer, now dead for sixteen years. None were available for him to admire, and he writes that he was recommended to visit the atelier of Heer van den Bergh in Amsterdam, who had recently executed works in that style. Unfortunately for us, Mr Timothy Morrison did not follow up this advice, but we can legitimately deduce that van den Bergh was known to produce paintings in the style of Vermeer, or perhaps, since we know of none, apart, I would suggest, from the *Lady*, he had recently produced a single example.

'We can get even closer to the Litvak painting by examining the circumstances of van den Bergh's life, which was the subject of a masterly French doctorat d'etat in 1970. Considerable documentation exists on this painter for several reasons: he made a good marriage; he was litigious and his will and inventory on death have been preserved. He was also peripherally involved in a notorious murder case in 1692, for which records have survived. The victim was a prostitute, named Elizabeta Vrielynk, who was his favourite model. Once we have been given this information, we can look for her among his works of this period. The first candidate is the most obvious one: it has always been entitled *Courtesan*.'

A close up of the *Courtesan's* face appeared on the screen.

'Then there is the *View of a Courtyard*, now in Dresden.'

I showed the whole painting and then a close-up of the woman, seated with a basket of fruit in her lap, placing the images side by side.

'What I am doing here,' I commented, 'is the contrary of all art criticism. I am not looking at technique or skill or style. I am looking for the real thing: the woman who is here represented. Is the courtesan the woman in the courtyard? I think that in these two cases we can see the same distinctive and attractive features. Here is another example I have found. It is a work in a private collection which was lent to the exhibition of Dutch genre painters at the Met four years ago. It is an interior scene, a vanitas picture, which is dated 1688. She, I think, makes the clearest link between the two other works and the *Lady*.'

The three close-ups of the woman's head were joined on screen by the Litvak head. The resemblance was remarkable.

'I now want to leave the work of art as an identity document and return to more familiar territory.' Here I took details from these paintings to illustrate van den Bergh's style and techniques. I showed how the brush strokes of the *Lady*, the characteristic loose dabs of paint, could be paralleled with similar techniques in van den Bergh's works. The slides flashed in a rapid exchange from Vermeer to van den Bergh and back.

So even at its inception, I argued, the painting was meant to look like what it was not. At that stage it was an honest fake in financial terms, as its value was set as a painting in the style of Vermeer, and may have fetched far more than an original. Later, as I went on to show, different intentions captured the work. It was retouched in the nineteenth century after Vermeer had become fashionable. These additions were made, almost certainly, with the purpose of deceiving, of emphasising the Vermeerian elements, particularly in the yellow tones. It was at this time that the false signature was added, I argued, as van den Bergh never used false signatures. I won't go here into my analysis of the social changes that produce an evolution in taste which selects certain painters of the past to make their works the icons of a later time. I refer you to my paper published in a collection with the trickily unacademic title *The Arts of Deception*, by the Yale University Press. I went on to show that the financial motivation for the 'improvements' of the work was reinforced by the even more powerful factor of pride of possession.

In support of my thesis, I turned to the evidence of science. 'Those of you who are experts on this period will be aware that until now no scientific tests are recorded in the literature about the Litvak Vermeer. This is not because the picture has been above question.

Many of the points that I have brought to your attention today were first raised in a series of articles in the 'sixties. It is rather because the Foundation which owned the painting was resistant to the running of such tests. However, I can now reveal that in fact the work has been subjected to scientific analysis over the years. I was alerted to the existence of such material by an article by the Director of the Litvak Foundation which affirmed that all such tests supported a mid-seventeenth-century date for the work. But where were they? By various means, not dissimilar to those employed by investigative journalists, I managed to obtain copies.'

I placed on the overhead reader a transparency of the paint analysis, so that my audience could see the date and place of the test.

'You will see,' I said, 'that this test does indeed confirm such a date. It has been generally accepted that 1666 is a convenient position in Vermeer's oeuvre to place the *Lady*, on stylistic grounds. Nothing here would contradict that. Although I have to say that nothing strictly confirms it, for the date range is too great to pinpoint the picture to a particular year. To achieve this level of certainty, we must go to dendrochronology. Among the tests to which I had access at first I could find no trace of this most important and accurate analysis, and, without betraying my sources, I have to tell you that, if I had not had help from insiders, I would not be able to give you this information now. Only recently was I shown the results of the dendrochronological test that was done in 1989, which reveals that, whether my hypothesis of van den Bergh is correct or not, Jan Vermeer of Delft certainly did not paint the *Lady in a Pelisse.*'

I was not dissatisfied with the ripple of excitement that passed through the hall. I placed a new transparency on the overhead reader.

'If you look at this chart you will see the left-hand scale represents the tree ring growth for the seventeenth century, starting here at 1610 and running through to 1700. The pattern in the centre of the chart is that of the Litvak panel. You can see that it corresponds very well with the period 1625 to 1685. The saw cut falls on the ring for

278

that year. We can assume a year for seasoning of the wood before cutting, and then a period in storage, before it was actually sold for use. This occupies the five years before 1690 to 91 when I suggest van den Bergh produced his painting.'

Academic violence, the ruining of reputations, is done in a civilised way. Throughout my lecture my delivery was bland, even boring, and an outsider would not have realised that anything remarkable had been announced. Those initiates of the enigma of academic papers knew what my words meant. Indeed, many of them, those who were experts in seventeenth-century painting or in Dutch genre subjects, would have known that my discovery could only mean suppression of evidence, which could only mean by Minna. I left the *Lady* and went on with my paper, taking another twenty minutes or so to conclude my argument.

I received congratulations and comments which were excited as well as interested. Art historians love controversy and here they could sense one that had the possibilities of scandal as well. Only Henrik said outright what others were wondering, 'Was Minna in the hall?' Nobody was prepared to comment on Minna and her reaction in my presence.

Julian said, 'Oh, yes, she was there. I met her on my way in.'

The adrenaline had ebbed. I felt tired and a sense of anticlimax. I needed to sleep for a couple of hours. Julian and I detached ourselves from the group and made our way down the marble staircase. Standing in the hall was Minna, shrugging on an overcoat with a fake fur collar and military-style brass buttons. If I had been alone, I might have hesitated there to allow her to leave and so avoid a confrontation. Julian's stride did not falter and I was carried on down by her will.

Minna glanced up and made no attempt to avoid us, holding her ground until we reached her level. Confrontation was what she wanted. I had feared to see her because I was afraid of seeing the pain I had caused, even in the pursuit of truth. I was saved from this, for she manifested none of the emotions I would have felt in her place. She was, simply, furious.

'Well, Nicholas,' she said. 'I told you that you were wrong when you started all this and you wouldn't listen to me.' She was not just angry at the invasion of her territory and the demolition of one of her citadels, I realised. She was indignant, too, at the defiance of her authority. 'The painting is a Vermeer. I do not accept any of the doubts you have chosen, for your own reasons, to throw on it. Its attribution will remain.'

'You can swear black is white, Minna, but that isn't scholarly debate.'

'Scholarly debate, pah.' It is impossible to reproduce the explosive contempt of the sound that erupted from her mouth. 'What you have been doing today is not scholarly debate, it's a crime.'

Part 5

Perjury

36

When we left Moscow I feared Julian would be depressed by Anatoli's rejection. However, once home her spirits remained high and I felt she had rid herself of her obsession. In addition, the stalking by the Uzbek's men had ceased. She was coming and going normally and the atmosphere of siege had dissipated. Her decision to go to Moscow had been right. Somehow, I was not quite sure how, the problem had solved itself.

From my point of view, too, the conference had been a triumph. The consensus was that my case for a re-attribution of the Litvak Vermeer was very persuasive and Minna had serious questions to answer about suppression of the scientific data. An article in one of the broadsheets about the painting set out the evidence in a reasonable manner, without personalities obtruding. I was approached by an important journal to write up my discoveries. I heard from Henrik that a colleague of his, now in America, was going to take up the question of the dendrochronological tests with the Board of the Foundation. Minna would find it hard to withstand such demands, especially as he would be supported by Anthony Watendlath, who had phoned me as soon as we returned, already briefed on the events of the conference.

'I hope you heard, too, about the tribute I paid to various anonymous donors of information,' I said.

'I did. I had no idea that these materials were being effectively hidden from researchers. It was a scandal,' he replied. 'You can be sure that steps are being taken here at the Foundation. Anyway, I'm delighted you managed to penetrate our defences in the name of truth.'

Only one small incident suggested that the past had not been entirely sloughed off. One afternoon I had been out to lunch and, since I was close to home, I went in to pick up a file that I had left behind that morning. As I opened the front door of the flat, I heard a male voice and Julian's murmured reply. I was, irrationally, convinced that this was Anatoli. I opened the drawing room door at once and to my astonishment revealed Tom Naish with a pile of papers on his knee, leaning forward to take a sip of coffee. He was the least likely person I would have expected to find there and at least a proportion of my amazement must have been visible in my face. He looked uncomfortable. Julian betrayed no unease. She finished pouring the thick liquid into a tiny cup and said, as though she was expecting me, 'Would you like some coffee? Take this one.'

She went out to find herself another cup and Tom, who had recovered from his brief awkwardness, sat back in his chair.

'I was checking with Julian some of the details of the attacks on her during the winter.'

'Anything new?'

'If you mean, do we have anything on the culprit, the answer is no. I'm more interested in the case in order to build up my data on Russian Mafia groups in Britain and their operating methods than in any hope of catching the men who mugged her. We're not even sure whether they were Russians or if the job was contracted out to locals.'

Julian had returned from the kitchen. 'The knife is very characteristic of the Russians, though, isn't it?' she asked.

Tom shrugged. 'Not necessarily. Anyone can use a knife. I'm still not convinced one way or another. And we're nowhere near finding whoever was concerned.'

'Perhaps something'll turn up,' she said. This was very different from her previous attitude, which had been to resist all speculation.

'It may. What you've told me today fills in a lot of background, but

I'm not sure there's enough to convict.'

'Nick was a witness,' she said, eagerly. 'If you ever had a suspect, he would be able to testify. He saw it all.'

I tried to recall that momentous evening which seemed so long ago. The car had been a BMW with only one tail light functioning, driven by two men. I could say nothing about their age or appearance. The mugger himself in his dark jogging clothes with his woollen hat pulled low over his forehead was a little clearer. He had been tallish, white, probably young. But I had no recollection of his face. I couldn't state his age with certainty, or describe any distinguishing characteristics.

'I doubt if I could say anything very convincing for a jury,' I objected.

'If they found the right person, it would all come back to you,' Julian said with determination.

I finished my coffee and put down my cup. Tom was in no hurry to leave and was not going to continue his business as long as I was there. 'I'll let you get on with it then,' I said. I picked up my folder from the hall table and my keys from the drawer. The knife that Henrik had given Julian rolled to the back with my mother's torch.

After I had left, I debated with myself whether I should phone Tom to tell him about the kidnapping in Moscow. It was circumstantial evidence that the attacks on Julian had been organised from Russia and by the Uzbek. However, I could not see that there was any hurry to give him this information, or that it would help in any practical way. The urgency had gone out of the matter.

Since my meeting with Anatoli and our conversation in captivity, my curiosity about Julian's past had eased. I had been reassured because all the details seemed to tally with what Julian had told me about the Bank and its directors. The nature of their relationship, hers with Anatoli, had become clearer, too. His disparaging remarks about her had shown that, at the most basic level, Julian and I worked in a way that she and Anatoli had not. Unless she faked it day after day.

When I saw Julian that evening, she made no reference to Tom's visit. I intended to ask her about it, but I waited, choosing my moment carefully. So it was not until we were in bed, viscid, sleepy, my face in her hair, that I said to her, 'There hasn't been anything new, that you had to tell Tom? Someone following you? Phone calls?'

She immediately arranged herself for sleep, curling her back to me. 'No, no.' Her voice was muffled. 'Nothing new. Don't worry, Nick. It's just the same old stuff.'

When, after several weeks, I had still received no message from Anatoli to say he was coming, I ceased to expect a fax from Moscow. It was one of those promises made to be broken and, since Julian no longer showed anxiety to see him, I did not mind. At some later stage, I thought, I would persuade her to come to a settlement with Anatoli, if there were still financial questions outstanding between them. This would detach her formally and regularise her position. Thus the whole episode could be put behind her.

My hope for a withering away of the Russian connexion was destroyed one Monday evening on the tube between Green Park and Hyde Park Corner stations. I was strap-hanging in the rush hour, on my way home, reading the morning paper which I had not had time to look at earlier. The headline that caught my eye was on an inside page under the International News. *Russian Banker Knifed in Moscow Street*.

I read the article at speed, swallowing it whole and reaching the sentence I feared to see near the end. *The dead man was a director of the Stary Bank. It is assumed that it was a Mafia killing, although most of the Mafia murders of businessmen in the last few years have been shootings. The Bank may have resisted demands to pay protection money or may have reneged on a deal with the Mafia.* Nowhere was the dead man named.

I went back to the beginning of the column. It rehearsed the well known statistics of Russian bankers and business men who had been killed in the last year and quoted various authorities on the dangers to life, human and economic, of the scourge of the Mafia. I folded my paper, as if by concealing the article I could cancel the information it contained. However, I could not hide it from Julian and this would reawaken everything that I had hoped had been laid to rest.

I could tell that she had not seen the paper, by her carefree tone calling, 'Hi, Nick,' as I came in. I handed her the article without comment. Her reaction was immobility, absorbing the shock. She said, desperately, 'It doesn't have to be Anatoli. It could be Igor or Dyadya.'

This was true. My assumption had been that the murdered man was Anatoli because of what had happened to us both. The Uzbek had got him at last, I had thought. Julian could more easily convince herself that it was as likely to be one of the other two because she did not know of the kidnapping.

'Of course,' I agreed with her. I did not want to seem to be wishing Anatoli dead, so I did not comment on the coincidence of the knife. The weapon itself suggested that the killing was connected with the attacks on her.

When the initial shock had worn off, she became manically energetic. I was sent out to buy all the day's newspapers to see if there were other, more detailed, reports. As it was late in the day I had to trail around several newsagents to find a complete set. She was sitting with the telephone on her lap when I got back.

'I can't get through at all,' she said in exasperation.

'Who've you tried?'

'The numbers for Anatoli that Igor gave me. Then I rang *The Times* and asked for the number of their Moscow bureau, because I thought they might have his name, the name of the dead man. But it's hopeless. Either it's engaged. *"All lines to Moscow are engaged. Please try later, please try later, please try later."* Or it rings and rings and there's no answer, so you think you must be on some kind of dummy line.'

She attacked the papers next, scanning the foreign news pages rapidly and throwing them aside. Soon she was afloat on a sea of billowing newsprint. For someone usually so orderly this display of carelessness was almost stranger than if she had broken down in tears.

'Julian, let's have a drink and something to eat and think about what we're going to do.'

'Ok.' Her acquiescence was verbal, not real. She discarded the *Standard* with a cry of impatience.

'There could be something in the financial pages,' I suggested.

'I'll never find them in all this.'

'I'll put them all in order and we'll go through them together.'

She regained control. I reassembled the papers and we began again to search them for news. Her mood puzzled me, for I did not recognise what was distressing her as grief; it was more like rage. Her reaction was odd, discordant.

Eventually, we found one more reference to the murder in the *Telegraph*, but it was no more informative than *The Times*, for no name was given and no clue about the dead man allowed us to guess which of them it could have been.

Julian slept badly. I was conscious of her lying tensely silent beside me at different moments in the night. She was up early, dialling and redialling to Moscow, two hours ahead. I had a heavy day of appointments, so all I could do was leave her to her enquiries. When I tried to phone home, the line was always engaged. By the evening the only progress that she had to report was to have reached *The Times* bureau in Moscow and to have left messages for the correspondent concerned to call her back. He did so later that night, which I was sure was due to the fact that I had phoned the editor, whom I know, and asked for his help. He had done no more than promise to ask Moscow to give us all the information they could. But in the end this lead was of little use. The correspondent had not seen the body. A local stringer had picked up the report and had written it up in the context of Mafia killings, which always played well in England.

None of our efforts bore fruit and Julian began a second day of anxious enquiries, answering any call for me with suppressed impatience. She handed me the phone as I was leaving in the morning, saying brusquely, 'It's for you.'

'Who is it?'

'I don't know. It sounded like Minna.'

It was Minna. I dealt with her as quickly as I could.

'What did she want?' Julian asked.

'I think she knows she's defeated. She wants to talk to me privately. So I've asked her for a drink here on Friday evening.'

Julian nodded indifferently, taking the phone back from me.

That afternoon when I came back to my office from a seminar, I found in my tray a fax from Anatoli, timed three hours earlier.

He made no reference to the reported killing and wrote that he would be arriving in London in two days' time. He gave his flight number and finished *Can you meet me?* I phoned Julian at once to put her out of her misery and was astonished by her reaction.

'He's coming the day after tomorrow?' she repeated and she sounded not overjoyed but afraid.

37

Anatoli's plane was to land in the late afternoon, at four twenty-three. Julian insisted that the request to be met, although it was addressed to me, meant that she should go to the airport.

'Do you want me to come with you?' I asked.

'No, I'll go . . . No, yes.'

'Darling, what does all that mean?'

'It means yes, if you're free, you can come with me. You can drive. But Minna's coming for a drink, isn't she?'

'That's much later. I've plenty of time to go to Heathrow and back. What are you going to do with him? I mean, do you propose he should stay here? In a hotel? Shall I book a table somewhere for dinner? For two? For three?'

She looked even more undecided, as if she could not envisage what would happen after their meeting. Perhaps she expected a re-enactment of their first encounter at Francesca's, a flash of lightning which would immediately change the world.

'I'll see what he wants,' she said vaguely, after a pause. 'Don't make any arrangements.'

I tried to convince myself that she intended to settle it all in the car on the way into London, with me as driver and witness, a drawing up of a balance sheet and a division of the assets. This would be the clean way to do it. The fear remained that she would desert me and I would watch them leave together and for good.

The fax had put Julian's mind at ease, but not released the

tension strumming in the flat. Anatoli was alive, so who was the victim in the Moscow street? Dyadya or Igor? Who was the killer, who the killed? Had Igor sided with Anatoli and been killed by the Uzbek for his betrayal, leaving the two senior partners facing one another, armocked in the last stages of their battle for control? On the whole, this was the explanation I favoured. An alternative hypothesis was that Anatoli was the victor, outwitting his captor and arranging a violent revenge. He was capable of it, I was sure. I had received evidence of his ruthlessness when we were incarcerated together, the blow to the guard's head, the burning of the horses. I did not discuss the various possibilities that went through my mind.

On Friday morning I went to the office. The phone rang as I was leaving home and I picked up the receiver in passing. A man asked for Miss Bennet. I called Julian, and continued on my way to the lift. Although the speaker did not greet me, I recognised his voice. It was that of Tom Naish.

I try to remember my state of mind that day of Anatoli's return. Was I really as unaware as I appeared to be? The answer is yes. All the evidence was there, like the scientific data on the Litvak Vermeer, but I had not looked at it. So when what happened, happened, it was less a surprise than a shock, almost recognition.

Julian took her coat in the car to Heathrow. It was a raw evening and she would need its warmth on the walk from the car park to the terminal. During the drive, it lay across her lap like a sleeping animal. I had already phoned to find out if the plane was on time, for she had insisted that we should be there for the touch-down.

'It'll take him hours to collect his luggage and go through passport control,' I had protested.

'They sometimes land early,' she had affirmed. 'And you can get through very fast. He might only have hand luggage. Or his bags may be the first off the plane.'

So we were there when the *Landed* sign flashed on the monitors. She was right; we did not have to wait long. About fifteen minutes later, Anatoli emerged through the controls, carrying only a small valise.

The bruises on his face had gone; the swelling had subsided; the smashed cheek had healed to a neat scar. Only his nose looked a little distorted: a bit of western surgery needed there. He was dressed, expensively, in a cashmere coat worn open over a jacket and tie and flannel trousers, looking like any prosperous banker. Julian spotted him instantly amid the families pushing trolleys loaded with suitcases and duty-free carrier bags, and moved forward to greet him as he came out of customs. I remained where I was, to let them have their meeting uninterrupted.

Anatoli put his hand out, resting it on her shoulder. She lifted her cheek. They exchanged kisses, coldly, old friends meeting after a year's separation. Anatoli dropped his hand. Julian drew back. He was speaking, searching for someone else in the crowd. They both seemed ill at ease, needing a third person to break the tension between them. With relief, I realised that my imagined reunion, the race into one another's arms, was not going to take place. A third person stepped into the sphere of embarrassment that surrounded them; I recognised the ubiquitous Tom Naish.

I came forward now, frowning. There was some confusion. I had consulted Tom about the dangers to Julian from Dyadya and here he was, in the wrong context. Other men joined him. We now made a circle, with Julian and Anatoli at its hub, which blocked the flow of passengers out of the customs halls. They divided like water round a rock, pressing on to their own reunions, ignoring us.

'Come with me, sir,' I heard Tom say.

'Tom,' I said. 'There must be a mistake.'

'Nicholas, keep out of this.'

'No, no mistake.'

Julian and Tom spoke simultaneously and I saw their complicity: the lunch meetings, the phone calls, leading up to Julian's kiss on the victim's cheek.

'But what . . .'

293

One of Tom Naish's companions had his shoulder between me and Anatoli. 'We are asking Mr Vozkresensky to accompany us to answer a few questions. Nothing more.'

'What about? What questions?' I was surprised by the indignation I felt. Had I survived the Uzbek's attack and saved Anatoli in Moscow to see him arrested, kidnapped once again, by Tom Naish? 'Is this really necessary, Tom? Couldn't you have called him tomorrow? If there's some question about the Bank, does it have to be settled here, like this?'

'Attempted murder's a serious matter, sir.'

'Murder? Who's been murdered?'

'Attempted murder. We are talking about the attempted murder of Miss Bennet on the night of 11 September last.'

My rejection of this was instantaneous. Anatoli was a ruthless man, but he had not arranged to have Julian killed, of that I was certain. It made no sense at all. As she herself had said, if he had wanted to kill her, she would be dead. His attitude to her was the cruellest, the indifference of an ex-lover. It would be easier to bear death, I thought; at least the separation is involuntary.

And here I saw the explanation of what was happening. It was not a question of Anatoli's guilt, but Julian's rage. She had plotted this. It explained her calm, her acceptance of not seeing him in Moscow, her meetings with Tom Naish. And at the same time I saw that the past was not over. My fury was so great that, at first, silence was necessary to contain it. I was afraid that if I voiced my anger at her deceit I would destroy everything. I did not want to do that, yet. The world had shifted and all the landmarks in it had taken up new relations to one another. I saw the past and the future in a new perspective.

Anatoli was led off by Tom Naish and we drove back to London, each of us entombed in silence. Heavy clouds darkened the sky. I kept my eyes on the moving tail lights in front of me and did not look at her, yet I could feel her tense body beside me, as if sensed by an alternative receptor in the brain. Incidents coalesced in my memory to form the pattern of this evening's betrayal.

Tom. I had put her in touch with him to ensure her safety and she had taken him as her weapon of revenge against Anatoli. I thought of the mysterious meetings and phone calls between them in the last few weeks. That led me back to the period before our visit to Moscow. She had done her deal with Tom then. Her part of the bargain must have been to entice Anatoli back onto British soil, so that the arrest could be made. That was why she had been so insistent on persuading him to come to London. My thoughts went further back. For a long time she had resisted going to the police. She had been charmingly uncooperative with them at the time of the mugging and the break-in. What had changed her mind?

Ahead of us the traffic was slowing to a half. We were in for a long crawl over the Hammersmith flyover. We decelerated into immobility, rolling forward every few minutes. It began to rain. My rage calmed. I glanced at her. She was facing straight ahead, impassive. I had hoped for some expression as a clue to her state of mind.

'Julian,' I asked. 'Why've you done this?'

She made no attempt to deny her part in the capture of Anatoli. 'Why do you think? Can't you see anything?'

'Revenge, because he left you,' I said flatly. 'As simple as that.'

'It was because of Sveta.'

'Sveta? What has she got to do with it?' The car slid forward and I almost hit the bumper of the dark red Passat estate in front of us. Children waved like prisoners from within.

'You can't imagine the pain,' she said, 'when I saw him with Sveta in Paris that evening we dined together at La Belle Pelletière. Do you remember? He'd left me without explanation, without saying goodbye. I didn't know what had happened. I heard nothing, nothing. Perhaps he would come back. Perhaps he couldn't get out, like Dyadya. Everything was provisional. There were the attacks on me; I didn't know why. But I suspected that Sveta ... When I went back to Paris with you, I thought I would try to find out where he was. You've seen yourself, he can be very evasive if he wants to. I found no news of him anywhere. Then that evening Sveta was playing Chopin, the same song I'd heard before. Anatoli was there with her. Did you understand?'

I understood that one of my happiest moments with Julian, sitting with her wrist in my fingers, was when she had experienced the acutest pain. In the train on the way home through northern France, by the isolated cemetery, she had first agreed to go to the police and started to tell me her story. In Moscow she had used me to persuade Anatoli to come to England, and she had intended to use me again, as the witness of the mugging who would testify against him. I had been lied to and manipulated throughout.

'You don't really think he was responsible for the attacks on you?'

'Of course, I do,' she snapped angrily. 'He was the only person with any interest in getting rid of me. He wanted me gone from every point of view, financial, emotional . . .'

'Why have you never suggested this before?'

We had reached the crest of the flyover by now and were inching our way down. I was mesmerised by the lights in the rain. Those in front of us flashed red, on and off, on and off, as the brakes were released and reapplied. The white lights of the traffic on the opposite side slid into long streamers on my oily windscreen. The wiper blades shifted the water and skewed the light, pulling it out into curving strands.

'We must put all this right, Julian,' I said.

'We have,' she replied. 'You said we should call the police and I've done it. I've put everything into their hands.'

'Fine. But that's not the same as making these accusations against Anatoli. He didn't try to kill you. We've known all along it was the Uzbek. When you think what happened in Moscow . . .' But she didn't know what had happened in Moscow. She did not pick this up.

'If you mean that, when you asked him, Anatoli agreed it was Dyadya, of course he did. He's not likely to have said to you, 'You've got it wrong. I'm the one trying to kill her.' Of course, it was Anatoli.

He had to kill me. I know too much. I'm in the way. He needed a clean sheet.'

I am always open to reason, and Julian was supremely reasonable. She spoke without emotion as she described why Anatoli should want to murder her. I felt the creeping sensation of doubt. Could it have been Anatoli who was responsible for the mugging? It was true he no longer cared for her and was irritated by her financial meddling. I had constructed a complete hypothesis to explain what had happened and I was reluctant to give it up. I had to like Anatoli. I did not want him to be a murderer.

Victor was on duty at the desk. Who knew more about whom, I wondered, as Julian, all smiles, stopped to chat. The lifts were out of order and we walked up the four flights of stairs to the flat. I saw the papers I had put out on the table before we left and remembered that Minna was coming round. Discussing art seemed impossible after what had happened that evening, but so did ringing her up and putting her off. That would have appeared like a failure of nerve. I said to Julian, 'Minna'll be here quite soon. I don't suppose she'll stay long.'

Julian disappeared into our bedroom. I did not follow her, but sat down in front of the television. I flicked through several channels, looking for the news, but found nothing. I turned the machine off and picked up my papers. I could not concentrate on them. I kept thinking of Anatoli imprisoned by the British police. I had abandoned him at the airport without making the slightest effort to help him.

I dialled Jamie's number. The least I could do was to get some help for Anatoli. Luckily, my cousin was at home. I explained the situation and asked him to arrange for the best solicitor.

'Can you get someone there tonight, as soon as possible?'

I put down the phone with a feeling of spite. Tom Naish would not be expecting such prompt support.

I glanced at my watch. No Minna for another hour and a half. Julian had now changed into a red dress. She took the key to her own apartment out of the drawer in the hall table. 'I'm just going next door,' she said.

Elizabeth Ironside

'Julian?'

'Yes?'

'What are we going to do?'

'There's nothing to be done.' She went out.

38

I told the story of what happened next many times in various forms to various people in the months to come. Not many of them believed me.

After Julian left I was studying my papers when I was roused by a knock at the door. I went to open it, expecting to see Minna's robust form and found myself face to face with a man I didn't recognise. He was tall, as tall as I, but lanky and a good deal younger than me, with a gaunt, large-boned face, without flesh, so that the skin sculpted the angles of his temples, eye-sockets and jaw. As soon as he spoke, his accent placed him.

'I've come to see Julian,' he said. I stood back to let him into the hall. He walked in, looking round.

'So you weren't killed in Moscow,' I said. 'She'll be relieved.'

'You think so?' Igor sounded amused. 'She'll be surprised. How did you hear about that?'

'It was reported in the British press. But no name was given, so we didn't know who, which of you, it was.'

Igor was smiling. 'She thought it was Anatoli?'

'Yes.'

'She thought he'd slipped through her fingers at the last moment.' I must have shown my surprise at his words. 'You didn't realise what she was doing? There's a lot you didn't realise.'

'Do you want to sit down?' I gestured at the door to the drawing room. I could have taken him straight across to Julian's apartment, but I saw an opportunity to learn about what was going on that wasn't filtered through her. He went in ahead of me and something about the back of his neck, boyishly thin, seemed familiar to me. Had I seen him somewhere in Moscow? Had he been at the Mafia restaurant? He sat down in one of my mother's chairs without taking his raincoat off. His hands were in his pockets.

'Let me get you a drink.'

'You wont have any cold vodka.' He stated it as a deplorable but unalterable fact about British households. 'So I'll have whisky, please. With ice, no water.'

I poured us both the same, making Igor's strong. I remembered Julian's descriptions of his drinking.

'Perhaps you could tell me what's going on. What happened in Moscow?' I asked.

Igor took a large swig. 'What's going on is that Julian is trying to take over the Bank, at the London end.'

I sat down opposite him. I did not have to simulate laughter. 'No, no,' I said. 'That's impossible. I know Anatoli and the Uzbek have been struggling for supremacy. I'm not quite sure where you come in all this. But I can't believe Julian is a player at that level.'

Igor was unmoved by my scepticism. He pulled a packet of cigarettes from his mackintosh pocket and lit up without asking permission, using matches, carefully replacing the spent one in the box.

'What do you think has been happening all these months, then? What's she been doing, according to you?' he asked.

'She hasn't been doing anything. She was stunned by the loss of Anatoli.'

'Fff.' He exhaled a jet of nicotine, contemptuous of my naiveté. 'It's true she was fucked up about Sveta. Sveta broke them up, Julian and Anatoli, and made things very bitter between then. But Julian hasn't been fighting to get Anatoli back, she's been doing her best to get him out.'

'Out?'

300

'Out of the Bank. She wants revenge and she's been trying to cut him out. She had her hands on a lot of what was going on here in London, in any case. But she wanted more. She wanted his balls. Not just to control his property, but to damage him in person.'

'I don't believe a word of this,' I said.

'What do you know?'

What did I know? My knowledge had already been undermined by an earthquake this evening. But what Julian had done at the airport was rapidly appearing venial, an act of passion, in comparison with Igor's monstrous accusations. Her betrayal of Anatoli to Tom Naish could have been done in good faith. She could have believed he was responsible for the attacks on her. At the worst, she could have been acting with the fury of an abandoned lover. Now Igor put all her actions into a new light, of ruthless calculation, which forced me to reinterpret everything she had ever told me. I rubbed my hand over my forehead.

'I can't sit here and listen to this without her. She must be able to defend herself.'

'She'll defend herself and you'll believe her. You might as well hear me first.'

'Begin at the beginning. The mugging ...'

'That wasn't the beginning. The beginning was Julian and Anatoli setting up the London end of the business together.'

'She didn't know what was going on: she refused to know. When she did begin to suspect, she wanted to get out, but she couldn't bring herself to leave Anatoli.'

'True, true, she was like you; she didn't want to know. Money was what fell from the sky when Anatoli walked past. But when I had made her see, she was in there: the drugs deals with the Colombians using the Vladivostok route, for example, that was Julian. She saw that transport was the thing. Dyadya had always controlled the railways; he could move anything, so why not really high value goods.'

'You're trying to shift the guilt onto Julian and it simply isn't

301

plausible. The arms dealing. How would someone like Julian have known where to begin. It's nonsense. Two or three years ago, no one here knew who a Chechen was.'

'Exactly. She got us into that shit through Mr Iman, you know about him? Her first guest, she always called him. They got on well together. Anatoli and I wouldn't have touched it. We knew about the Chechens in Moscow, but she didn't. She got us in *because* she didn't know what a Chechen was. And then she convinced Dyadya to go ahead. He isn't a Russian, he's an Uzbek, and couldn't care a fuck if Russia breaks up. Her timing was incredible. We went to Istanbul in the spring of 1994. You know when the Chechen war broke out? That autumn. It was no coincidence, I promise you.'

'No, it wasn't like that. It couldn't have been.'

Even as I resisted, the picture changed in front of my eyes. I remembered that this was one story that she had told in detail, reworking her own history. The facts were the same, but the interpretation was different. What had been authentic, Julian's past told by herself, now appeared a forgery. It was not simply a question of my deliberate blindness in refusing to understand what she was. She had fabricated an image with the intent to deceive.

'It certainly was. Then Anatoli met Sveta again in Paris. Sveta's a very nice girl, good pianist, great singer and all that, but she's not beautiful and she's not clever like Julian. But that's Anatoli for you. Somewhere he's soft. He had a conscience about those years she'd spent in Soviet madhouses and wanted to make it up to her. I've spent years in the camps, but he's never felt the need to make it up to me. And he was fed up with Julian interfering in everything. He wanted a woman who was beautiful, sexy and fun, and that's all. So he abandoned Julian and London and moved his base to Paris. But Julian had all the knowledge, contacts and papers. At the very least, the stupid bastard should have kept them both in play. It's not as if it's difficult to run two women in different cities. He's had plenty of practice.'

Anatoli had said she liked to take control, I recalled, and I had thought he meant emotionally, sexually.

'The mugging,' I repeated. 'Who did it? Who was trying to kill Julian?'

'That was Dyadya,' Igor said. 'Can I have another whisky?'

I rose to pour him one. I put ice in his glass and tipped the liquid over it plentifully. He watched in silence, not speaking again until he had taken a deep drink.

'I think he did mean to kill her. She was beyond his control, a completely unguided missile, Pershing plus. It's odd that he didn't get her, though. I've never heard of one of Dyadya's hitmen failing before. I think what happened was that she swivelled round, and when the knife went in, it entered on her right side, not the left. Normally, they go straight for the spleen . . .'

I did not want to hear about the assassination methods of Igor's branch of the Russian Mafia. 'And the flat?'

'No, that wasn't Dyadya. That was something else. He still had his guys watching her, but she'd signalled to him by then, to fix something.'

'With Dyadya?'

'Well, it wasn't all settled until she got to Moscow, but she'd already realised she'd have to make peace with him.'

The night we first slept together, I remembered every detail of it. The textures of the ris de veau and the daube on our plates, the sound of the footsteps in the street, the scent of the lilies in her hall as we entered, the sight of Julian's transparent skin. And her voice saying, *It must be the effect of the mugging. I thought I'd settled everything.* Then the nightmare evening in the Mafia club in Moscow; Julian and the Uzbek sitting together; the authority with which she had faced him. Why had I never questioned, never analysed? That must have been the moment when the deal was struck.

'The business with the flat and the farce you were involved in, that was me,' Igor was saying. 'I wanted her to think it was Dyadya. I was trying to keep the pressure up and make her choose me. Once Anatoli was out of it, she had to chose between me and Dyadya.' He was nursing the last mouthful of whisky in his glass. 'Didn't it ever

303

occur to you there was something odd about those attacks? Violence without conviction. I never meant to hurt her.'

'The wrecking of the flat was very convincing, I can assure you.'

'Yeah, well, no one got killed.'

'Let me understand what you're telling me,' I said pedantically. 'You're saying that Julian has been a fourth partner in all your activities, has been the cause of the break-up of your partnership, has had Anatoli arrested. I still don't understand where the murder in Moscow comes into your story. Who killed the Uzbek?'

Igor was lighting a cigarette and did not answer.

'Let me guess. You're going to tell me that the Uzbek was also Julian's lover and she had him killed, because . . .' I searched for the most implausible reason I could think of.

'An interesting idea.' I should have realised that Russians have no sense of irony and an endless capacity for speculation, taking up any absurdity if they can weave some debate from it. 'I don't *think* he was ever her lover. She was quite fond of him, though. With her, it's all acting. She was Dyadya's little girl, she was my best friend, she was Anatoli's devoted little wife, with you, well you know about that. I'd have said there was only one person she really cared for out of all of us . . .'

He paused, but I did not ask the question he was waiting for. Instead, I repeated, 'So who killed the Uzbek?'

'That was me.' Silence again.

'Why are you telling me this?'

'I want you to see Julian, to know what she is and what she's been doing before . . . before we go any further.' He lifted his glass to receive the whisky I was pouring into it. I didn't bother with ice this time. 'I knew her before you. I know her for what she is. You can't see what's in front of your eyes. You put her on a pedestal, a wronged woman, devoted, betrayed, a sort of female counterpart for you. You think what Emily has done to you, Anatoli did to her.'

Igor's knowledge of my life, which could only have come from Julian, was the most convincing evidence of how close they had been.

She used to tell me about Victor, Igor about Anatoli. Why had I not guessed she was telling someone, Igor, about me?

'You created a new person to hang your ideas on and for a while she liked it,' he went on, then paused to watch my reaction. 'She told me, you see, all about you.'

So my rival all those months had not been Anatoli, but Igor and his drunken, intimate conversations. He must have been coming to London, every few weeks throughout the winter with his briefcase full of dollars. Julian had spent her mysterious days with him in quiet hotels in Bayswater. I could imagine them at restaurant tables, eating and drinking, while she described the food we ate; lying together on the bed in some dingy room, while she described our love-making, every private gesture exposed. I shut my eyes and groaned.

'And you're still refusing to see,' Igor was saying. He was helping himself to whisky now. 'I'm going to open your eyes. I'm here tonight to tell Julian her plans haven't worked. Dyadya's dead and I'm not. She made a deal with Dyadya when she was in Moscow and the deal was that she would fix Anatoli and Dyadya would get rid of me and they would share things between them.'

'No, no, no.' I must have been a bit drunk. I had eaten nothing all day except a sandwich consumed in haste in the department at lunchtime and the whisky, even though I had only had two glasses to Igor's four, had gone to my head. My voice sounded too loud, and less than convincing in its repetitions.

'I offered her the same deal and she turned me down for Dyadya. The stupid bitch. She preferred Dyadya for business and you for pleasure. Well, I've dealt with him.'

'She's a fiend, a fiend,' I said. 'A demon', Anatoli had called her. How had I reached this point, enslaved by such a woman? Even Emily looked innocent beside her. I got out of my chair and stumbled furiously towards the door.

'I'm not having anything more to do with this. You and Julian can sort it out together.'

I had not so lost touch with reality that I had forgotten Minna.

Only my work was important. I must pass Igor and his farrago over to Julian to deal with, so I could see Minna in a sober and authoritative state. I led the way across the landing. The door to Julian's apartment was open and we went in. The lights in the hall and drawing room shone in the gaping emptiness. The windows were sinister black rectangles. There was no heating and the air was frigid.

'Julian,' I called sharply.

This part was the hardest to describe; the hardest to live through.

We heard her footsteps above us in the gallery. She reached the top of the stairs, when she must have seen Igor draw out from behind me. She stopped, one hand holding the newel post. She was wearing her coat against the cold in the flat; it hung loosely open to show her red dress beneath. She said nothing, paused, waiting.

'Julian, I'm back.' Igor overtook me and ran up the stairs towards her.

I saw the joyous reunion that had not taken place at the airport was happening now and in the same moment I realised where I had seen Igor before: lying naked, face-down on Julian's bed.

They met in an embrace that held for a second and then split open the world. They whirled apart. I saw Julian stagger. Igor turned and ran downstairs. She had her hand inside her coat, holding her side, as she followed him.

'Igor,' she said. He did not respond. As he passed me, without speaking, I heard a skittering on the floor. Julian lurched forward and crashed down the last half dozen steps, lying at my feet, face down, her hair thrown forward over her head, exposing the nape of her neck, like Cordelia's battered doll.

'Julian, Julian.' I rushed forward. Frantically I was trying to help her up. This time there was no will to rise. I put my hands inside her coat and felt the warmth and dampness soaking into her dress and had no need to look at my hand to see what had caused it. I tipped an object with the toe of my shoe and bent down to retrieve it: a knife.

'Nicholas.' In the door of the apartment stood Minna. 'Nicholas,' she said again. 'What on earth have you done?'

39

I was arrested the following day.

Absorbed by grief, by all that had happened in the previous twenty-four hours, I did not understand my own danger and not until I was cautioned did I realise that I was the obvious suspect.

Although Minna's first words to me amounted to an accusation, in the atmosphere of crisis our mutual hostility seemed to have been forgotten. Even though I knew Julian was dead, I behaved as if she were still alive and there was still a chance of saving her. I put the knife down on the stairs and pulled up her clothing, to reveal the wound in her side. The visible loss of blood was not great, but I knew that her body cavity was filling up with the flow from her ruptured spleen. Minna bent down beside me. She had no medical background, but she knew death when she saw it.

'It's no good, Nicholas. We must call the police.'

'An ambulance, if we could get her to hospital . . .'

'All right, an ambulance. Where's the phone?'

We went next door to my flat. I picked up the phone, hesitating for a moment, wondering where to find the number of the hospital. Minna took the receiver from my hand impatiently and dialled 999.

'Police,' she said.

'Ambulance, ambulance. The address is . . .'

I watched her with the sensation that one gets talking on the telephone to Moscow when you can hear the gap, the time taken by speech to reach its destination a thousand miles away. Everything reached me with a perceptible delay; my own words echoed in my head and Minna's actions were taking place on the other side of a double-glazed window. I had registered Julian's death, but my mind had not even begun to work out its meaning and consequences. I was still trying to comprehend the past, what she had done to Anatoli, what she had done to me.

The police filled both apartments with their voices and activity. They carried bags of equipment which they dumped on the floor, opening them with clumsy speed. I did not go back to Julian's apartment, but sank into a chair in my mother's drawing room, occupied with my own thoughts. Minna picked out and cornered the senior officer with the skill of a champion sheepdog bitch and I allowed her to take charge. I could see her standing on the landing in a position that commanded a view of both flats. As she spoke, though I could not hear her words, I could see her occasionally glancing at me.

She must be telling him about Igor, I thought. It was only then that I remembered him. Minna had arrived so soon after his swift, yet unhurried departure that she must have seen him, either up here or below. I should have done something at once; I should have followed him and caught him. Why had I not chased after him, or at least phoned to Victor to call the police, to stop him, forcibly, from leaving the building? Julian had been my priority and I had not given him a thought. Now I leapt up. I looked at my watch and saw with astonishment that it was only just after nine. So much had happened that I felt it must already be the early hours of the morning. There was still time.

But the delay was enough to catch me.

I interrupted Minna's conversation to insist that someone tried to find Igor. Minna ignored what I was saying and introduced the police officer, whose name I immediately forgot.

'A tall blond Russian,' I was saying. 'He's very thin, early thirties, very pale grey eyes, height one metre ninety, about the same as me.'

Misunderstanding followed. This was the first they'd heard of Igor.

'Minna, you must have seen him as you arrived,' I said.

'Seen whom?'

'Who are we talking about, sir?'

'The man who . . . He killed, knifed Julian. Then he just walked out. It's already more than an hour ago.'

I was trying to think of where he might have gone. Would there have been a BMW, parked in the square with its engine running, waiting to pick him up, as for the jogger on the first night? Or would Igor make a more democratic getaway, eschewing the flashy chauffeur-driven cars beloved of the Uzbek? I imagined him dissolving into the darkness of the streets, walking anonymously among the crowds at the tube station, stepping off the Circle Line, unremarked, at Queensway or Notting Hill.

I can't pretend that the police ignored my story, though there was no rush to follow a trail which was cooling by the minute. The senior officer abandoned Minna and led me into the dining room. He allowed me to begin at the end of the story, to describe the meeting between Julian and Igor, their violent embrace, Igor's calmly precipitate departure.

'He was a visitor for Miss Bennet,' he repeated. 'You took him over the landing to meet her. He stabbed her as you watched and left.'

'Yes.'

'You didn't try to stop him?'

'I was dealing with Julian. I was trying to stop the bleeding. Then Minna came. She must have seen him. And Victor, the porter on duty. He must have seen him coming in as well as leaving. Perhaps he saw which way he went. He'll know what time he left.'

His pouchy face, made of pockets of flesh hanging from points of purchase around his eyes and nose and jaw, showed no sign of what he made of this. He had been noting what I said; then he nodded to someone standing behind me, out of my view, who left the room. He began to question me in earnest.

I remember the last time the police came, after the break-in, Igor's fake burglary, Julian had answered their questions without giving any explanations. At the time I had noted how minimal were her replies; I now understood why. It was all too complicated. Impossible to convey the motives, only half-understood at the time, that had drawn along the train of events. So, like her, I made no effort to interpret my story.

I answered his questions and watched him write down Julian's name, age, address; my own name, age, address, relationship to the deceased; Igor's name, age, address: not much that I could help with there. My account was interrupted from time to time by people knocking on the dining room door. During those intermissions I sat looking at the flowers, placed there by Julian earlier in the day, reflected in the high polish of the table. I felt as if I was dead too. Without her, I didn't care what happened. I didn't care whether they found Igor or not. I was without feeling and, even stranger, without thought, emptied out, so that I had become a shell. In the last twenty-four hours, I had been given fragments of information, about Julian, about Anatoli and Igor, about the Bank, but I no longer had any interest in fitting them together. They only had significance in relation to Julian; without her, it did not matter who had allied with whom, or who had won in their bloody power struggle.

I overheard an interchange which took place in the hall, behind my back, the briefing of a new arrival.

'What's the story?'

'Some guy has knifed his girlfriend.'

'Dead?'

'Yup. The doc's been. They're taking the photos now.'

How had they come to the conclusion that Julian was Igor's girlfriend? I had said nothing about his motivation or his relations with her. I had simply described the events of the evening as they had happened. I had not mentioned that suddenly revived memory of the naked figure on Julian's bed. Perhaps, for the police, all violence between the sexes was automatically seen as sexually motivated. And the casual interpretation was not so far wrong, I thought. If they wanted to see it like that, well and good. It would save me from stories that strained credibility about rivalry within the Russian Mafia, money-laundering, drugs trading. I did not fully understand what lay between Igor and Julian (I would have time to work that out later), but I had seen all along, in Julian's account, his obsession with and desire for her.

I could hear voices and movement next door. A photographer emerged and stood by the lift, closing the flap of his bag over the bulk of his lenses, the last images of Julian's impassive, supremely photogenic face, rolled onto his films. Some time later I heard her body being removed, the characteristic shuffle of men manoeuvring a stretcher. I caught a glimpse of a bagged form before the doors to the stairs closed. Eventually they all left, sealing Julian's flat. Still in my clothes, I lay down on our bed and fell at once into a dreamless sleep.

The next day I woke suddenly and completely and for a few seconds everything that had happened was cancelled. Julian was still alive in my mind. Then the physical discomfort of my clothes, my aching head, recalled me to the nightmare of reality. I got up and undressed; I showered, but could not be bothered to shave. As I made myself some coffee, I worked out what would happen next. The police had their job to do of finding Igor. They would enquire at hotels in the area where he usually stayed. They would have been visiting them, street by street, during the night. Perhaps they had already found him, were questioning him at the police station. When they arrested him, I would have a chance of learning the truth about what Julian had been doing. In the meantime, I began the complex task of deciding what, how much, to believe of his story, of fitting his account of her activities with hers, and with my own observations.

I was prevented from reaching any conclusions by the doorbell which announced the return of the police. There were two of them, the pouchy-eyed one from last night, and another.

I wanted to know, before they began, whether Igor had been found. 'No, no sign of him. No one seems to have heard or seen him.

Except you, of course. We haven't been able to trace his movements at all.'

'But you're watching the flights to Moscow? Can you get hold of passenger lists?'

He did not reply and I recalled that I did not even know Igor's surname. And he could take another route, cross the Channel, fly to Cyprus or New York. It was becoming clear that it wasn't just a question of arresting Igor and letting justice take its course. The police were going to need much more help from me. I would have to tell them about Julian and Anatoli, about the Bank and its activities. And once started, there was no end. Everything needed explaining. I saw resistance in their stolid expressions, a refusal to believe. I did not blame them. It was for that reason I had not wanted to embark on the story. It was hard to know where to begin.

I need not have worried. They did not want to ask about Julian's past, they concentrated solely on the hours immediately preceding her death. They wanted to hear, again, what we had been doing. Here I made my next serious error: I did not mention Anatoli. My aim had been originally to help him, and that purpose would not be served by involving him in this business, in which, as far as I could see, he had no part. So the story I presented to them was true, but simplified. I said we had been out in the afternoon, to the airport to meet a friend, and had returned about six. Julian had gone across to her own flat while I remained, reading and preparing for my meeting with Dr Horndeane in my own.

'Had you had any sort of disagreement?' he asked

'We never quarrelled. It was impossible to argue with Julian; she simply withdrew. She never had rows.'

'What happened next?'

I explained that Igor had arrived, I had let him in, thinking he was Dr Horndeane. He had been with me for less than an hour. No, I had not met him before, but I knew of him as a friend of Julian's.

'What did you talk about for so long to a stranger?'

I hesitated. 'We talked about Julian.'

'What in particular about her?'

This was my opportunity to explain about the Bank, the three partners, the Mafia. But I did not take it. I did not believe anything Igor had told me; I was not sure I even believed Julian. I did not understand what had been going on. How could I explain what I did not understand? So I left it all out.

'He came to talk to her about something, I don't know what exactly. But he was annoyed with her. He spoke of her in an unsympathetic, uncomplimentary way. He didn't rage or threaten. I had no idea that he was going to do what he did.'

'When he made his attack, where did he get the knife from?'

This was a good question, one I had not attended to. I shut my eyes and watched the scene replay. I hadn't seen an attack; I had seen an embrace. My mind had interpreted what I saw according to my preconceptions. Only afterwards I had understood. So where had he kept the knife?

'It must have been inside his raincoat pocket,' I said. He had not taken off his mackintosh in my flat. He was still wearing it, open, when we walked over to find Julian.

'When Dr Horndeane entered she found you holding the knife . . .'

'That was because I had just picked it up. I almost fell over it, where it was lying beside her on the floor.'

'And what sort of knife was it? Can you describe it for me?'

I tried to recall, and succeeded. The brain takes in and records information even at the time of immense emotional pressure. 'It was about a foot long altogether, including the handle, with a very sharp point and I think it was double-edged. The handle was short in comparison with the blade, maybe only four inches long.'

'Had you ever seen the weapon before?'

'No, of course not. He must have had it in his pocket and drawn it out the moment he reached her.'

'You're sure about that?'

'Yes.'

'Now, I want to ask you about a knife you or rather Miss Bennet acquired in Russia.'

I couldn't think what he was talking about.

'We understand that when you were at dinner in Moscow in March, a friend bought Miss Bennet a knife.'

Henrik. How on earth could they know all this? Minna?

'Yes, you're right. It was a Dutch art historian called Henrik Gevaert who gave it to her.' I remembered Henrik's expression as he looked into the pearly-white breasts of the woman selling roses and souvenirs.

'And what was that knife like?'

I frowned. 'I don't really know. I don't think I ever studied it closely.'

'Do you know where it is now?'

'I've no idea. I imagine Julian left it in Moscow. It's not the sort of thing she would particularly value.'

'You don't know its whereabouts now?'

'No.'

'Would you permit us to make another search?'

'Of course, go ahead, if you want to. But I can't see what that knife has to do with anything that has happened.'

The interview continued for hours, as they nagged on and on about Igor, the knife, the timing of his departure. After about four hours they left. I was to be available for questioning at all times. They would have to come back to check certain points with me.

'What happens to the body?' I asked. 'What about the funeral?'

'We're a long way from that, I'm afraid. There'll be the inquest next week and we'll take things from there. What about next of kin, sir? Have you notified her relatives of what has happened?'

I shook my head. I had until then done nothing to tell anyone about the catastrophe that had hit me. And who would I tell? I knew Julian was an only child, her parents dead. Who besides me would care?

After this long and wearing session, I came out of my stupefaction sufficiently to ring Prisca's number. Only the answerphone replied and I could not bring myself to say after the beep, 'Julian's been murdered. I'm being questioned by the police.' I hung up without leaving a message.

They came for me about six in the evening, less than twenty-four hours after Julian's death. I had not expected it. They should have been pursuing Igor. If they had got him, he could have answered all their questions. But when he spoke, the pouchy-faced officer whose name I never registered, I had a sense of the inevitable. This was what was meant to happen. I could see a pattern: I had met Julian on the night someone had tried to kill her and now he had succeeded. I was set up to be the killer.

40

Thus the whole astonishing process of the trial began, astonishing because I could not believe it was happening. I lived each stage, the police station, the statement, the remand, the committal proceedings, the prison, as if it were happening to someone else. The sense of distance was increased by the sharp demarcation between freedom and captivity.

I was taken from the magistrates' court to prison in a private security company bus, like no other vehicle I had ever been in before. As it made its way through London, I sat on the hard seat of a cell in the semi-darkness and thought about Julian. Quite soon I must wake up from this nightmare; she would be restored to me, alive; we would be back in the flat together, talking about where to go for dinner, what concert to hear at the weekend. But when the bus came to its final halt it was inside the prison walls and I and my companions were escorted into the Reception Block. Here a series of alienating procedures progressively cut you off from your past. Each stage was another door closing on normality. First we were photographed. Something in the automatic cameras of the police and prison authorities imposes criminality on the face, coarsening the features and brutalising the expression. I was assigned my prison number; then strip-searched and sent to a cell. I was now Ochterlonie SX5860, someone other than the Nicholas Ochterlonie, writer and academic, Julian's lover, Emily's husband.

This rupture with my own life did nothing to ease the sense of

317

predestination that came at the arrest; in fact, it enhanced it. More and more I had the feeling that I was on an unstoppable train heading for some unknowable but disastrous end.

Prisca was clear what the catastrophe would be.

'You're facing life imprisonment, Nicholas,' she said as she sat opposite me across one of the formica-topped tables in the Visits Room at the prison.

We met here, in a routine that she imposed to cheer me up and galvanise me into defending myself. She came almost every day, flogging through the south London traffic from her office in the House of Lords. She submitted to the tedious process of waiting to be let into the prison, showing her Visiting Order, indicating my name and number and desire to see her, queuing with the mothers and wives and girlfriends and children to be let in, one by one. The Visits Room had the air of a gloomy cafe with small tables in rows, supervised by video cameras supplemented by several warders watching the exchanges with bored and cynical glances that swept the area like searchlights. Prisca was always already seated at our table when I was led in to meet her.

I had become one of her causes and united her crusading vigour and her family feeling. I was able to give her plenty of material for her prison reform dossier, which had long been one of her interests. Sometimes her research into prison conditions overrode her concerns about my case and she cross-questioned me about life as a remand prisoner, comparing my experience with best practice. I could not complain of ill-treatment, only boredom, discomfort and the misery which derived from my thoughts, not my surroundings. I was celled up with another prisoner, on remand for grievous bodily harm. We were locked up together for about twenty-one hours a day. The three hours out consisted of an hour of free association in the evenings, which I could have done without, half an hour of exercise ambling about the prison yard, occasional trips to the prison library, the visits of my lawyers or Prisca herself. Other diversions from our full-time occupation of lying on our beds were the three expeditions to collect our food from the basement for our meals, which were eaten in our cells at hours I had never previously regarded as times for eating. I told Prisca about what was happening to me as if it were a drama playing on a television switched on in a corner of my room, an episode vivid and self-contained, with no connection to my own life.

'I don't know what's the matter with you,' she said, angrily. 'You seem incapable of making any effort on your own behalf.'

I tried to explain my sense of doom, the oddity of the pattern, the knifings that had begun and ended my time with Julian.

I had hardly begun before Prisca interrupted. 'I've no time for that sort of thing,' she said. 'You always say you hate abstraction, you like particularity, and yet you come out with this rubbish. You're condemning yourself by your own actions. Your problem is that you're suffering from shock and some kind of retreat from reality. You've got to get over it. You can indulge in all the grief you like once you're out of prison.' She waited for a response and, when I said nothing, she sighed. 'I'm changing your solicitor.' On my arrest I had rung my family lawyer, the same man who was dealing with my divorce. 'You need someone who specialises in crime, in cases like this. I took Jamie's advice and I've found the best people to go to and they'll get us the best barrister. Someone should come to see you tomorrow, once you've told the authorities about the change.'

I studied Prisca's face, determination etched into the lines around her nose and eyes. She was like a piece of sculpture saved from some pagan temple which is still touched as a talisman. Her brow and cheeks and nose were paler, as if polished, than the darker skin around her eyes. I had never really noticed that before.

'Nicholas,' she said more gently. 'You're not going to get out of this by the operation of abstract justice. You've got to tell them everything. Begin at the beginning and tell them all you know.'

'The problem is,' I explained, 'I don't know what I know. All right, all right, Prisca. I'll try. Let me explain to you. I know what I observed myself directly, of Julian. I know what she told me about herself and

319

her relationship with the man she used to live with, a Russian banker called Anatoli Vozkresensky and with his partner, the murderer, Igor. What I don't know is what is the truth. That's why, to begin with, I just told the police what I knew I knew. Igor came to see her; he stabbed her; he left.'

'You'd better begin by going through it all with me.'

Once I had been charged, I understood that Igor's disappearance had left me in a very vulnerable position, for there was no one else to accuse. The police would have to understand the complexity of the situation, so, at length and with great patience, I told them Julian's story, not everything, not Igor's version, not Anatoli's, as part of my statement. By that time they had discovered their own records of the mugging and the break-in, so I explained to them that throughout our time together, she had been at risk from the Russian Mafia.

Initially, I think, my story impressed them sufficiently to stem their scepticism. It was so circumstantial and so detailed that it was unlikely that anyone could improvise such an elaborate tale. But their earlier disbelief returned when they failed to find any corroboration of what I had said.

My lawyers, the new firm organised for me by Prisca, had little more faith in me than the police. They applied themselves to my case with a professional vigour which never quite hid their doubts. We are paid to believe you, they implied, but you might have made life easier for us by coming up with something more convincing. The partner in charge of my case, George Goodson, interviewed me for the first time with the assistance of a beautiful black colleague, called Christina Martens. Solicitors' visits were held in special interview rooms, not amid the communal hurly-burly which Prisca, as a relative, faced every day. An hour spent with the lawyers was a time of semi-privacy that I enjoyed for itself; the conversation was a secondary benefit.

I had organised my account carefully, bearing in mind Prisca's insistence on the importance of frankness. I summarised as concisely as possible my relationship with Julian and the danger she had been in. The story that I recounted was partly my own. It was also partly Julian's story. I was retailing, secondhand, what she had told me of her life with Anatoli. But that account did not altogether tally with what had been revealed at our meeting with Anatoli at Heathrow, still less with what Igor had told me. I had to decide how much I believed. I would have preferred the first version, Julian as victim, but some sense of self-preservation suggested to me that I would only make matters worse for myself by censoring the story and I simply told them everything I knew and let them make what they could of it.

Ms Martens worked silently at her laptop, while Goodson, of an older generation, made notes on an elegant black leather-backed pad. Neither of them displayed surprise at the account I gave with a comparable lack of emotional emphasis.

Goodson leaned back in his chair when I had finished and said, 'Let me get this perfectly straight. Our story is that Miss Bennet was killed by a Russian banker, a colleague of her former lover, who regarded her as a rival in the illegal operations of their organisation.'

Put like that I could see there were credibility problems.

'Yes, I suppose so. But I am not sure of the motive, only of the act. The motivation is speculative.'

'But how does all this fit with the statement you made to the police?'

'I've told you more than I told them. I began by not saying much, just that Igor was there, that he did it. It was so complicated, too difficult to explain, especially, as I've told you, I'm not certain of the truth myself. I can see it was a mistake not to have tried to explain everything right from the beginning.'

'I can't say that it has added to your credibility. You start with one story; you give them another when you're arrested, and now you tell us something else.'

'They're not different stories,' I protested. 'They're expansions.'

'The police are not so subtle. For them one story is one story, and another another. We'll have to do what we can to find some witnesses who can support what you say, anybody, a taxi driver, someone passing in the street. A bit of corroboration is what we need.'

He asked more questions, made a few more notes in minuscule writing and the two of them left with a list of names: Igor, Francesca, Barnaby, Anatoli, Colin Trevor, Tom Naish.

A week later Ms Martens returned, alone. She was uncomfortable. At first I thought it was empathy that had produced her distress, for the news she had to convey was not good. They had had no success so far in identifying any of the people I had mentioned and I would have to search my memory for more details. I could see her problem, but I could not help. Barnaby and Francesca, for example. I did not know the surname of either of them. If I had ever known which firm Barnaby belonged to, I had forgotten it.

'They don't believe me,' I complained to Prisca when she came next day. 'Even my own lawyers don't believe me.' I had been telling her the story every afternoon, during the twenty or thirty minutes of visiting time, elaborating another episode while she asked questions.

'Of course they believe you,' she said. 'They're looking at how to present your case in court. They've already retained a barrister, Roger Ignatius, no one could be better. They're aiming at the best outcome for you.'

'No,' I said. 'They think I did it. They think I'm not completely sane and that I'm trying to escape the responsibility of what I've done by blaming an alter ego, a creation of my own mind.'

Prisca never flinched from debate. She did not dismiss what I said, replying calmly, 'Well, it is one rational explanation of what happened.'

'And do you think that I've made up the whole story, the attacks on Julian by the Mafia, as a cover story for what I've done?'

She was a better judge than anyone. I knew her well and had confided in her, as far as I confided in anyone, for years. She had met Julian, yet I had never hinted to her at any stage before the murder that Julian was at risk. If she didn't believe me, no one would.

'No,' she said slowly, 'I don't think it is a fabrication, either conscious or unconscious. I believe you.' She looked down at her hands, swivelling her watch on her wrist so that the face came into view; she had a heavy programme which demanded strict time keeping. 'Frankly, Nicholas, I don't think you have the imagination to create such a story which, even if it isn't verifiable, is intricate and complete. You have never been attentive to human relations. I am sure you are as capable of lying as the next person, especially to save your life, or rather your liberty. But your story doesn't even promote that end. Reason suggests that it must be true.'

'Well, the lawyers don't think so. They clearly think I'm mad.'

'The next thing is to confirm any part of your story we can. I'm sending private detectives to Moscow. Not that firm you used, you'll be glad to know. Someone a little less high-powered who's glad to have the job. She's going to find out about the Bank.'

'I hope she doesn't get herself into the sort of trouble that I did when I was there.'

'I've warned her to be very careful. I think she realises it's a dangerous place out there.'

'Then we must sort out this question of the knife.'

'What about it?'

'You say he took the knife out of his pocket. Minna swears it was the one Julian was given in Moscow.'

'How can Minna tell one knife from another?' I asked. 'I can't. I don't know where he got the knife from.'

Later, lying on my back in my cell, I decided that Prisca was the only person who believed in Julian's connexion with the Mafia because she had never liked her. I had seen the instinctive recoil of the two women that night with my father. In spite of this, or perhaps because of it, she made me tell her all I could about her and speculated endlessly about character and motive. Nothing I said was admissible evidence in court, because it was hearsay; but Prisca claimed it was vital background information, and I liked to do it. I missed Julian endlessly and to talk eased that unimaginable pain. When she was alive, I had thought that the impossibility of ever knowing her completely or having her entirely was the worst torture

323

I had endured. However, it was nothing to knowing that I would never know her or have her again. I saw her all the time: her bony wrists and cold dry hands, her hair falling forward as she bent over me, the transparent skin of her abdomen, the vividness of her smile breaking in her impassive face.

Prisca would not permit me to dwell on these memories. She did not want to hear of Julian's beauty. She wanted her story, then Anatoli's, then Igor's.

'Why did he do it?' she asked. 'He had to have a reason.'

'I don't know why; I can only guess,' I said wearily. 'I only met him that evening. And that was the terrifying thing: it happened without reason, like a thunderbolt. I had no idea when I led him across to meet her of what he intended to do.'

'Think about what he said. People tell you what they want you to believe, what they want to believe themselves. It may not be the truth, but it is a version of it, so you can use it to construct your interpretation, a glimpse of what happened.'

'Talking to you, Prisca, is like looking in a pair of mirrors, reflecting ad infinitum. All I know is the simple truth: the act. He stabbed her.' I stroked my cheek, unshaven, rasping. 'I thought they were embracing.' And I had realised that my rival was not Anatoli at all, but Igor.

'We have to construct a scenario, a motivation. What did he say?'

'I've told you. He said that Julian was an active participant in the Bank's activities and after her bust-up with Anatoli she was trying to take over the London end. To achieve this she had done a deal with the Uzbek.'

'And did that mean cutting out, not only Anatoli, but Igor too?'

'Igor said, implied, that he had offered her a similar deal, but she had rejected it in favour of alliance with the Uzbek.'

'And the killing in Moscow. According to you she was in agony, not knowing who had won the battle, Igor or the Uzbek.'

'I suppose that was it. I thought that she was desperate with fear that Anatoli had been killed. She must have known it was likely to have been a shoot-out between Igor and his old godfather, the Uzbek, and she was anxious about the success of her plan.'

'But all was not necessarily lost for her, even with the Uzbek dead. She would presumably have hoped that Igor would renew his offer. You had no sense that she expected danger from Igor's direction? She seemed to think she had him well wrapped up.'

'I don't believe any of it. I don't know what to believe.'

I was grateful for Prisca's faith, as all attempts to verify my story failed and Julian's past evaporated as if she had never lived. Only her death confirmed her existence. As far as the police were concerned, their case was clear-cut; they had an accused, a witness, an arrest. For them, the simple story and the obvious suspect were the best. They had no need of the complication of the Mafia. I had not wanted to tell them and now they did not want to hear. My lawyers came every week with stories of failure.

The first problem was not so much the absence of Igor as the presence of Minna. Igor could not be found; Minna claimed that she had never seen him. When she had arrived on that evening she had found the lift doors open on the ground floor and Victor had explained that the lifts were out of order. She had clambered up to the fourth floor where she had found the doors of both apartments ajar, but nobody in sight. She had briefly peered into my mother's flat, calling my name, but not for long enough, she insisted, for anyone to escape without being seen.

I could see, after what had happened in Moscow, that she would take pleasure in her role in the police enquiry. I had, effectively, murdered her *Lady in a Pelisse* and now she would have revenge by seeing me convicted for another murder, a rather less important crime in her eyes than my original one of contesting the authenticity of the Litvak painting. I had to acknowledge that she was not necessarily lying, in denying that she had seen Igor. It was difficult for me to judge how much time elapsed between his departure and her arrival. She could be telling the truth; but I was not convinced of it. Her pleasure in shutting her eyes, at not seeing, would be too

325

great and too convenient. My conviction for murder would not invalidate my charges against the painting, but it might make it easier for her to resist them for a while. A paper presented by someone who soon after was imprisoned on a charge of murder might be regarded as the work of someone not entirely sane. I wondered if she would be able to suppress my contribution to the conference from the publication of the proceedings. I would not be around to fight my corner.

I explained all this to George Goodson, who said admiringly, as if impressed by my imagination, 'So the one big witness against you is malicious.'

'I don't think she can be trusted to be fair in my case. For the reasons I've given. What about Igor?'

'No news, I'm afraid.'

Prisca in her work on finding corroboration had seized on Anatoli, for she had got out of me what I had deliberately withheld from the police, that he had been in England at the time of the murder, under arrest by Tom Naish.

'Why didn't you mention him at once?' she reproached me.

'Because he had nothing to do with what happened. He was in prison himself.'

'Don't you see you haven't a single person willing to stand up and vouch for what you say. At least he's here. He can answer questions. He can give us Igor's name, Barnaby's. He can explain things.'

'I didn't realise that Igor would never be found.'

A week later, Prisca was gloomier.

'It's extraordinary how all these people disappear like mist.'

'That means that Anatoli's gone. What's happened to him?'

'He's back in Moscow, presumably, because he's not in this country. Oh, there's no doubt he exists, but we're not even going to be able to prove that. Anatoli got himself an excellent lawyer who had him out of your friend Tom Naish's clutches within a couple of days.'

'That was me, or rather Jamie.'

'What was?'

'The excellent lawyer. I rang as soon as we came back from Heathrow.'

'From what I can gather, the arrest was part of a plan to roll up some of the Bank's networks in London. Julian was co-operating and the charge of attempted murder was going to be used to pressurise Anatoli into talking. I'm not sure whether it was just a local operation, or a much bigger one involving other police forces abroad. Probably the latter, I suspect, because Tom Naish is beside himself with rage at having lost him. Without Julian, he had nothing to go on. And he was probably humiliated in front of his colleagues by allowing the sting to fail here in London.'

She put her flexible fingertips into her eye sockets and gently massaged her eyelids. 'There's something about this case,' she said. 'We just can't get any purchase on anything. No Anatoli . . .'

'He wouldn't have been willing to get involved anyway.'

'Not just that. Tom Naish is refusing to give us any help. He claims that publicity will ruin his work and warn off another big Mafia group whom he hopes to catch. National security.'

'I'm not sure that anything Tom Naish said would do me much good.'

'Perhaps not, but he knows that what you say isn't a complete fantasy, yet he won't stand up and say so. We have no one, no one at all, not one witness.'

'There is Colin Trevor,' I said on another occasion to Ms Martens. 'He wasn't exactly helpful to me, but we might try to get some information out of him. I went to him when I wanted to find out about Anatoli. I wasn't looking for Igor, at the time. I didn't know he existed. But Trevor might have turned up something about him.'

This venture failed too.

'I've heard from George Goodson about his approach to Colin Trevor,' I told Prisca. 'Do you remember? He was the private detective.'

'Yes.'

'Completely fruitless. First he denied any knowledge of me. Then he cited client confidentiality and refused to comment. When a great deal of pressure had been brought to bear on him, he agreed that he had seen me once. He said that he had rejected the case. Finally, he admitted that he had destroyed the file and that he would never agree to get involved in the case or to give evidence, "for fear of the safety of his family". He wouldn't say more than that.'

41

Although this Kafkaesque situation did not last long, it dominates my memory of the time I spent on remand. After a while, my sense of living rather than observing my own existence returned. The first sign was the irritability I began to feel towards my cell companion. I was confined with an almost mute young black man, which was, by chance or forethought on the part of the authorities, a sensible pairing. Neither of us enraged the other with conversation. However, the disadvantage of this silent companion was that he was hyperactive. His fretful movements from the bunk above mine broke into my self-absorption and I began to wake up to my position.

The first breakthrough came when George Goodson turned up for the weekly meeting instead of Ms Martens, whom he used to pass on bad news. He was standing behind his chair, smiling, as I entered the interview room. He wore a superb suit, Savile Row, and a bow tie, flat and narrow, so that he looked like a distinguished East Coast academic. He gestured welcomingly to the seat on my side of the table.

'You'll be glad to know,' he said, 'that this elusive Russian bank really exists.'

I felt a spasm of rage, which had as much to do with my crumpled clothing and stubbled cheeks as his patronising manner or his implicit surprise that anything I had said was true. I don't think any of these feelings were visible, or audible, when I replied, 'That's very good news. How did you, er, discover it?'

'It was Christina Martens's idea, clever girl. She contacted the commercial department of the Russian Embassy here in London and at our Embassy in Moscow. A tortoise race, she called it, to see which would come back to us sooner, if at all.' He sat down and took out his slender pad. It was an affectation of his never to carry a briefcase. 'The Brits beat the Russians. Fax in yesterday replying to our letter of a month ago. It was set up in 1992, one of the hundreds of banks established after the downfall of Communism. It was an important one right from the start; has dealings with a number of big European banks, involved in privatisation joint ventures. Rapidly became one of the biggest going and is now among the top ten local banks with a capitalisation supposedly running into billions of dollars. I say "supposedly" advisedly: apparently the figures are not always reliable or verifiable. But these are more or less good guys. Only bit of dirty business known: some tough tactics in the Ukraine to do with aluminium transports. Nothing too serious, given the competition. Otherwise, as pure as the driven.'

He paused and I said, 'Well, thanks. For the effort, I mean.' All this was no more than I had told him already, so I could see no cause for enthusiasm.

'More good things to come. The names of the directors are . . .' He balanced a pair of reading glasses on the end of his nose and peered through them with a camel-like tilt of the head in order to read out: 'R.Y. Muzafarov; A.F. Vozkresensky; I.A. Romanov. So there we are.'

I.A. Romanov. At last a name. But what good did it do me?

'This gives us something to work on,' George Goodson said, in reply to my unspoken question. 'I'll be in touch.'

More background was filled in by Prisca. I had described the street, the house, to which I had followed Julian during my stalking period. With a supreme effort of memory I had recalled the number, 15. She had gone to knock on the door and bring back more confirmation of my version of Julian's story.

Francesca had opened the door, a tall, emaciated woman with a

330

large bust displayed in a Wonderbra and T-shirt. She had been unaware of Julian's death and had led Prisca inside, calling to Barnaby, repeating the horrifying news, talking incessantly. Barnaby had risen from a welter of newspapers to shake her hand. He was, according to Prisca, a vain man struggling to retain his youth and figure against the forces of time and alcohol. He had broad, florid face and pigeon-shaped torso, tapering down to a neat pair of feet, shod in embroidered slippers. He had acknowledged his organisation's relations with the Bank and was willing to sketch some of the deals they had been involved in together, but he could contribute nothing about Igor's whereabouts now or then. Neither he nor Francesca could recall his presence at their dinner table. Anatoli they claimed to know well; they had met him at least half a dozen times, though not in the last year.

'No, longer,' Francesca interjected. 'At least a year and a half. Almost two years, I'd say.'

They remembered him as charming, amusing. 'Very attractive,' was Francesca's comment; 'Very astute,' Barnaby's. They had seen him with Julian at Glyndebourne, at a weekend in the country near Bath. He spoke good English, had a great sense of humour. The Uzbek, too, Barnaby had once met in London, a long time ago. But Igor, no. Barnaby was clear that there was another director, though he had not taken part in their negotiations. Francesca denied ever encountering him.

I heard Prisca's account of her meeting in much the same spirit as I had listened to George Goodson. It might reassure my lawyers that I was sane, and that I had not fabricated the whole legend, but it did nothing to prove my innocence.

This quality, innocence, was something that had to be taken on trust, and not many people were willing to. Pessimistically, I had expected this. The very fact of being present at a murder, mixed up in a police enquiry, remanded in custody, was enough to taint me, even before conviction. Prison screened me from most of the embarrassment, and I was only faced with the suspicion of my family.

331

Elizabeth Ironside

Emily behaved well. She refused all interviews and protected the children from reporters. Her only appearance in the press was a picture of her broad, floral-skirted backside scuttling indoors, scooping the children ahead of her. She made no contact with me. I was glad of this and withdrew all the delaying tactics to the financial settlement, so that the divorce could proceed unhindered. All the children were at boarding school now, even Cordelia, and Em was free to live her fulfilling life on my money.

My father did not visit me, nor did he, later, attend the trial. He wrote that his health was playing up and my step-mother had forbidden him to leave Scotland. When telephoned by a reporter for an article entitled *Professor Charged with Lover's Killing*, he made the single statement that he was sure I was innocent. Thus far my close family 'stood by' me.

In contrast, Jamie and Sybil visited me whenever Prisca could not; they both sat through every day of my trial. Prisca supported me in everything.

Apart from them, the only person who came was Victor. He contacted the prison authorities to ask if he could see me. I agreed and one afternoon he and I sat awkwardly together in the Visits Room. Victor's distaste for the place was written in the distressed creases of his face. I took his presence as a sign of solidarity and felt a warm gratitude towards him.

'How's . . . Mary?' I asked. 'And Rose.' I couldn't remember if Rose was the daughter or the granddaughter, but I could hear those names repeated like returning waves in the tide of Julian's conversation.

I had somehow managed to say the right thing, a legacy of Julian's charm. He looked more at ease, leaning forward confidentially.

'They're all right, ok, thank God, you know what I mean?'

'Well, that's good. No more problems at home?' This seemed to be the right track. I recalled the rows, raised voices, crashing china, slamming doors of Julian's soap opera. But no one had ever got hurt. I was no longer in a position to regard the violence of Victor's life from a disdainful distance.

332

'No, thank God.' He looked around at the furniture for something to touch; then rapped his head. He hunched closer across the table. 'Nothing, nothing at all. I was worried . . . After, you know . . .'

He had been worried by the break-in too, I remembered. He was easily upset by violence. Julian had tried to conceal her gashed legs from his view. I could not account for the depth of his concern.

'A terrible, terrible business.' He could not bring himself to speak of Julian's death directly.

'Yes,' I agreed.

He sat shaking his head. I had no sense that he was accusing me of responsibility for what had happened.

'She was a lovely lady. My friend. She used to say, "My friend, Victor," and we were. Friends.'

Tears were magnifying the milky-coffee coloured whites of his eyes. I had a vision of Julian leaning on her wrists against his desk in the entrance, one leg kicked out behind her in an absurd 'fifties model girl pose; she was laughing. Despair at her loss overwhelmed me again.

'I'd better be going.' Victor pushed back his chair. The dandyish side of his personality was in evidence: he was wearing a bright red and gold tie with a Hermès chain pattern, dressed up even for a prison visit. I experienced none of the hostility that had welled up in me at the sight of George Goodson's bow tie.

'Very nice of you to have come, Victor.'

'I just wanted to see you. I'm glad you understand about Rose.'

I didn't know what he was talking about. I needed Julian to explain it to me. 'Of course,' I said.

'That's great. Great.'

'Fine, Victor.'

'It makes it easier for me. I feel bad about the court case.'

'Er, yes.'

'Bye for now. Good luck.'

An explanation of some elements in this unexpected visit came a little later. We were approaching the date of the trial, set for mid-

October, and George Goodson had called a meeting with Roger Ignatius, the barrister, to pull together all the threads, as he put it. The interview room was crowded with the leaders and their acolytes. They projected efficiency and optimism. Briefcases and computers snapped open and closed. An air of business prevailed over the passivity and defeatism of the prison atmosphere.

But nothing could conceal the absence in the centre of my case: Igor was not there. Nor, it would seem, had he ever been. Enquiries at the Home Office had at last been answered. No one named I.A. Romanov had either applied for or been granted a visa to Britain in the last five years. The private detectives despatched to Moscow had discovered that the police there had no leads on the murderer of the Uzbek, Muzafarov, and that case was on hold. The Bank had suffered no ill effects as a result of the violent death of one of its founders. I.A. Romanov and A.F. Vozkresensky were still listed as joint presidents of its board, but neither was accessible, or even visible. No approach, direct or through third parties, had elicited any response.

Roger Ignatius was a man of about my own age, jovial, well-fleshed, with soft curly hair and a rubbery baby face. Dismissively, he slapped closed a file that lay on the table.

'This case depends on impressions, not technicalities. All this stuff on the Mafia is basically unusable. It's hearsay. We haven't got the witnesses and we're never going to get them. What we've got to do is say to the jury, Look at this guy: a professor, a serious person, never wielded anything more violent than a pencil sharpener in his life. Do you really believe he behaved in a manner so out of character as to stab his girlfriend?'

He looked around the stuffy room. No one spoke. The consensus in expression was, 'Yes.'

'And before they say, Yes,' he went on, 'we've got to undermine the witnesses for the prosecution. The art historian, well, she's a tough nut, but we can try professional rivalry. If she can be riled, forced to turn nasty in the witness box, she could lose the sympathy of the jury. What do you think?' He turned to me. 'Is that a possibility?'

'Very much so. She's quick to get angry. Any suggestion that she's not right will do it. She's always managed to lose my sympathy very fast.'

'Good, good.' He nodded encouragingly, as if the whole thing were put on to keep my spirits up. 'And what's your reading of the other witness, the porter?'

'Victor?'

'Is that his name? Yes.'

'What does he say?'

'Well, nothing. That's the point.' He snapped his fingers over one shoulder. 'Let me have the papers from the committal proceedings. In the prosecution's statement their two chief witnesses are named as Horndeane, who says she saw you with the knife, and the porter, who says that no one came in or went out at the relevant time, except her.'

So that was why Victor had come.

Ignatius put down the papers and drew one hand forward through his curls.

'Look,' he said. 'Let's be frank. We have to admit you face a very sticky wicket. Your story is virtually unverifiable in legal terms. You were caught . . .' He stopped himself. 'Sorry. You were found with the murder weapon in your hands, so that it's plastered with your fingerprints and no one else's. No one else was seen entering the building. I've got to say this: it's a pretty incredible story, yours. And I shall have a job to make the jury believe in it. The prosecution is going to say that it was a lovers' quarrel. Our chances of getting you off are only fifty-fifty.' He stopped.

I knew what he wanted to say, but was not allowed to. *'If you pleaded guilty with a defence of provocation, I would believe you. The jury would believe you. The chances are you'd get off with ten years, out in five with good behaviour . . .'*

They all looked at me with a detached curiosity. They really didn't mind. They could argue it any way I liked. They'd do their best for me.

'I'm sorry,' I said. 'That's how it was.'

42

A trial is a play. It has everything necessary for drama: a stage and an audience, a protagonist and a chorus, a troupe of actors, a struggle between good and evil, a denouement. It even conforms to classical rules: unity of time, place and action. But it is even more exciting than a play, for although the parts are fixed and the lines are known, there is an element of improvisation. The ending is unwritten and the punishment is real.

I pleaded not guilty to the murder of Julian Bennet.

I looked round the courtroom briefly and observed Prisca was, as usual, in the front row, with Jamie and Sybil beside her. Roger Ignatius was already there. His ruddy face was not improved by his wig; he looked like an actor pretending to be a barrister. His opponent, Dominic Allwood, QC, prosecuting, with his gloomy horse face, was far more convincing. Best cast of all was the judge, Mr Justice Strowger, who dominated the scene both physically and morally from his position above us all. Elderly, he must have been in his seventies, and looked older. He had a small, wrinkled, hairless face, lacking even eyebrows and eyelashes, balanced on a thin, wattled neck. His mouth was pursed by a shrewd, humourless sphincter and his eyes were bright between heavy lids. He had a leathery, ancient, reptilian look about him, as if he knew of every possible cruelty, every perversion, every crime and nothing could surprise him any more. The jury, who were sworn in once my plea was made, appeared as a row of busts on a shelf. I ran my eye along the line, noting its composition, five women, one Asian, two, a man and a woman, youngish, the rest stolidly middle-aged. I could have worked harder at estimating their varied social status and associated prejudices, but this would have implied a reaction to me and a judgement on my story. I preferred to concentrate on the ritual of the opening, in which the judge, clerk, barristers all played their parts with the professional ease of actors, ultimately untouched by what was going on.

The prosecution opened with a speech to the jury explaining its task was to prove that the accused, who was assumed to be innocent, had indeed committed the crime, and theirs to be convinced 'beyond reasonable doubt'. The prosecutor's voice was matter of fact, without indignation in his tone, and his performance was all the more effective for that. He described Julian's killing, when, where and how it took place and went on to give the details of the case against the accused. The chief witnesses for the prosecution were to be Minna and Victor, supported by others who would testify to certain details, such as the provenance of the murder weapon, finger prints. Everything centred on the night of the crime and no wider context was admitted. It was not necessary. Was the accused there? Did he do it? were the only questions he wanted to answer. The prosecution case, in its simplicity, was that the accused had a row with his lover and killed her in a jealous rage. The details of the killing were hardly open to debate. The murder weapon was a Russian knife, given to Miss Bennet by a Dutch art historian on a recent visit to Moscow, an event witnessed by Dr Horndeane, who discovered the accused with the knife in his hands only seconds after the murder. The mysterious third person, whom the defence would allege was the murderer, had been seen by no one and had no existence, except in the mind of the accused.

Although I had been able to find no witnesses to my truth, the prosecution had been able to find plenty of evidence for its fiction. The only way to tolerate it was to hear it impersonally, as if it concerned someone else, and to admit that if it had been like that, it might well have ended in the way they said it did. I had to concede it

was skilfully done. The art lay not so much in the simple recon-
struction of the murder, as in the subtle painting of my character in
the darkest tones.

The subtext, never stated directly, but which the jury could easily
read was insidiously damning. The accused, Nicholas Ochterlonie,
had several counts against him. In the first place, he did not have a
proper job. He was temporarily employed by London University, but
he had trained as a doctor and psychologist and worked as a writer
and philosopher and art historian. In the second place, he had left
his wife and was living with his lover. These two facts implied a lack
of respectability derived from secure employment and a stable
marriage. The accused was, moreover, psychopathically jealous. The
impression was of a mad professor, not so mad that he could not be
held responsible for his actions, but just mad enough to make a single
violent act plausible.

The accused became obsessed with the victim, his neighbour, and
made constant enquiries about her. Eventually, after her apartment
had been severely damaged in a break-in, he persuaded her to move
into his flat. As no one was ever charged with the damage and, as no
illicit entry was ever discovered, the police concluded that it was an
inside job. The accused became irrationally convinced that Miss
Bennet was having an affair. He spied on her, sitting in his car outside
the house to watch her comings and goings. In the later stages of
their relationship he did not permit her to leave his flat, keeping her
imprisoned there for weeks at a time, only allowing her out under his
escort.

His extravagant concentration on his lover and unreasonable
demands for her attention led directly to the tragedy of the killing,
which was all but witnessed by Dr Horndeane. As she was there by
arrangement and not by chance, the prosecution could not logically
call the murder a premeditated act. But the subtext implied that the
accused had brooded on it for so long beforehand, that the act
combined the cunning of a planned murder with the violent impulse
of a crime passionel.

When I remarked to Roger Ignatius about the development of my character, he dismissed my complaints. The prosecution never adduced more than the admissible facts, he insisted. If they had, he would have protested. I said no more, though I had no doubt of the image that the jury would be given. However, I was pleased that, by able cross-questioning, Ignatius succeeded in modifying, if not essentially changing, the picture.

Minna's performance in the witness box was at first a success. By physique and age, hers was inevitably a character role rather than that of a leading lady, and she played her part with all the authority with which she handed down rulings on art attributions. Allwood led her through the minutes immediately after the murder.

'When I arrived the porter apologised to me that the lifts were out of order and showed me where the stairs were. I climbed to the fourth floor, and when I arrived I found the doors to both flats open.'

'Did you meet anyone at all, apart from the porter, between your arrival and reaching the apartment of the accused?'

'I did not,' Minna said, solemnly, as if her life depended on it.

'Please continue.'

'I rang the bell of Professor Ochterlonie's flat and, when there was no response, I knocked. As I was standing there, I heard noises from within the flat opposite.'

'What sort of noises?'

'Gasping sounds, not loud, but they were distressful. I put my head round the door of Professor Ochterlonie's flat and called, "Hello?" I could hear nothing, and see nothing unusual inside. So I approached the other door, pushed it open and walked in.'

'How long were you inside the flat.'

'I wasn't really inside. I just pushed the door sufficiently to see inside.'

'Could you still see the landing and the exit to the stairs?'

'Yes, I could. No one could have passed me without my seeing.'

'Please tell the jury what you saw when you went into the other apartment.'

'The accused was standing over the body of a woman with a knife in his hand. I didn't recognise who it was at first. She was sprawled, face down, on the floor at the foot of the staircase.'

Ignatius did good work here.

'Would you describe *exactly*, Dr Horndeane, the relative positions of the accused and the body of Miss Bennet when you entered?' he asked.

Minna was less eager to be precise. 'She was lying on the ground, face down, as I said, at the foot of the stairs.'

'Yes, and where was the accused? Facing you, with his back to you? In front or behind the body, from your view point?'

'Facing me. He was in front of the body.'

'That is, the body was behind the accused. He had his back to it?'

'Yes.'

'Would you care to estimate the distance between them?'

'There was some little distance, say six or eight feet.'

'And how *exactly* was the accused holding the weapon.'

From Minna's reluctant replies the picture of the murderer looming over his victim, the weapon in his clenched fist, changed. The body was, in fact, behind the accused, some distance away. The accused could not have stabbed the murdered woman from that position. Moreover, Minna was forced to agree that he was holding the knife by the blade as if he had, as he claimed, just picked it up from the floor. What she had seen was entirely consistent with the story that the accused was not the murderer, but a witness like herself.

'How would you describe the behaviour of the accused when you came upon him?' Ignatius asked.

Minna pondered. 'Calm,' she replied.

'Calm,' Ignatius repeated. 'Not frightened, not threatening, but calm. Was he co-operative?'

'He was,' she conceded. 'He seemed shocked, a bit slow to react.'

'You say you asked for a telephone to call the police. Did he make any attempt to leave, to escape?'

'No. He took me across to his own flat.'

'In fact, he made the phone call himself.'

'He was phoning for an ambulance. I called the police.'

'So he showed no sign of guilt. Only anxiety for the injured woman.'

'He showed anxiety, yes.'

'But you did not. You didn't call an ambulance?'

'I could see she was already dead.'

'Did you examine the body?'

'No, I didn't touch it.'

'Was there a lot of blood visible?'

'There was blood on the knife.'

'But nowhere else?'

'I wasn't looking anywhere else. I saw blood on the knife.'

'So you just assumed that she was dead.'

'She was dead.' Angrily.

'Now let's come to the visitor, Igor Romanov, who was with Miss Bennet and Professor Ochterlonie before you arrived.'

'I saw nothing of him.'

'But you found the door of the flat open, as if someone had recently and hastily left?'

'The door was open. I drew no inference of who had left or how recently.'

This was not so good. Ignatius then raised the question of our disagreement on the provenance of the *Lady in a Pelisse*. It seemed inconceivable that Minna would not have realised that the painting would be mentioned, but she reacted as if taken off guard, with great venom. Ignatius managed to incite her to rage to such a degree that the jurors could see that, although our debate was a mere academic point, she was not an unbiased witness and, even more important, that the subject of our disagreement had been concealment of evidence.

'Would you tell us, please, the reason for your visit to Professor Ochterlonie on the evening of the murder.'

Minna looked very put out. 'It was a social call.'

'I understand it had been arranged a day or so earlier, in order to discuss an academic matter that was in dispute between you and the accused.'

Minna hesitated. 'We would probably have talked about that question, if we'd had the chance.'

'So the call was arranged at your request to discuss an academic disagreement?'

'I suppose you could say that.'

'It was?'

'Yes.'

'Would you sum up, in layman's terms, the nature of the academic dispute between you and the accused.'

'There was no dispute.'

'I thought we had just agreed that you had asked for the meeting that evening in order to discuss the matter. Was the issue that Professor Ochterlonie had questioned the attribution of one of the paintings belonging to your Foundation?'

Minna appeared more and more annoyed. She no longer answered the questions fully and with the enjoyment that she had responded to Dominic Allwood.

'It was,' she said reluctantly. 'But the points he raised were trivial ones.'

'Is it true, too, that at his Coulounieix lectures last year and at the Moscow Conference on Art and Perception in March, Professor Ochterlonie adduced as evidence scientific data which he claimed was known to you and which had been suppressed?'

Minna exploded. 'There was no suppression of evidence. It had evidently been mislaid. Or scholars had simply not found the material. The accusations were mischievous.'

The Judge's style was one of non-intervention. He sat above the fray, his tortoise eyes blinking under the overhang of his wig. Up to this point he had spoken little. In this interchange he several times ordered Minna to answer the question and she did not receive the direction well. However, a bad-tempered, unsympathetic witness is

343

not necessarily an untruthful one. The jury probably didn't like her, but they would believe her, nonetheless.

Victor was an even more telling witness against me. He had dressed in his very best for the part, in a camel blazer, a light blue shirt with a dark blue silk tie. He looked nervous and kept glancing at the public gallery where, following his eyes, I saw a grey-haired white woman with a coloured child, her hair plaited and beaded, on her knee. At first, Victor's voice was low and faltering and the judge had to instruct him to speak up, as he acknowledged who he was, what he did, how long he had been employed, that he had been on duty on the night in question. He had known Miss Bennet for more than four years, he said. She was a wonderful lady. Professor Ochterlonie he had know for a long time because he used to come to visit his mum. He had only moved in to live permanently less than a year before, before the murder. He was a very nice gentleman, always polite.

Victor was transparently easy to read. When he was happy answering a question, he responded at once and looked directly at the barrister addressing him. When he was reluctant to reply, he spoke more slowly, lowering his eyelids and looking obliquely away from the questioner. So he vividly conveyed his admiration of Julian and his dislike of incriminating me, which were even more damaging than Minna's hostility.

'Who,' Allwood asked when they reached the night of the murder, 'Who entered the building that evening after you came on duty?'

'It was a quiet night,' Victor replied, casting his eyes down. 'Many of the residents were away for the weekend. Dr Horndeane came. She was the first.'

'No one came before her?'

A pause. 'No.'

'And what time did she arrive?'

'Just after eight, I'd say. I didn't notice the time exactly.'

'But, let's be clear, no one else came to see Miss Bennet or Professor Ochterlonie earlier, at any time?'

A long pause. 'No.'

'Quite specifically, a tall fair Russian man in his early thirties?'

Victor turned his head away. 'No, sir, no.' He sounded grieved, as if he would have seen him if he could, but he was bound, in honesty, to admit he had not.

'And what happened next, as far as you were concerned?'

'The police arrived.'

'What time was that?'

'I didn't look. About eight thirty.'

'Describe what happened.'

'They came in and asked for Flat 8. Two uniformed officers. I told them the fourth floor and they went up. Then, quite soon, all hell broke loose. People were arriving, asking for Flat 8, all going up there. I knew something was up.'

'Once again, this is crucially important, did anyone, anyone at all, even a resident known to you, leave the building between Dr Horndeane's arrival and that of the police?'

'I didn't see no one.'

Listening to Minna and Victor, it was easy to understand why Roger Ignatius wanted me to admit to the lovers' quarrel, claiming provocation. It was the obvious interpretation, the easiest one to match to the facts, the most believable story. I could see how easily he could have made Julian into an infuriating woman who could enflame jealousy. But I did not want her portrayed in such terms. However, doing what he could with the brief he had been given, Roger Ignatius skilfully chipped away at the prosecution evidence and for a period I thought that he had sown sufficient doubt for me to escape. It would not be a vindication of my story, an honourable acquittal, but it would be freedom nonetheless.

One prosecution witness, a scene-of-crime officer, turned out to be particularly useful to us. He had been a member of the team called out on the night of the murder and had been detailed to search the flat while his colleague was occupied with the body. He had only found one interesting cache: in the main bedroom of the apartment

345

of the accused, stored inside an unlocked tortoiseshell box he had found a Russian pistol and two hundred thousand dollars in hundred-dollar bills. When questioned by Roger Ignatius, he agreed when he found them the possibility of a Russian Mafia connexion had come into his mind.

Why so?

Because such a large sum in dollars suggested unlaundered black money, for which the source was either Latin America where narco-dollars circulated, or Russia where large sums of cash needed recycling into the white economy. The presence of a Russian pistol was not conclusive; such weapons were found the world over, but the conjunction of the two, cash and gun, was at the very least suggestive of a Russian origin.

Why had this lead never been followed up?

The scene-of-crime officer could not answer this. It was not his job. The police opinion had been that they had found the obvious suspect to arrest. There was no need to confuse matters by introducing unnecessary questions about Russian or any other kind of international criminals.

Another prosecution witness who helped my cause was the finger-print expert. He testified that my prints had been found on the murder weapon and this evidence was the crux of the case against me. However, under Roger Ignatius's cross-examination, he admitted that mine were not the only ones there. Two residual, smudgy and unidentifiable prints were also recovered from the handle. He could not say whether they were the same as those found on one of the glasses and the bottle of whisky in the drawing room of my flat.

All the good work that Ignatius had done evaporated when I took the stand. The accused is the first defence witness to testify. Ignatius wanted to make my account as straightforward as he could, to get over the credibility problem, he said, and I was to help him by making my replies direct and unconditional. This seemed a good policy and I intended to co-operate fully. But as soon as the questioning started I could feel that the atmosphere was unsympathetic, as an actor must

346

sense the rejection of a play by the audience. The jury did not like me. One after the other, their lips tightened with doubt, as it occurred to them that I was too clever, quite clever enough to have made up the whole story. All I could do was trudge on with my set lines. I looked too cerebral and the story that I told, of Russian bankers and their rivalry, was too complicated. It lacked the comprehensible story line of the prosecution's case. Oddly, only under cross-examination by Allwood did I perform well. I was a match for his nitpicking and could not be shaken in my story. Whatever else, I had the conviction of consistency.

Barnaby was called as a witness to testify to Anatoli's existence, his job, his relationship with Julian. He also confirmed another director of the Russian bank was a certain I.A. Romanov. Victor had already been cross-examined by Ignatius about Anatoli's cohabitation with Julian. He was vague in his reply, almost closing his eyes. There had been a gentleman, he agreed, Russian he couldn't say, foreign, yes. He was never there on a permanent basis. He came and went. Ignatius asked him about Igor's visits. The question produced the troubled frown, the sideways look, the reluctant admission that he could recall no such person.

The account of the attacks on Julian was more persuasive. Ignatius demonstrated that they had begun some time after she had separated from her previous partner, the Russian banker, Anatoli Vozkresensky. These incidents, with which the accused had no connexion, had threatened her life and culminated in her murder. They had been reported to the police, at least the first two had been. Police and medical witnesses were called to describe what had happened.

Prisca's private detectives had traced the Rolls-Royce whose driver described to the court the accident that had occurred one night in early February. It was just before midnight and he was driving down the ramp into the underground parking to put the Rolls into its reserved place on the first floor for the night. A motorbike had been coming the wrong way, out of the in-coming ramp, and had driven headlong into his car. The rider had been thrown over the Rolls and hit the ground behind. Astonishingly, he had jumped up and run away, leaving his bike blocking the road. The chauffeur had examined the damage to his car, which was slight, dragged the motorbike clear of his path and parked the Rolls. He had seen two people, a tall thin man and a girl in a fur coat, running out of the exit and had assumed that there had been some kind of 'trouble'. He had not reported the incident. He had not wanted to get involved, he explained.

The chauffeur, the policemen, the bulldog and the terrier who had investigated the break-in, all dealt with reality. There was no fantasy in these practical men as they answered questions about the mugging or the break-in. The 'dent to the front bumper and slight scratching of the paint work on the roof and boot', the 'heavy damage to furniture, fixtures and fittings made with a sharp instrument such as a knife or razor', the 'narrow knife wound in the right side . . .' all carried conviction. These events really happened and there were credible witnesses to their results.

A pattern emerged from Ignatius's questioning: the final attack that had killed Julian Bennet was one of a series. Was it reasonable to believe that these episodes were simply random coincidences: a woman who is mugged by a nameless jogger, has her flat burgled, is attacked in an underground car park, is merely unlucky, and these things had nothing to do with her ultimate fate?

This argument had its effect. The jury could believe in the existence of Anatoli Vozkresensky, but Igor it could not cope with at all. He was invisible. I struggled to make him real, but he was a man without substance. And no wonder. I had only seen him once myself. In his final statement, Roger Ignatius argued that life is more complicated than fiction, and that the untidiness of his story was evidence of its truth.

Allwood, however, saw neatness rather than disorder as the mark of reality. In cross-examining me, he undermined my story with an alternative scenario. The attacks on Julian were not chance affairs, nor had they been orchestrated by some anonymous Russian criminal; they had been the work of the accused, as part of his attempt to dominate the victim. It was not the old lover, but the new one who was responsible. Finally, the Russian pistol and the bundles of dollars? The professor himself had visited Moscow recently. Why look for an unseen culprit when an explanation was at hand?

I joked to Roger Ignatius, during one of our last periods of consultation, 'The prosecution's case is so convincing, I believe in it myself. I think I must have done it.'

I could imagine the quarrel that we did not have that evening. I was accusing her of deceit, reproaching her for her ruthless trapping of Anatoli, her betrayal of us both with Igor. I could imagine her leaving me to my rage, walking across the landing to her own apartment. I was following her. I opened the drawer in the hall table to find my key, and saw the knife, left there on our return from Moscow. But I couldn't get any further. I knew that if she had defended herself, I would have believed her, as I always did. Any justification would have been good enough. The next image was Igor's foot, in its grey Russian shoe, which I saw as I bent over her. Then the sound of the blade on the wooden floor.

Ignatius did not laugh, though he maintained his bonhomie and optimism to the end. I accepted the verdict as inevitable.

43

When you become a convicted rather than a remand prisoner, life changes. You pass from Purgatory to Hades; you are no longer waiting, you are a permanent inmate. I was only allowed one visit a fortnight and, as I had been moved to another prison, out of London, reaching me was much more of an effort. I wouldn't have blamed Prisca if she had skipped a few, but she never did. I had shut down links to other people since Julian died, as the only way to survive their proximity. I was celled up with a middle-aged, ex-employee of British Rail who had cracked open his wife's skull like a breakfast egg in a quarrel over where to go on holiday. He was a fussy, routine-bound man, with whom I had nothing in common. I depended on Prisca.

'We must get you out,' she told me. 'You'll go mad here. What do you do all day?'

'It's not so bad. I'm getting used to it. As a murderer I have a certain status. I read.'

'You don't work?'

'Ah, work is a privilege. Sex offenders do the laundry. Some of the murderers work in the kitchen, perhaps because they're thought to be skilful with knives. I know that one or two of the men in for assault and battery are cleaners. I'm on the waiting list to sew diplomatic bags, I'm told. In the meantime, the prison library is working on a book list for me. I'm category B, which means I'm not thought to be violent. I'm quiet and co-operative; I expect to be on the enhanced regime for good behaviour soon. Prisoners who just want to read are no trouble at all. The authorities encourage it. So I thought it was an ideal opportunity to write up the case of the *Lady in a Pelisse*.'

'You're not to accept the verdict. We're going to appeal.'

Her determination filled me with awe. 'Prisca, you're a lawyer. You know, better than me, that you can't appeal just because you think I'm innocent. You have to have some reason to do so.'

'That's not a problem.' She brushed aside my ignorance of the ways of the law. 'I saw Roger Ignatius, straightaway and he had already called for a transcript of the judge's speech.'

'Why? Was there something wrong with it?'

'He was certain, as was I, that there was an error in the summing up, sufficient for an appeal.'

The immediate grounds of appeal were technical: the judge had failed to give an adequate direction on the burden of proof. What this meant in practice, Prisca explained, was that Roger Ignatius was going to argue that the element of doubt in the case, particularly the origin of the previous attacks on Julian, had been inadequately explained in the judge's summing up. The judge had also not set aside as irrelevant the suggestion, made by Allwood in his final statement, that I might well have been responsible for those attacks.

I recalled the hope I had felt during several days of the trial and allowed it to re-emerge. 'Is there any chance?' I asked. 'Are you doing this because you think I have a real possibility of getting out or because you can't bear to be defeated and you need to do something?'

'Ah, you know me too well. I won't let go any chance, even the slightest, but I can't pretend it's very hopeful. The bind is this: even if the Lords of Appeal find that Strowger misdirected the jury, and I'm sure he did, if they think that in practice there hasn't been a miscarriage of justice, the appeal will fail. Basically, that means you can't get off on a technicality.'

'So we're no better off than we were.'

'No, we've bought time. I always thought if we'd had a bit more time before the trial I would have turned up something.'

'It's all there,' I said. 'But it's in Russia, and it's not going to be made available to us here.'

'I'm not thinking about Anatoli or Igor in Russia. I've accepted we can't get anything out of them. But there's the question of Igor's presence in the building on that night. If he was there, he must have been seen. I'm going to interview everyone in the block myself. Then there's Colin Trevor and the pressure that was put on him. I'm going to get a statement out of him. I'm going to pull some strings to make Tom Naish dance.'

'It's been done, Prisca. We've tried all that.'

'I'm going to get my private investigators to find someone who was around in the square that night. Even if he wasn't seen in the building, it would help if someone would swear to seeing him in the area.'

When she came back a fortnight later, she was more downcast than I had ever seen her.

'I can't understand it. Not a single person will admit to seeing Igor. In fact, if you believe all your neighbours, hardly any of them was there.'

'It was a Friday evening; they were all away for the weekend. I told you it wouldn't be any good. In any case, you never see anyone in that building. I visited my mother there innumerable times when Julian was living opposite her and we never met. The only person who saw everybody was Victor. There is only one way in and one way out and that's past his desk.' My lack of surprise renewed her combative spirit.

'Then Victor must have seen Igor and I must see Victor.'

'He's stated on oath that no one came or left except Minna. It's no good, Prisca.'

'There has to be an explanation. It's probably very simple, if we could only see it. The question that wasn't asked. Did he go to the bathroom, for example? Could Igor have hidden in the building, say on an upper floor, and got out later, the next day even?'

'I talked to Roger Ignatius about that sort of thing. You know he was desperate to find something. I'm sure the police searched the building, visited every apartment, before they left that night. But go ahead. Why not?'

'It's hopeless being so pessimistic,' Prisca said severely. 'You've got to take some responsibility yourself. You've got to think. That's what you're supposed to be good at.'

I had plenty of time for that. We were locked in our cells by eight o'clock every night and I spent the evenings lying on my bed, remembering. However, I preferred to think about Julian than to search for an explanation for the inexplicable. I would recall the first time I saw her, the first time she invited me for a drink, the first time we had dinner together, the first time we made love. I listed the dates, the places, the times of day, what she wore, what she said. The past was the land I lived in, a refugee from the present. Only occasionally did I turn my mind to how I had arrived in my present position and whether I could escape from it.

Prisca returned from her visit to Victor without success.

'I was sure, as a woman of colour, I was going to get something out of him when no one else could. But he didn't change his story.'

'He adored Julian,' I said. 'They had this thing going. He told her everything, at least . . . I now wonder whether anything she ever said was true. She used to tell me all these stories about Victor and his family. I suppose they weren't fabricated. What's his house like, his family?'

'The house is very ordinary from the outside, one of those semi-detached Edwardian places in Camberwell. Inside it's crammed with furniture, very neat, highly decorated in colourful taste. His wife is white, called Mary, a retired nurse. We all sat in their front room and his granddaughter watched a video of *Little Women* with her thumb in her mouth.'

'I saw them at the trial. I used to hear how Mary and the daughter, what was she called, Josie, used to quarrel. They used to have the most appalling rows, apparently.'

I was carried back to journeys with Julian in taxis, coming home

from a restaurant or a film, holding her hand, hearing the next
episode of Victor's life, a row between Josie and Mary, Rose's
birthday party, the dog. Did they ever get the dog? I couldn't
remember. Perhaps that part of the story was interrupted. 'So what
happened?'

'I made an appointment. I explained who I was. He didn't make
any difficulty about seeing me. He was happy to talk. I let him go on
about you, about her. I learned a lot.'

'What about?'

'You both. He was – is – very fond of the two of you. He admired
her, was in awe of her in some way. But the way he described her,
reading between the lines, enraged me. She was an emotional tyrant,
one of those cold, controlling women who will always find a slave.
You were such a bloody fool, Nicholas.'

'You're quite wrong. She wasn't cold at all.'

Prisca made an angry sound of disagreement, like a suppressed
sneeze. 'He regretted what had happened. To you and to her.'

'That's what did for me at the trial. It was so clear that he didn't
want to harm me; he just couldn't help it. Did you learn anything
new? Did he admit that he went out for a smoke and was afraid to tell
anyone?'

'No, no, nothing like that. He just reminisced about her. When I
brought him round to the night of the murder he broke down in
tears, insisting he would have done anything to help her, but there
was nothing he could do about it. Nothing so far, but we're still
working on it. God, look at the time. All this way for an hour together.'

Prisca had failed, but my own flippant words, spoken to conceal
my pessimism, awoke a cascade of memories. Victor. Igor. Julian
and Igor. It was not just that last night, all the other nights had to be
accounted for. Why could Victor never remember having seen Igor?
If I had not seen Igor myself, lying on Julian's bed, I might have
concluded that all her stories were false, and that Igor had never
visited the apartment at any time, so Victor would never have had a
chance to see him. But I knew Igor had been there; indeed, he must

355

have had his own key. Victor must have seen him. If he didn't recall him, it was because he didn't want to.

'It's better not to ask,' he'd once said. When had that been? I relived my intense curiosity about Julian in those early days. I remembered my attempts to find out something about her, my frustration with Victor's reticence.

'Some people pay us not to talk,' he'd said.

Then I saw it all. Victor's co-operativeness, his reluctance to do harm, his apologetic visit when I was on remand, had distracted me from seeing that he was under as much pressure as Colin Trevor. He was paid not to see and not to talk. And the person who had paid him was not Julian, nor even Anatoli, but Igor. Once I had made this connection, everything fell into place. I waited impatiently for Prisca's next visit.

'I've understood about Victor.'

'Wait, wait. What about Victor?'

'Victor was paid. He was paid not to talk. He told me once . . .'

'What are you talking about?'

'He's not a man who is reluctantly telling the truth; he's someone who is reluctantly lying. He was paid to keep his mouth shut and it must have been Igor who paid him. Right at the start he would never answer my questions about Julian. He even tried to warn me off; I see that now. Once he told me that some of the residents tipped him to protect their privacy, to stop him being tempted to speak to journalists. At least, that's what I took him to mean. I see now he meant something much more specific.'

Prisca was looking thoughtful. 'And why do you think it was Igor who paid him?'

'Work it out. It has to be Igor. Anatoli couldn't have cared less. He liked to be seen with Julian. When I was shut up with him in Moscow, the thing he mentioned about Julian was the sensation she used to cause when she walked into a room. That's what he kept her for, as far as I could see.' I laughed. 'It wasn't sex; he thought she was cold; like you.'

'With more evidence for his opinion,' said Prisca.

I remembered Victor's expensive tastes. 'Victor always drove good cars, bought expensive clothes. I expect he lavished things on his granddaughter. There was more money there than there ought to have been.'

Prisca agreed to speak to him again. She made copious notes in her huge handwriting, covering page after page of her tiny notebook.

'Will this make a difference?'

'Who knows? With other things, it could tip the balance.'

44

Prisca arranged for Victor to come to the Lords because she wanted to tackle him alone, without the presence of Rose or Mary. She intended to overawe him with grandeur and hoped that the authority of the place would reinforce her cross-examination. He had seemed less willing to be helpful than the first time, but, when she persisted, he had conceded to the interview. So she heard the story of Victor and Igor, and Rose and Sleepy, which even Julian had never been told.

They met at the entrance gate where he was checked by security. She led him up the winding stairs to her office, invited him to sit down and made coffee for him on her little machine. Victor was, as usual, dressed for the occasion, but ill at ease, fearful of what was to come.

Prisca gave him milk and sugar and, handing him his cup sat down in front of him. I could imagine her leaning forward, ignoring her own coffee, resting her jutting chin on her angled palm and telling him straight out, 'Victor, I've asked you to come here like this because I wanted to talk about something that I am sure you would prefer Mary and Rose not to know about.'

Victor's gaze flashed upwards and then slanted down, not looking at her.

'I've been making some enquiries of my own, quite separately from the police or anyone else, and I now know all about what happened.' She waited to see what he would do, whether he would deny it to the end. 'And I know that you have been paid over a long period never to mention Igor.'

Victor's reaction had been low key, but nonetheless striking. It was a sign of his dislike of dishonesty that he did not resist, or perhaps a sign of his terror. He said nothing, setting down his coffee cup with a hand that was perceptibly trembling. A sheen of sweat spread over his forehead and cheeks and he leaned back in his chair. Prisca was aghast at the success of her techniques of interrogation. She feared that he was about to faint, or worse, to have a heart attack and hastily ran out to find him a glass of water. He took it from her and drank it, slowly, while his breathing slowly adjusted itself to a normal rhythm.

'It wasn't the money,' he said at last. 'I never did it for money. I couldn't help it.'

'Will you tell me about it?' And he did.

'I met Igor when Julian and Anatoli first moved in. They were such a nice couple. I always liked them. She was lovely, well, you know all about that. She always chatted to me, asked me about the family. He was sort of commanding, do you see what I mean? He had that smile, didn't he, white teeth under his moustache, as if he'd eat you. Igor was different; you didn't see him. I remember the first time he came, almost as soon as they arrived. Anatoli was away. He, Igor, had to ask what floor and I thought, all these Russians, they're all over the place now, do you see what I mean. But after that I didn't really notice him again.'

Igor was simply one of the hundreds of familiar faces, friends and relatives of the residents of the block, which recurred, passing from the front door to the lift. But he had special needs. He had to be able to go in and out discreetly. He wanted to know if Anatoli was in, had arrived back unexpectedly. He needed Victor. It started easily enough. Victor was used to husbands, wives, lovers, who wanted tasks done with discretion, things delivered, messages or parcels taken, guests let in or out without any comments made to others. Igor required the same services.

'He was an odd one. I could never make him out. And what did she see in him? I never thought there was anything between them, you know, sex. But I couldn't understand why he always came when Anatoli was away. In the end I thought perhaps she was in the same boat as me, he had some hold on her. We never talked about it, but I think she understood.'

Igor had paid well, too well. His tips came in brown envelopes, thick wadges of dollar bills, which Victor had been canny enough to change at hundreds of different banks over the years, so that he never set up a routine that could identify him. But Igor demanded a standard of loyalty, a commitment that Victor would never betray him, that could only come from fear.

'He was a bit like the Arabs,' Victor said, 'who didn't know the value of money, who were right out of scale. We'd had an Arab prince living there a few years back, who'd had six bodyguards and three or four servants, just for one man. Every time he left the country his private secretary gave money for us porters. He used to come down and leave this envelope full of fifty-quid notes.'

But that had only happened once or twice a year. Igor's gifts were frequent, secret, for Victor alone. The first two or three envelopes he had received with glee. He had patched up his car, had it serviced; sent Mary shopping up West; bought some toys for Rose. But the dollars kept on coming and he couldn't understand why.

'All he wanted was news of Julian. He used to ring as soon as he arrived in London and I had to tell him where Anatoli was and what she was doing. "He's away, expected on Saturday, sir. She's on her own." Or "He's here today. Shall I let her know your number?" I'd say.'

He felt uneasy. The money was too much for the services performed, so Victor knew it must be a lien on the future; something that Victor might not want to sell. The next time he tried to refuse. When Igor came through, stopping at the desk to slip the envelope under his book, he pushed it back.

'No, no, sir. It's too much. Really. Anything I can do, any time. It's no trouble.'

Ignoring what he said, Igor was already on his way to the lift. Determined to release himself from the trap he was in, Victor handed the envelope back to him when Igor left in the early hours. The Russian held the envelope in his hand, his eyes glazed, as if he needed time to recognise it.

'That was the first time I realised he drank. He never showed a thing, never stumbled, never spoke funny. But he was far gone, man.'

At last he said, 'Ok. If that's the way you want it. But you'll change your mind.'

Victor got up from his chair at this point and Prisca watched him walk behind her to the window, to look out over College Green and St Margaret's church.

'This is nice,' he said. 'How did you get here?'

'By car, I have a parking ... Oh you mean, *get* here.'

'Yes. You, there can't be many like you here.'

'It's long story. In the first place I married someone, that got me started. Then I worked. I was lucky and one thing led to another.'

'But you had education. You can tell you had education.'

'Yes, I had that.'

'Well, that's what I want for my granddaughter. I want her to be someone. My daughter, Josie, she never liked school, left as soon as she could. She never had no ambition. But Rose. I don't know how Igor knew about Rose. He was spooky, he knew things no one never told him.'

Julian, I thought, Julian would have told Igor, just as she told me.

One day, soon after this, Josie collected Rose from her nursery school at the end of the morning, as she always did. She was a bit late; that was usual, too. On the way home they popped into the Seven-Eleven to buy some bread for lunch. Josie had brought the dog with her, a dirty white poodle-cross called Sleepy, to give it some exercise. She was towing dog and child along the pavement towards their house, when they stopped at a crossing, idly waiting for a car. Instead of driving past, or even stopping to let them go, it drew up alongside them and two men got out. Josie had not foreseen danger.

She didn't recognise them, but she took them to be friends of her boyfriend, come to find her. An instinctive coquettishness had made her straighten her back, thrust out her bust, as they approached. Without hesitating in front of her femininity, they seized child and dog and bundled them into the back seat. In seconds, the revving car had made a u-turn and driven off. Josie had been left hysterical on the side of the road.

The twenty-four hours that followed were the worst of Victor's life. 'I didn't go into work. I didn't sleep or change my clothes. I couldn't understand who could've planned the kidnapping. But they were coloured, the guys that did it, and that made me think that my money had got them envious, do you see what I mean. I thought if I get her back, and I have to take money from Igor again, I won't spend it no more. I'll save it like, for Rose. I looked everywhere for her; I was frantic. I telephoned everyone I could think of, preachers, pub-owners, trying to find out who done this thing. I drove from one bar to another; I walked the streets. But I didn't go to the police. I was afraid, you see. I thought about those dollars; some of them were still in a shoe-box at the back of a cupboard in my bedroom.'

A day later Rose was found playing on the slide in a local park. She had approached a woman who was watching her own children and said she wanted her dinner now. She had recited her address and been led home. There was no evidence that she had been harmed in any way. Some mild questioning had produced the report that she had found the people who had looked after her 'nice'. She spoke approvingly of the pizza she had been given for her tea.

Sleepy had been less fortunate. Her body, the throat cut, had been returned by a separate route. Victor found her in his locked car that evening when he opened the door to set off for the night shift. The killing had indelibly soaked the interior with blood. Red paw marks on the side window marked the death throes. He still did not realise whom he was dealing with. He still expected some kind of demand for payment, and instructed Mary and Josie not to go out, not to answer the phone, above all to keep Rose inside.

He only understood that night when, at about one in the morning, Igor left the apartment building.

'How's your granddaughter?' he had asked.

'I felt a cold hand squeezing my heart,' Victor said to Prisca. 'I didn't know what to say.'

'She's ok,' he managed at last.

'Good, very good. Let's keep her so.' And he tossed the same envelope onto the desk.

After that, he had never doubted that if he ever revealed anything about Igor to anyone, his granddaughter would be killed. He had kept his part of the bargain until confronted by Prisca's powers of persuasion.

When I next saw Prisca she told me the whole story in detail.

'They were an exceptionally nasty bunch you got yourself mixed up with.' In an English context, the death of a dog was more shocking than the gunning down of a bodyguard in Russia. 'It may be enough to get you out of here,' she said. 'It's evident that he was under pressure and lied to the court. We may also have got a witness to Igor. My detective lady is on the track of a taxi driver.'

This character took form and flesh later in the week. I phoned Prisca who told me that they had now discovered the mini-cab driver who had delivered Minna to the square, a Maltese driving a Sierra estate car for Central Cars.

The detective work had been meticulous, worth every penny, Prisca averred. The investigator, a woman, had waited on several days outside Minna's flat in Hampstead to discover if she habitually used the same taxi service. On identifying the mini-cab company, she had been able to trace the journey made to Knightsbridge on the murder evening. She had noticed, with excitement, in the company's records, that the driver had picked up a fare immediately after dropping Minna at 20.09 hours, and taken him to Waterloo, depositing him there at 20.27 hours. She then contacted the Maltese driver who was understandably somewhat hazy about the evening in question now months ago. Once he had identified the day as the evening before his daughter's eighteenth birthday party, he had summoned up some vague memories. He thought it was a man who had approached him. He hadn't really seen him. He might have been wearing a light raincoat. The fare had bent down and spoken to him through the near side window and then got into the back of the car. He hadn't seen where he had come from. He could have come from out of the same building which Minna had entered, but he could have just been walking on the street. He might have had a foreign accent.

'Not perfect,' Minna said on the phone. 'But pretty good. Someone, roughly answering Igor's description, left the square immediately after Minna's arrival, and the journey and times are logged in the cab company's records.' She was jubilant.

We had uncovered another web of motivation and action, but I had little hope that it would produce any change in my circumstances. I had in any case accepted my situation.

'You're becoming institutionalised,' Jamie remarked when I told him that, grateful as I was to Prisca for all that she was doing, I still couldn't believe it would do any good in practical terms. 'All those years at boarding school was just preparing you for this.'

I laughed at the old joke. 'There's one difference,' I said. 'At school, awful as it was, you could still choose your friends. Here your companions are forced on you.'

The next time I saw Prisca, I asked her, 'Why are you doing this?' We were sitting decorously opposite one another in the Visits Room. Our immediate neighbours were passionately embracing across the table. They had not spoken a word since they met. 'I mean, why do you pursue this case so unremittingly? You did everything you could before the trial. You could have given up then. Why fight a hopeless cause?'

She swivelled a signet ring on her little finger. 'I can never give up, you know that,' she said lightly. That seemed to be the answer. It lay in her character, not in me or events. Then she added, angrily, 'And I'm doing it because of her. I detested her.'

365

'Julian?' I knew she had not much liked her; I was surprised at the depth of dislike she revealed. 'How could you detest her? She was always loved. Charm was her thing. What did she do to you?'

'It's not what she did, it was what she was.' She sat still, making up her mind to speak. 'Well, I might as well say it. It might help you to come to terms with what happened. She was everything I despise.' Her face had tightened, the lines around her mouth deepened. 'She reminds me of myself. Not now, but when I began. I was ambitious, like her and, like her, because I was . . . ' She could not bring herself to say 'beautiful'. 'Well, looked as I did, I had choices.'

I remembered Prisca when she was young, when I had first known her. She had been twenty-six; I had been seventeen. She had worn her hair cropped then, exposing the Nefertiti lines of her face, the colour of bronze. She was tall and adored clothes. Montfort loved her to dress up and encouraged her sartorial extravagance for the pleasure of the admiration she aroused in other men. It had only been a brief episode. As soon as she had got rid of him, she grew an enormous Afro and wore the longest, loosest, plainest garments she could contrive, a style, at once ethnic and idiosyncratic, which she maintained to the present.

'I could have become like her. For a time, I *was* like her. But thank God, I gave it up. She was a succubus, a woman who defined herself entirely by her relations with men. She was dependent, manipulative, enticing but fundamentally cold. But it's not a theoretical dislike. One meets plenty of women like that and I don't waste my time disliking them. It was what she did to you. She found you at a vulnerable moment, when you'd lost your wife, your children, your usual existence and she seized you. She used you and exploited every weakness of your situation and your character.' She saw me beginning to protest and she went on quickly, to prevent me from interrupting, 'And even worse, she exploited your goodness, perverted your trust, destroyed you. And I don't just mean landing you in here. That was the least of it. And it's that bit I hope to undo.'

45

While time inched forward towards the date set for the appeal, I tried to work on the *Lady in a Pelisse*. There was no reason for Minna to get away with her faking just because I was locked up. The authorities at my new prison were sympathetic and special arrangements were made for me to work. Instead of being assigned to sew diplomatic bags, I was allowed to study in the prison library and books were sent from London for me. I installed myself at a small table under the barred window, and from eight to ten thirty and two to four most days I was locked in to pass the time as I had always done. However, I did not work with my usual surge of ideas and flow of words. I would sit for hours watching the changeable west country sky through the cell window, the clouds forming and reforming in ranks in their north-eastward flow, until the turning of the key awoke me to the end of my study session. I would often find I had not written a word.

Everything led back to Julian. Even the keys grinding in the locks which divided every segment of my day reminded me of the key to her flat which had begun it all, of Anatoli's false key which had released us from the dacha, the hypothetical key that had let the wreckers into her flat, the key that Igor must have kept. Each key took me to another point in her story.

Even more evocative was the postcard of the Litvak *Lady* which I kept with my notes. As a reproduction it was not very good. The colour tones were distorted, but the luminous, innocent gaze and the moist mouth still had enormous power. I used to gaze at it for hours in the prison library, thinking about her alter ego, Julian.

As time passed, events clarified, gradually settling into a thick layer of sediment at the bottom of my mind. Now at some distance from her, I could begin to reach a personal conclusion about Julian's life. I acknowledged to myself that she had not been what she seemed, or what I had taken her for. I now accepted that she had loved Anatoli and hated him, too. She had wanted revenge for the pain she had suffered and had conspired his downfall with Tom Naish. What she (or he) had expected to come of their plan I could not guess. I wondered whether, in her case, the key was the act of arrest, when she had handed him over, and what happened next was unimportant to her. I knew very well the compulsion to revenge, the urgency to act. She had wanted to see the knife strike and the body fall.

In this view of her, she was exactly what Prisca detested, a woman who lived through and on men, whom she manipulated to counterbalance her lack of power. Was there more to her than this? Had she been a powerful and independent creature, an executive director of the Bank's operations, motivated by money not emotion? Was this, in any case, more admirable? At this point in my thoughts, I was plunged into the same whirlpool of muddied water that had engulfed me on the evening of her death. I remembered her oddness about money, her extravagance and her meanness, the oblique way she had told me about the Bank's criminal activities, tempting me to see more, worse, than she said.

I snapped my notebook closed on the painting. I wanted her, like me, to be innocent.

Prisca was full of optimism about the appeal. I did not allow myself to think about it, still less to hope for my release from prison. I did not want to go to court to hear the case and tried to persuade Prisca that it could be done without me. However, George Goodson and Roger Ignatius would not permit this. It was inconceivable, they said, for an appellant not to appear in court, and it would undermine my case. I submitted to these arguments.

The Art of Deception

I was shipped up to London on the day before the hearing to be delivered to the Law Courts in the Strand early in the morning. I was surprised to see that, in spite of the revolution that had taken place in my own life, everyone remained the same. Roger Ignatius looked as incongruous under his wig as he had last time round, and more ebullient than ever as he briefed me on the characters and histories of the three Lords Justices of Appeal who were to make up the tribunal.

I concentrated for the entire two-day period in court on such extraneous details, refusing to pay attention to the substance of what was happening around me. Roger Ignatius spent long hours on his feet, reading passages from his documents and answering questions from the tribunal. I was struck once again by the element of drama and role-play in pleading. He knew his part and he acted well. He was never at a loss and could improvise as well as learn a script. But all the time there was an edge of overacting in what he said that revealed the boundary between the true and the false, the felt and the acted. By the evening of the first day, when I was taken away to the police cells, I had a sense of how things were going, but, like Cordelia watching a film on television, closing her eyes at the frightening bits, I did not want to look.

I felt nothing but disbelief when the judgement was announced, that after so much horror and bad luck, it should turn out like this. What had it all been for?

The appeal was allowed on the grounds that the conviction was unsatisfactory. The court was adjourned for a fully reasoned judgement to be given later. I emerged blinking into the grey drizzling air of the Strand in the late afternoon, a free man again. Prisca, Jamie and Sibyl were there to greet and embrace me. Prisca dealt efficiently with reporters. They were much more eager to talk to and photograph her than me.

'I didn't think you would want to go to your mother's flat, at least for tonight,' Prisca said. 'So I booked you a room at the Goring. I picked up a suit for you, though it might not fit too well. You look as if you've lost weight. You haven't been eating properly. Then we're all going out to dinner together.'

I had been imprisoned since the day after Julian's death a year ago. I should feel some joy in freedom, I told myself, as I showered and changed that evening. If nothing else I should savour the contrast in my surroundings: the marble beneath my feet, the thick towels that I had wrapped around myself while I shaved. But I felt nothing, neither elation nor even comfort. I was as empty as a spilled glass. No external change seemed to fill the hollow core. I would have to do better this evening, I thought. Prisca and my cousins had been euphoric when we left the Law Courts. They had fought for me and won. The least I could do was to show gratitude, to reward them for what they had achieved.

My hotel room was hot. I opened the window and looked over the garden, a green space jailed by the surrounding buildings. My life was starting again, but I had no idea what direction I wanted it to take. I had felt safer in prison. There, at least, I had no choice in what I should do. It was all Emily's fault, I thought, bitterly. If she had not chucked me out of my good life as a householder and father of a family, none of this would have happened.

That evening we drank a great deal of champagne. My cousins were triumphant, celebrating a victory for truth and justice. I was simply relieved that the waiting was over and would probably have felt the same if I had been on my way back to my cell. I managed to put on enough of a show that my hollowness did not show. Just as I had experienced no pleasure in the luxury of the hotel, so I found the food difficult to eat. The dull, stodgy prison meals had required no decision. Faced with richness of choice and taste, I took the plainest food available. Even that, whatever its composition, resolved itself in front of my eyes into the colours and textures of flesh and blood, saliva, semen and faeces. In our mood of euphoria, no one noticed my lack of appetite.

'The mind of a killer is a fascinating study,' Prisca remarked.

She was eating trout, concentrating on piercing its crisply fried skin, slicing along its back and separating it into fillets, having already removed its head.

'Can one tell, do you think?' she went on. 'Not after the event, but before. Not who did it, that's an obvious question, but who *will* do it? Could you? Did you see?' She did not look at me.

'No, of course not,' I said. 'There was a lot I didn't see.'

'Before now I've only ever known murderers retrospectively.' She was lifting out the backbone and removing it fastidiously to the side of her plate. 'That is, they'd already killed when I met them, when I was a prison visitor. I never knew them before the act. And that's the interesting bit.'

'Beforehand I had everything wrong. All the information was there, but I simply didn't read it properly.'

I had chosen a steak, because I couldn't be bothered to consider anything else on the menu. I had cut through the encrusted surface and now the reddish edge was gently weeping onto my plate.

'To do you justice, some of the information was faked.'

'You know I don't accept that.'

'Nicholas, you were duped, tricked all along the line. Either that or you're fooling us.'

She selected a forkful of flesh, dabbed it with sauce and put it in her mouth.

'Why aren't you eating? Isn't rare enough for you? You ought to write it up. It would be therapy for you, get you started again. You needn't bother with who did it; we know all that. The view you want is not who, but why. Could you see beforehand? Should you have guessed what was going on? You were the only person who had the information, who knew everybody, or at least knew about everybody.'

'It's not just a question of who is going to be the killer. It's also who is going to be killed.'

'The victim was always pretty obvious. Asking for it, in my opinion. Not that I dreamt . . . But I didn't know the half of it.' Prisca helped herself to a piece of French bread. She stabbed a curl of butter and pasted it into place.

371

'I can't write any more. I've been trying to work on my book on art and perception, but I can't concentrate. I think I need a holiday.'

The steak was tough. It required some energy to saw through it. Human flesh was equally fibrous, dense, knit together in a durable web of tissue. To puncture the skin and pierce the muscle was the work of force. I put my knife and fork down, wishing I'd chosen something else.

'Nonsense.' Prisca never took holidays and did not see why anyone else should. 'You've just got to get the whole thing out of your system. Write it up. Then you can come back to your academic stuff later. Refreshed.'

She ate the last mouthful of her fish and took a sip of wine. All that remained on her plate was a framework of fine bones.

'I suppose I could try. I'd want to explain how it seemed at the time, the signs that were there, but which I didn't understand, to do it without hindsight, innocently.'

'However you want to tackle it,' Prisca said, 'the important thing is to cauterise the past. Now, what shall we have for pudding?' She took the menu from the waiter. 'I think it's quite important for you,' she went on, 'to come to some kind of understanding of what happened, why it happened, why it happened to you of all people.'

I chose roasted figs, three soft black bulbs which sat in a raspberry sauce, a pink pool in the centre of the white plate. I broke into the first fruit with the side of my fork. It opened up like a wound to reveal its centre, a milder red, fibrillous, speckled with golden seeds. Food had recently taken on an extraordinary power to return itself to raw materials in front of my eyes. And not just the form of its origin, but transubstantiated into flesh, open, throbbing, bloody, female. If writing about what had happened would put an end to this, it would be worth doing.

'It all began like this,' I said.

'What do you mean?'

'It began that night two years ago, when you and I, Prisca, had dinner together to talk about Emily. Do you remember? That's when I met her.'

They talked about the trial and the appeal, recalling the details obsessively, commenting on the skills of the solicitors, barristers, judges involved. Prisca had trained as a lawyer, Jamie still practised, and they analysed the case with professional thoroughness, as if it had been a game. They ordered more coffee; Jamie had a brandy. Julian was not with us, so no one ate the petits fours.

'I had to be optimistic,' Jamie said, 'especially with poor Nick, but I can say now I think we were bloody lucky to get off at the eleventh hour.'

'It's terrifying,' Sibyl said. 'How close you can get to terrible injustice. Because you can't prove, and nobody will believe, the truth.'

'There are different levels of truth.' Prisca was expounding one of her theories. 'On the legal level you can only judge by what comes within the rules and nothing else. If the truth, or a truth, can be exposed within that area, fine. The fact that there was a material irregularity and a key witness changed his story is enough to end play.'

'It's not like that, Prisca,' Sibyl replied. 'It isn't a game. One story is fake and the other is real. Those events really happened. There's no choice about that.'

'Nobody denies they happened. It's the interpretation that differs. That's my point. Even when you have established the bare facts, there is the whole level of intention. The interpretation of that subterranean flow of motive and purpose is another level of truth. Julian's story, Igor's story. Where was the truth there? Was she killed for love or money, sex or power? Your choice of interpretation is more to do with your personality than hers.'

'I'm sure Minna was lying,' Sibyl said. 'She must have seen Igor. Think how often we walked up and down those stairs to work out the timing. She committed perjury. And that was because of the painting. If Nick hadn't been embroiled with her over the *Lady in a Pelisse* . . .'

'It was revenge,' said Prisca.

'The irony is that it won't make any difference to the truth about the painting,' Sibyl went on. 'They'll rerun the tests and the experts will draw their own conclusions. It's not as if locking Nick up for life would stop the process.'

'No, that's why I said it was revenge. It was a violent, impulsive act which you do because of the past, not the future. I think she made her first denial instinctively and after that she was stuck with it.'

I could hear Julian's voice, *I thought you lot, intellectuals I mean, were dedicated to the service of abstract truth.*

'Prisca's right,' I intervened. They turned to look at me with surprise. They had argued this over many dinner tables when I was in prison. They were not used to my being with them. 'The interpretation of the facts depends on your point of view. You all supported me and worked for me, for which I can never thank you enough. But in the end, you did it because we're cousins. Not for abstract love of truth.'

There was silence. I had cruelly reminded them that we had won on the rules, not on the evidence. Jamie and Sibyl both studied their plates. Prisca looked at me, startled, with that penetrating expression that always made me feel that she had understood more than I had said.

I poured more champagne. 'As Jamie was saying, I've been very lucky, particularly in you three. I know I wouldn't be free if it hadn't been for you. I thank you from the bottom of my heart for your loyalty and friendship.'

We said goodbye to Jamie and Sibyl. Prisca and I got into her car for her to drive me to Victoria, on her way home. When she stopped outside the hotel, drawing into the side of the road, it was neither a good time, nor a good place for the purpose, but I had to thank her again.

She accepted my kiss on her cheek, but did not return it. She was gripping the steering wheel in tense hands.

'Nick,' she said, 'Tell me. I should have asked you this right at the start. I don't know why I didn't. Was Igor really there that evening?'

Prisca always had the power to surprise. I answered her calmly, looking into her eyes.

'He was there. He told me everything, just as I told you.'

She looked at me frowningly. 'Something happened at dinner. There was a split second when I thought . . . I thought you *had* killed her.'

I sat very still beside her, wondering what to do. The temptation stirred within me to tell her the other story of what happened that night, that I had never recalled even for myself. I said nothing. She gave me time and I did not take it.

'I thought,' she went on, 'he was there, but he didn't kill her. You did. You changed the roles.' Again she waited for my response.

I got out of the car and walked round behind it to cross the road. She did not move off and I saw that she had wound down her window and was speaking to me. I went back to her.

'Prisca, you've had what all women want, the last word.' I bent to kiss her goodbye.

'Good night, Nick. Sleep well, if you can.'

I watched her go, swinging round the corner on the lights. I would never tell her, or anyone.